THE POLITICS OF HOPE

The philosopher and theologian, Jonathan Sacks, Chief Rabbi of the United Hebrew Congregations of the Commonwealth, is well known outside the Jewish community as a writer and broadcaster. He delivered the 1990 Reith Lectures on the BBC ('The Persistence of Faith'), and is currently visiting professor at Kings College London and the Hebrew University Jerusalem. In addition to his many academic distinctions, he holds honorary doctorates from the universities of Cambridge, Haifa, Middlesex, Liverpool, St Andrews and Yeshiva University in New York, and is an honorary Fellow of Gonville and Caius College Cambridge and Kings' College London. In 1995, he was awarded the Jerusalem Prize. *The Politics of Hope* has been cited by leaders across the political spectrum.

Jonathan Sacks

THE POLITICS OF HOPE

FOREWORD BY
Gordon Brown

VINTAGE

Published by Vintage 2000

4 6 8 10 9 7 5 3

First published in Great Britain by
Jonathan Cape 1997

Vintage
Random House, 20 Vauxhall Bridge Road,
London SW1V 2SA

Random House Australia (Pty) Limited
20 Alfred Street, Milsons Point, Sydney,
New South Wales 2061, Australia

Random House New Zealand Limited
18 Poland Road, Glenfield,
Auckland 10, New Zealand

Random House (Pty) Limited
Endulini, 5A Jubilee Road, Parktown 2193, South Africa

The Random House Group Limited Reg. No. 954009
www.randomhouse.co.uk

A CIP catalogue record for this book
is available from the British Library

ISBN 0 09 976541 1

Papers used by Random House are natural,
recyclable products made from wood grown in sustainable forests;
the manufacturing processes conform to the environmental
regulations of the country of origin

Typeset by Palimpsest Book Production Limited,
Polmont, Stirlingshire
Printed and bound in Great Britain by
Biddles Ltd., King's Lynn, Norfolk

Contents

III The Good Society

For Jonathan and Deborah,
Gilad, Michal, Avishai and Yoav

Foreword

I was delighted to be asked to write a foreword to the paperback edition of *The Politics of Hope*, for it is a book that has had a profound influence on my own thinking about civic society and about politics more generally over the past few years. I find that I come back to its wisdom time and time again – and now that it is back in print, I shall happily resume my practice of recommending it to my friends.

Not all will agree with Jonathan Sacks in every particular, but he would not expect us to do that. What he invites us to do is rather to join with him in a moral debate – a 'national conversation', as he puts it. His book offers not only a superb frame for this debate, but an opening contribution that is – as befits the man – at once deep-thinking, humane, learned and also immensely readable.

His invitation is one that I urge you most forcefully to accept. For the questions that Jonathan Sacks raises are, I believe, of the utmost human importance – and the answers he gives are ones that ought to be taken very seriously even by those who disagree. And if they do not accept his answers, they will surely end the book with the certain recognition of a strong onus upon them to spell out just as clearly the basis for their disagreement, and to come up with better answers of their own. In the national conversation that this produces, part of the author's purpose will already be achieved.

What sort of society do we want to live in? What kind of people do we aspire to be? On what basis can we, as widely differing individuals of all faiths and of none, join together to our greatest mutual benefit within a single society? How can we give a due respect to each person's own individuality, yet also sustain the social cohesion and the cooperative engagement in common purposes that are equally human essentials, and, in more practical terms, what new approach might offer a better route to solving the many entrenched human and social problems with which we are still faced in Britain today, where so many past approaches have failed? Can we now find a solution to the grave issues of drugs and drug-related crime, and fully restore social trust in institutions where this has been undermined? What is clear from this book is that we cannot begin to answer these more practical questions without giving very serious attention to the moral questions as well.

It must be important to people of every political persuasion not simply that we in Britain set out to achieve a better off country, but that we also aim for a better society too. But this means that we cannot avoid the question: what is a good society? And we cannot start to answer this question without looking more deeply into our own selves as individuals, as Jonathan Sacks asks us to do.

From my own perspective, the value and interest of this book rests not just with the questions it asks but with many of the answers it gives. Perhaps I am so drawn to it because it chimes in so many interesting ways with my own Scottish background. When Sacks talks about civil society, I am reminded at once of the town of Kirkcaldy where I grew up in the 1950s and early 1960s, a town with strong community and voluntary organisations at its heart. There I saw how in children's and youth organisations, in churches, in sports, community and voluntary organisations, and in trades unions, individuals were encouraged and strengthened, made to feel they belonged and, in turn, could contribute, as part of an intricate network of trust, recognition and obligation. And for me, this gives a real and personal meaning to what Jonathan Sacks has in mind.

But Kirkcaldy was also the birthplace of Adam Smith, and when I went on to the University of Edinburgh, the names of David Hume and Adam Ferguson were enshrined in its modern buildings (though I have to add that Hume's was a rather belated recognition, for in his lifetime the University denied a philosophy chair to the greatest philosopher of his age).

These great thinkers of the Scottish Enlightenment are often called the 'moral sense' philosophers. They believed that human beings are naturally both moral and sociable creatures and that society is not ultimately based in rational self-interest but rather in our common and innate feelings of human sympathy.

And here of course there is a direct and obvious connection with the distinction that Sacks draws between political and civil society, and with his suggestion that what constitutes the latter should be thought of not as a contract but as a covenant. A contract is rooted in self-interest and is maintained, as he says, through the external force of law. A covenant, by contrast, has a moral basis and is maintained 'by an internalised sense of identity, kinship, loyalty, obligation, responsibility and reciprocity'.

So what is this moral basis that underlies the constitutive covenant for civil society? In answering this question I turn to a book Sacks quotes from several times, *The Moral Sense* by James Q. Wilson. As the title suggests, Wilson takes his start from the Scottish philosophers. He argues that in all human societies people manifest the dispositions to be dutiful, to exercise self-control, to believe in fairness and to empathise with one another.

These innate dispositions are of course influenced and shaped by the surrounding culture. They coexist with more selfish dispositions such as greed and vanity. And the fact that we are all disposed to fairness does not in itself define what is meant by a fair society – as to that, there is certainly disagreement. But the dispositions are the necessary and universal moral core that makes society possible.

And the evidence shows that these basic dispositions begin to appear in very early childhood. By the age of four, for example, many children are disposed to share even when it is not in their interests to do so and even when their parents are not watching. They have already internalised a standard of fairness. Here indeed is a starting-point for a Politics of Hope!

So can we root Sacks' covenant in our shared dispositions to duty, self control, empathy and fairness? Does this lead, as I would argue, to social arrangements that not only require responsibility in return for opportunity, but demands we extend opportunity to all, a theory of social justice if you like? And can such a social covenant based on the four dispositions bring a modern civic society to life as, instead of merely passive observance of rules, individuals participate together in shared endeavours for our mutual good, to help where help is needed and to share social institutions that encourage these dispositions? How far can recent initiatives such as Sure Start and the Children's Fund, where the state gives power to the forces of compassion and care in our communities instead of the state taking power to solve social problems, encourage the civic renewal to which Jonathan Sacks is committed?

I am optimistic that from a million centres of energy and goodwill within our country the politics of hope can lead us towards the good society of Jonathan Sacks' dreams.

Gordon Brown
August, 2000

Preface

In the three years since *The Politics of Hope* was first published, I have been encouraged by the response it has evoked. Parts of it were serialised in *The Times*. It has been cited by senior figures in both the government and the opposition. Because of it I have been visited by, among others, labour organisers from the United States, mine-workers from South Africa, and community groups throughout Britain. I have been asked to lecture to think-tanks in Washington, economists and welfare activists in London and senior army officers at Sandhurst. The themes I raised – marriage, the family, community, citizenship, education, civil society, responsibilities alongside rights, and 'social covenant' as well as social contract – have become part of the mainstream of public debate. The book touched a chord, as I hoped it would.

It is worth saying why I wrote it. I did so in the summer of 1996, conscious that there would be a general election in Britain within a year, and that in all likelihood a Labour government would be returned to power after a gap of eighteen years. The significance of that moment was more than local and immediate. It was part of a larger awareness, better articulated in the United States than anywhere else, that a certain kind of politics had run its course. A new insight was in the making, and it was far broader than any specific of policy. It touched on culture, society and the nature of the individual. It had been articulated by philosophers, social analysts and moral theorists across a surprisingly wide swathe of sympathies and orientations. Nor was it party political. The case I advanced had nothing to do with left or right, Labour, Conservative or Liberal Democrat. That is not to say that it was not controversial; it was and is. Bill Clinton and Tony Blair had spoken about a

Third Way. My concern was something different. I call it the Third Sector.

My intuition was, and remains, that modern politics has been dominated by two entities, the individual and the state. They are embodied in two institutions, namely markets and governments. The shared assumption has been that between them they hold the answer to all social problems. The right prefers the market. The left prefers the state. Both, however, have found themselves faced with social problems that have resisted all attempts at a solution. Among them are rising crime, the breakdown of the family, educational underachievement, the growth of psychiatric disorders especially among children and persistent concentrations of hopelessness and social exclusion. These are simply not amenable to the usual repertoire of politics. The market favours the successful but offers no consolation to the losers. The state can create relationships of dependency that make things worse, not better. Faced with repeated failures of both kinds of strategy there is a temptation to despair.

Nor will the situation get any easier. We are currently in the midst of one of the great transformations of history. There have been two in the past: from hunter-gatherer to agricultural, and then from agricultural to industrial societies. Ours – the move from an industrial to a global information age – is the third. Globalisation will bring great benefits, but it will also intensify the strain on our social structures. Employment will become less secure as production, even clerical tasks, is switched around the world in response to wage rates and currency fluctuations. Communities and neighbourhoods will become more attenuated as high street shops give way to e-commerce, and face-to-face encounters are replaced by mobile phones, e-mail and the internet. Wage differentials will continue to rise as we move to an economic order dominated by intellectual capital, which favours the gifted few. The social bond will become ever more tenuous. The new economy, unlike its predecessors, is what George Soros calls 'transactional'. It is not based on long-term relationships with people to whom we can put a face or whom we know by name. Life, for most of us, will become significantly less secure.

That is why third-sector institutions are important. Imagine taking a child for a walk around London. You pass the Houses of Parliament, and you explain that they are the home of government, the arena of politics, and that politics is about the creation and distribution of power. Next you pass offices and shops, and you explain that these are part of the market, the realm of economics, and that economics is about the creation and distribution of wealth. Finally, the child notices the great dome of St Paul's. What, she asks, is that? You reply that it is a house of worship. 'And what does *it* create and distribute?' she asks. You might be inclined to answer that it is not that sort of thing, but you would be wrong. Places of worship – and more generally, families, neighbourhoods, schools and communities – do create and distribute something of great significance.

We can see what this is by a thought experiment. Imagine that you have total power, and then you decide to share it with nine others. The result is that you have one-tenth of the power with which you began. Now imagine that you have a thousand pounds, and then you share it with nine others. Again, you have a tenth of what you had. Power and wealth are, at any given moment, zero-sum games. The more I share, the less I have. That is why governments and markets are arenas of conflict, mediated on the one hand by democratic elections and on the other by monetary exchange. We need such institutions. Without them, as Hobbes said, life would be nasty, brutish and short.

Now, though, imagine that you have a certain quantum of love, or friendship, or influence, or loyalty, and then you share it with nine others. Do you have less than when you started? In fact, you have more. I call these *social goods*, and they have this characteristic in common, that the more I share, the more I have. We can now say what it is that families, communities, schools and congregations produce and distribute. The answer is social goods, the goods that exist in virtue of being shared.

This is a simple way of putting a proposition that has been arrived at independently in recent years by three quite different disciplines: economics, sociobiology and political theory. Economists like James Coleman, Robert Putnam and Francis Fukuyama call it *social capital*. Sociobiologists such as Robert Axelrod and Anatole Rapoport call it *reciprocal altruism*. Political theorists on the left speak of *communitarianism*; those on the right, of *civil society*. In many cases they invoke, by way of support, a fascinating branch of mathematics called Games Theory, and one of its methods known as the Iterated Prisoner's Dilemma.

These are big words for what is ultimately a simple idea, namely that in any competitive situation, long-term victory goes to those who have developed habits of co-operation. Whether we speak of animal species, businesses or societies – even, in a global age, of humanity as a whole – survival depends on the ability of individuals to work with others to achieve what none can do alone. That is why our social ecology must include strong third-sector institutions. Families are where we discover the bonds of love and trust. Schools are where we learn the collective story of which we are a part. Communities are where we are there for other people at times of need, and they for us. Congregations are where we join our prayers to those of others, making their hopes our own. Collectively they are the places where we learn to speak the language of 'We' as well as 'I'. They are where we learn moral literacy, 'habits of the heart', the give-and-take of rights and responsibilities, the grammar of reciprocity. Without them, society is too abstract to be real. Community is society with a human face.

Third-sector institutions are larger than the individual but smaller than the state. They are where relationships are sustained, not by monetary exchange (the market), nor by the coercive use of power (the state), but instead by loyalty, faithfulness, mutuality and trust. In the book I call these *covenantal*, as opposed to contractual, relationships. They are essential to the health of any society, because they are arenas of co-operation rather than competition. The market and the state mediate relationships between strangers; third-sector institutions turn strangers into friends. That is why they foster the pre-political virtues – civility, integrity, honesty, reliability – without which neither the market nor the state can function in the long run. Without them there is a systematic breakdown of trust.

That is what has gone wrong in the 'late capitalist' phase of the liberal democracies of the West. In a culture dominated by the market on the one hand, governments on the other, families and communities start to disintegrate. Relationships become contractual rather than covenantal, short-term and provisional, not long-term and supportive. Morality – our generic word for the shared codes of behaviour that hold families and communities together – fragments under the twin assaults of the market and the state. How, for example, can marriage survive in a culture which, on the one hand, embodies the consumer ethic of 'buy it, use it and throw it away', and on the other, invents surrogate fatherhood in the form of the welfare benefits of the state? The short answer is that it can't and doesn't. The most striking feature of British and American societies in the past forty years has been the dramatic collapse of marriage in favour of an open-ended variety of living arrangements, which, whatever their value, fail to provide children with the same security, stability or socialisation.

My approach to politics comes from personal experience. My late father came to Britain as a child, fleeing from persecution in Central Europe. His family was too poor to allow more than one child, my late uncle, to have a full education. My father had to leave school at the age of fourteen to support his parents and siblings. He never had much success, yet his four sons all went to university, entered the professions, and made their way in the world. As I reflected on how my own family, along with thousands of others like them, had broken free of the bonds of poverty in a single generation, I came to the conclusion that it was because of the strength of three things: family, community and faith. The Jews of the East End were poor in everything else, but they were rich in social capital. They had families whose members made sacrifices for one another. They had communities that were networks of support. And they had faith that gave them confidence, self-respect and trust.

Today, when I visit run-down neighbourhoods, I see the same poverty I remember from my childhood, but with one fateful difference. I see a poverty of hope. Its symptoms are all too evident. For some they take the form of anger: crime, violence and 'in your face' aggression. For others they become the expressions of despair:

drug abuse, alcohol addiction, depressive illness, suicide attempts. These are the casualties of our advanced consumer society, and to turn a blind eye to them is unforgivable. The global age may be fine for the rich, the successful and the talented, but it is currently claiming too many casualties to be a morally acceptable social order. The right may blame the state; the left may blame the market; but what will make a difference will be the patient, slow, hard work of rebuilding families, communities and neighbourhoods where hope is born. These are the places where we learn that, though each of us is vulnerable, when we share our vulnerabilities we discover strength. That is the power of the covenantal bond.

A good society is one that offers its members equal access to hope. That is my belief, and what led me to write this book. In it I tell the story – and it is a complex one – of how we came to deplete our reserves of social capital, and how we can rebuild them again. This is now our most important task, and the future will make it ever more urgent. We are entering an age of unprecedentedly rapid change, scientific and economic, and of all things, change is hardest to bear. I disagree fundamentally with thinkers like Anthony Giddens who argue that when society changes, our ethics and basic institutions must also change. Few things are more facile than this confusion of 'is' with 'ought' – what is happening, as against what ought to happen – and few more irresponsible. It is precisely when the world is moving at bewildering speed that we need the stability of families, communities and moral codes that are secure. Change is not threatening so long as we keep firm hold of the values for which we live. We can travel with confidence if we have a map. We can jump with safety knowing that there is someone to catch us as we fall. We can face the future without fear so long as we know we are not alone. It is those structures of togetherness, the third-sector institutions, that give us the inner resources to cope with change.

The pages of history are littered with the debris of civilisations that were once technologically supreme, but which soon vanished into oblivion. Those that survived were those that did *not* go with the flow. Instead they held firm to the values and institutions that sustained the 'structures of grace in society', the covenantal bond between persons. An impersonal world, dominated by states and markets, international corporations and global forces, is one where each of us is replaceable, none of us valued for what we uniquely are. It fails to speak to our deepest needs as social, meaning-seeking animals. Nothing in our present situation forces us to opt for the libertarian culture we have created in the past forty years. It is something we have chosen; therefore it is something we can unchoose.

The time has come for a counter-cultural voice to challenge the idols of the age: celebrity, power, wealth, success and the freedom to do what we like so long as we can pay governments to deal with the consequences, picking up the pieces of broken lives, above all the lives of many of our children. The road we have begun to travel, of ever more powerful states and markets, and ever weaker families and communities, is one that cannot but end in tragedy. For many, it already has. This book, then, is a principled protest against a society that seems, at times, to know the price of everything but the value of all too little, especially of the things that are lasting and long-term. It is a call to strengthen those human and humanising institutions that are based, not on the power of the state nor the transactions of the market, but on the covenantal bond between people. That is what changes lives and rebuilds the damaged landscape of hope.

For this new edition, I have made changes to chapter 1, and completely rewritten chapter 20. My thanks to my literary agent, Louise Greenberg; Syma Weinberg, Jeremy Newmark and Sara King-Scott of my office; and Arzu Tahsin of Vintage publishers. It has been a pleasure working with them.

Introduction

[S]ociety means a community of ideas; without shared ideas on politics, morals and ethics no society can exist. Each one of us has ideas about what is good and what is evil; they cannot be kept private from the society in which we live. If men and women try to create a society in which there is no fundamental agreement about good and evil they will fail; if, having based it on common agreement, the agreement goes, the society will disintegrate. For society is not something that is kept together physically; it is held by the invisible bonds of common thought. If the bonds were too far relaxed the members would drift apart. A common morality is part of the bondage. The bondage is part of the price of society; and mankind, which needs society, must pay its price.

Lord Devlin[1]

There is no such thing as society.

Margaret Thatcher[2]

MY ARGUMENT IN this book can be stated simply. There are two concepts of a free society, one liberal, the other libertarian. For the past fifty years the libertarian view has prevailed. Shared by British and American politicians on the left and right, it maintains that a free society is ideally one in which individuals are left free to pursue their own choices. The central question of politics is whether this is best achieved by governments doing as much as possible or as little: should we have a maximalist or minimalist state? The maximalists argue that the task of the state is to give

[1] Patrick Devlin, *The Enforcement of Morals*, 10.
[2] Margaret Thatcher, Interview, *Woman's Own*, 31 October 1987.

1

everyone as far as possible the resources with which to pursue their private vision of the good life. The minimalists argue that this is best done by the opposite strategy, namely by leaving as many resources as possible in the hands of individuals.

Philosophically, the debate has been between John Rawls and Robert Nozick.[3] Economically it has been between Keynes and Milton Friedman. Politically it has been between the Roosevelt–Beveridge vision of a welfare state and the 'small government' programmes of Margaret Thatcher and Ronald Reagan. But both sides share an ideal, however deeply they differ in the means they adopt to achieve it: namely, of an arena in which the state guarantees the freedom of the individual to realise his or her own choices. Morality has no part to play in politics beyond fair procedures and the transparency and accountability of governments. All significant moral decisions are to be made by individuals. Indeed morality itself is a purely individual concern. On both views the key players – the only players – are the state and the individual. Beyond that, as Margaret Thatcher once said, 'There is no such thing as society. There are individual men and women, and there are families.'

This is a tenable view, and there is only one thing to be said against it. It has been tried and it has failed. It has given rise to a social order – or more precisely, to a social disorder – more bleak than any within living memory. Today many parts of Britain and America are marked by vandalism, violent crime and a loss of civility; by the breakdown of the family and the widespread neglect of children; by an erosion of trust and a general loss of faith in the power of governments to cure some of our most deep-seated problems; and by a widespread sense that matters crucial to our future welfare are slipping beyond our control. More than a decade ago, Robert Bellah articulated the fears of many when he wrote that 'social ecology is damaged not only by war, genocide and political repression. It is also damaged by the destruction of the subtle ties that bind human beings to one another, leaving them frightened and alone. It has been evident for

[3] John Rawls, *A Theory of Justice*; Robert Nozick, *Anarchy, State and Utopia*.

some time that unless we begin to repair the damage to our social ecology, we will destroy ourselves long before natural ecological disaster has time to be realized.'[4] Since then, on most indices, things have become worse.

It will not be my intention at any stage of the argument to criticise the past, second-guess the leaders of an earlier generation, or adopt the false righteousness of hindsight. To the contrary it is my conviction that at every stage of the long journey towards the present, those who made political and moral choices acted on the basis of high and honourable principle. It is not simply that they did the best as they saw it. They did the best that could have been seen. But time has moved on, and so must we. The politics of the past have run their course, and we must search for a new way.

Fortunately this is less difficult than it seems. We are able to go back to the writings of those who set out on the path toward a free society and re-acquaint ourselves with what they had in mind. As soon as we do this we discover in many cases that their concerns are uncannily like ours, and they had wise things to say which we have since forgotten. Their view of politics was liberal rather than libertarian. Their central question was: how can we create a society in which everyone can participate, and everyone achieve the maximum possible dignity? Their answer was not to privatise morality and rule it out of order in political debate. Some important moral issues are private, but not all are. In particular, it is impossible to create a good society without a vigorous process of public debate and without some consensus about the kind of society we wish to create. Nor is the creation of a society a matter, simply, of state action on the one hand and the private choices of individuals on the other. It is at least in part the task of families, neighbourhoods, businesses, communities, voluntary organisations and religious groups, each of which has its role to play in linking us to something beyond the narrow ambit of self-interest, allowing us to become joint architects of something we build and share with others. Societies are made not just by states and individuals, but also and crucially by what we do, severally, freely and together in

[4] Robert Bellah et al., *Habits of the Heart*, 284.

a thousand local contexts and constituencies. If libertarianism is a politics of interests, liberalism is a politics of involvement.

The good news is that wherever this kind of politics has been tried, it works. It protects freedom because it diffuses power. It sustains liberty because it promotes the virtues on which self-government depends. It creates a more equal society because it bases human dignity on something more accessible to each of us than wealth or success. It creates a more humane society because it is built on a broader view of human nature than one that sees us simply as atomic individuals pursuing private projects. Compared to libertarianism, it yields a social order in which we are less vulnerable and confused. Above all, it is the most powerful available antidote to despair, because it leaves us less exposed to forces beyond our control, to decisions in which we do not have a part. These are my views, but not mine alone. Increasingly they have come to be shared by philosophers, economists, social commentators and literary critics. Most importantly they have begun to be adopted by politicians at both ends of the political spectrum – by Democrats and Republicans in America, and members of the Labour, Conservative and Liberal Democratic parties in Britain. There was nothing wrong with the politics of collectivism and the politics of private initiative, but their greatest days lie in the past and we are ready for something different and more challenging. My name for it is: the politics of hope.

I

Starting a
Conversation

1

The Blood-Dimmed Tide

> Mankind's moral sense is not a strong beacon light, radiating outward to illuminate in sharp outline all that it touches. It is, rather, a small candle flame, casting vague and multiple shadows, flickering and sputtering in the strong winds of power and passion, greed and ideology. But brought close to the heart and cupped in one's hands, it dispels the darkness and warms the soul.
>
> James Q. Wilson[1]

IN 1940, TEACHERS were asked to list the seven most serious problems they faced in school. Their answers were: talking out of turn, chewing gum, making noise, running in corridors, cutting in line, not wearing school uniform, and dropping litter. In 1990, a group of teachers was asked the same question. This time their answers were: drug abuse, alcohol abuse, teenage pregnancy, suicide, rape, robbery, and assault.[2] This is an indicator, a particularly vivid one, of what is going wrong with our world among the many things that are going right.

We begin the twenty-first century on the brink of extraordinary possibilities. Never have we had so much freedom and affluence, diversity and choice as we do today in the liberal democracies of the West. The average shopper in the average supermarket is confronted with an array of goods that, a century ago, would have been beyond the dreams of kings. Journeys that would have taken months then, today take hours. We have sent space probes to distant planets, photographed the birth of galaxies, created instantaneous global communication and decoded the human

---

[1] James Q. Wilson, *The Moral Sense*, 251.
[2] William Bennett, *Index of Leading Cultural Indicators*, 83.

genome, the mystery of life itself. The boundaries of human opportunity expand daily.

Simultaneously with these advances, though, we have experienced disturbing phenomena, among them random outbursts of violence, football hooliganism, road rage and a general loss of civility. There has been a huge increase, among the young, of suicide attempts, depressive illness, eating disorders and stress-related syndromes. So widespread have these become that a psychologist, Oliver James, has described contemporary Britain as a low-serotonin society, serotin being the chemical register in the brain of states of wellbeing.[3] Contemporary society is a magnificent building but the cracks are showing and they grow wider by the year. Something is amiss. The question is, what?

The short answer, though it is anything but simple, is that we have begun to lose our moral bearings. Our world is moving at great speed, but we are not quite sure where we are going or why. Within a single lifetime, intuitions that were once quite clear have become vague to the point of indeterminacy. We no longer feel we know what to tell our children, or even ourselves. Moral insight has not kept pace with scientific advance. The result is that we have unprecedented knowledge of what is, unprecedented doubts about what ought to be.

Concern about our moral situation is deep and growing. 'There is little doubt that most people believe that Britain is in severe moral decline.' So began a newspaper editorial in 1996. It continued: 'Some regard the situation as hopeless; the majority are uneasy. Few seem to know what to do about it. A Gallup poll last week painted a grim portrait of a nation ill at ease with its conscience, worried about issues of religion, sexual morality, honesty and a willingness to make sacrifices for others. Institutions are under attack, respect in decline, behaviour appalling, the outlook bleak. Anomie is rampant. Three-quarters believe society is less moral than it was 50 years ago. Half think the church does not provide adequate moral guidance. Only one in five believes there is a broadly agreed set of

[3] Oliver James, *Britain on the Couch*, 1997.

moral standards; most maintain it is left (wrongly) to individuals.'[4]

These fears are genuine. We inhabit a more chaotic, disordered world than the one we remember or the one our parents knew. Crime rates in Britain, which had fallen during the second half of the nineteenth century and remained at a low level until midway through the twentieth, have risen precipitately since, from under 1,000 for every 100,000 of the population in 1955, to 10,000 in 1991, a rise of ten times in thirty-five years. After a brief lull in the late 1990s, they began to rise again, to the point where an American news bulletin, in the summer of 2000, warned viewers about to travel to Britain that it had become a more dangerous place than the United States. 'You are more likely to be burglarised here,' said its London correspondent, 'almost twice as likely to be robbed and two-and-a-half times more likely to be assaulted.'[5]

Meanwhile, in the United States itself, whole neighbourhoods have become an underworld of drugs, theft, assault and casual brutality. One American writer noted, 'By 1970 a baby born and raised in a big city had a greater chance of being murdered than a World War II GI had of dying in battle. Today, a twelve-year-old American boy has an 89% chance of becoming a victim of violent crime in his lifetime.'[6]

Directly or indirectly, these fears touch most of us some of the time. For the last nine years we have lived in a quiet suburb of North London. Within days of our arrival a neighbour and his family were held at gunpoint throughout the night while burglars ransacked his home. They coped stoically with the shock but soon afterwards they moved, unable to bear the house and its memories. A member of our local congregation, a woman in her eighties, was attacked and thrown to the ground on her way to the synagogue by a group of teenage girls. Quite apart from the direct harm and lasting trauma to the victims, crimes like these damage the values of trust and openness in neighbourhoods. People become more guarded. Doors are no longer left open to friends. We think twice about going out at night. The elderly stay at home. Buildings that were

[4] *Sunday Times*, 7 July 1996.
[5] CBS Evening news, 28 June 2000.
[6] Myron Magnet, *The Dream and the Nightmare*, 50.

once freely accessible to the public – churches, colleges – are now locked against strangers. Shop windows are barred and shuttered, and at night many high streets and arcades look like scenes from a battle zone.

In another age we might have looked to the family, in Christopher Lasch's phrase, as a 'haven in a heartless world', but today the stable family has itself become a casualty. The divorce rate in Britain has risen to four in ten of all marriages, and in the United States even higher. Childbirths outside marriage, which remained at around 5 per cent throughout the nineteenth and early twentieth centuries, had risen to 39 per cent by 2000. There has been a vast increase in the number of children who grow up without a father, or with a succession of stepfathers, or whose parents separate. Our experience of childhood is one of the most powerful determinants of whether, throughout the rest of our lives, we view the outside world with trust or suspicion, confidence or fear. In their most formative and vulnerable years more children today than in the past will grow up without the experience of an enduring relationship between their parents, and fewer resources with which to build them themselves.

The teenagers I meet are markedly more guarded and anxious than my friends and contemporaries were thirty years ago. They worry about whether they will find a job and, if so, whether they will keep it. They wonder about whether they will get married and, if so, whether the partnership will last. Around them they see the sharp discords of affluence and poverty, elegant shops in whose doorways at night the homeless sleep in cardboard boxes. Many of them have seen their parents' or their friends' parents' marriages disintegrate under the pressures of too much work or too little, workaholism and unemployment. They have seen moments of hope, like the peace processes in Northern Ireland and the Middle East, end in disillusion. They inhabit a world whose most cherished goods – success, wealth, physical beauty, sporting prowess, fame – are inequitably, sometimes even arbitrarily, distributed. Around them they find a society which maximises envy and minimises consolation.

They are surrounded by images of violence and sex without a

connecting narrative of justice or fidelity. Their mood is dark and it is mirrored in the art that most speaks to them, films like *Pulp Fiction*, *Trainspotting* or *Natural Born Killers*, music like Heavy Metal or Gangsta Rap, stars like Kurt Cobain, who committed suicide after singing 'I hate myself and I want to die', television channels like MTV with its non-stop succession of provocative and disconnected images. Theirs is the first generation of children in a century to have less high hopes than their parents. In a recent American survey, 60 per cent of respondents said that they thought children were worse off today than in the past. A special commission of politicians and medical, educational and business leaders met to deliberate on the health of young Americans. They concluded: 'Never before has one generation of American teenagers been less healthy, less cared for, less prepared for life than their parents were at the same age.'[7] A massive report by Sir Michael Rutter and Professor David Smith documented a sharp rise over the past forty years in depression, psychosocial disorders, drug and alcohol abuse, and actual and attempted suicide among young people.[8] The 1960s were sometimes described as the decade of the 'death of God'. The 1990s were the decade of the death of optimism.

Contemplating this ravaged landscape many observers adopted an apocalyptic tone. Eric Hobsbawm ended his history of the twentieth century, *Age of Extremes*, with this bleak judgement: 'The structures of human societies themselves, including even some of the social foundations of the capitalist economy, are on the point of being destroyed by the erosion of what we have inherited from the human past. Our world risks both explosion and implosion. It must change.'[11]

Similar warnings have been sounded by social philosophers like Alasdair MacIntyre, David Selbourne and John Gray, MacIntyre speaking about the coming age of 'barbarism and darkness'.[10] The

[7] William J. Bennett, 'What to do about the children', *Commentary*, March 1995, 23–8.

[8] M. Rutter and D. J. Smith, *Psychosocial Disorders in Young People*, Chichester, John Wiley and Sons, 1995.

[11] Michael Novak, *Awakening from Nihilism*.

[10] Alasdair MacIntyre, *After Virtue*, 244.

Catholic thinker Michael Novak, in his 1994 Templeton Prize address, held before his audience the prospect of the demise of liberal democracy in the West. 'No one,' he said, 'ever promised us that free societies will endure forever . . . Free societies such as our own, which have arisen rather late in the long evolution of the human race, may pass across the darkness of Time like splendid little comets, burn into ashes, disappear.'[11] As the twentieth century neared its close, the lines most often heard were the famous words of Yeats:

> Things fall apart; the centre cannot hold;
> Mere anarchy is loosed upon the world,
> The blood-dimmed tide is loosed, and everywhere
> The ceremony of innocence is drowned;
> The best lack all conviction, while the worst
> Are full of passionate intensity.

I share many of these concerns, but there is another face of Britain. It was evident during the mourning for the late Princess Diana, and on the eve of the millennium itself. Vast crowds gathered in London and elsewhere, but they were orderly, gentle, hushed, restrained. At times of tragedy, like the massacre at Dunblane, the mood of national concern is palpable. There are moments when you see Britain not as a nation of individuals living disconnected lives in pursuit of self-interest, but as a people united by a sense of fellow-feeling and kinship, joined by a covenant, un-articulated but still immensely strong, of shared suffering and fate.

News lends its own perspective to events, and it is not necessarily a balanced one. What catches our attention is the unusual, not the norm, the plane that crashes, not the thousand that land safely. If 40 per cent of marriages end in divorce, then 60 per cent of couples stay together for life. For every child involved in crime there are two, or even ten, engaged in voluntary service to others. For every story of violent attack there are a hundred unreported tales of neighbours and strangers helping one another, stories rarely publicised of friendship, steadfastness, the unostentatious pursuit of

[11] Michael Novak, *Awakening from Nihilism*.

duty, a myriad 'ordinary virtues'. The very fact that violent crime is news tells us two things: that it remains exceptional, and that evil has not lost its power to shock. Our fascination with disorder testifies to the underlying strength of order.

There are – there always were and will be – individuals who injure the social bond by acts of violence and brutality. But the bond survives. Britain, like other liberal democracies of the West, is still a powerfully moral nation. Our sense of connectedness, one to another, remains. But our self-knowledge has become temporarily obscured. We have lost the habit of telling the story that explains us to ourselves as moral beings. The result is that we see the bad more clearly than the good. We can explain self-interest. Conflict, we understand. But that other aspect of ourselves, no less real and active, which makes us weep when other people suffer, has moved out of focus so that we only recognise it at moments of great tragedy. But it has not disappeared, and it is this still vital core of moral energy that sustains society and humanises our political and economic institutions.

The new century heralds an era of immense and potentially destabilising change. We do not know what tomorrow will be like, but we do know that it will not be like today. The old sources of personal security – a job for life, a marriage for life, a sense of boundaries and predictability – have become ever less secure. Under such circumstances it becomes all the more urgent to draw the moral map in the midst of what otherwise seems like chaos, to bring stability back into our most enduring personal relationships and to strengthen a society in which we know that others will be there for us in times of crisis and need.

The case I want to argue in these pages is that we have at our disposal a resource of unparalleled power with which to confront the problems of a new age. That resource, neither mysterious nor difficult to understand, is morality, specifically the Judaeo-Christian tradition. For several centuries it has been under attack. There are intellectual, political, economic and social reasons why this should have been so. As a way of organising human behaviour it has been displaced by a quite different set of assumptions, the scientific ethic of the Enlightenment, with massive consequences for the way society is structured and individual lives are lived. This once held out great promises, and indeed it has delivered many. But it has now become dysfunctional. Its side-effects are becoming acute, and the more it is applied, the greater the pathologies it produces. More seriously, it acts as a screen against the kind of thinking that might allow us to chart a way out of our impasse. Faced with an increasing range of human tragedies, it either ignores them or explains them away.

It is no accident that the word 'demoralisation' refers both to a loss of moral meanings and a loss of hope. We are made most anxious by things outside our control. Ancient civilisations were dominated by fears of natural catastrophe – drought, floods, famine – and much of their creative energy went into personifying these forces as gods who might be placated by incantation, ritual or magic. Today we are no less fearful of vast forces – technology, the erosion of the biosphere, the globalisation of industry, the internationalisation of terror – but we have no narrative structure through which to personalise them, rendering them intelligible and capable of being influenced by what we do. Our hopes are invested in governments, from which we demand more and in our more sombre moments anticipate less. At the core of our culture is an echoing discrepancy between what we believe and what we know. We believe that we are faced with unprecedented choices. We know that too much of what happens to us is beyond our control, the result of economic choices or political decisions taken far away by people we will never meet nor be able to identify. Beyond the narrowing circle of the self lies a world in which we are not the makers but the made. This is the genesis of despair.

Against just such a backdrop, some four thousand years ago, there emerged a different conception of human life. It suggested that individuals are not powerless in the face of the impersonal. We can create families, communities, even societies, around the ideals of love and fellowship and trust. In such societies, individuals are valued not for what they own or the power they wield but for what they are. They are not immune to conflict or tragedy, but when these strike, the individual is not alone. He or she is surrounded by networks of support, extended families, friends and neighbours.

These relationships do not simply happen. Much of the energy of communities such as these is dedicated to ensuring that they happen, through education, social sanction, and careful protection of human institutions. Children are habituated into virtues and rules of conduct. They learn to value the 'We' as well as the 'I', and this is rarely easy to achieve. But the rewards of such an order are great. It creates an island of interpersonal meaning in a sea of impersonal forces. It redeems individuals from solitude. Morality is civilisation's greatest attempt to humanise fate.

The power of this vision is that it locates the source of action within ourselves. It restores the dignity of agency and responsibility. It leads us to see our lives not as the blind play of external causes – the genome, the free market, international politics, the march of technology – but as a series of choices in pursuit of the right and good, choices in which we are not left unguided but for which a vast store of historical experience lies at our disposal. It reminds us that the acts we perform, the decisions we take, make a difference: to our family, to our friends and associates, to our sense of a life well lived. It teaches us to cherish and sustain the relationships – marriage, the family, friendships, communities – which give us strength as we face the uncertainties of an open future. It removes the randomness of a life lived in border skirmishes between our desires and those of others. It allows us to see ourselves as on a journey, begun by those who came before us and whose histories we share, to be continued by those who come after us of whose hopes we are the guardians, a journey towards a remote but intelligible destination, the good society. Above all it tells us where to begin if we seek to change the world.

Rabbi Israel Salanter once said: 'When I was young, I wanted to change the world. I tried, but the world did not change. So I concentrated on changing my town, but my town did not change. Then I turned to my family, but my family did not change. Then I realized: first I must change myself.' This, the authentic moral voice, is a perspective we are in danger of losing. Against it is set a world view that argues the opposite, that if you want to change the individual you first have to change the world. We are the product of social, economic, psychological or genetic causes. Our personalities are relatively fixed, and transformation can only come about through social engineering or cultural revolution. Moral striving is at best irrelevant, at worst repressive and psychologically harmful. The only agents who can effect change are governments. As individuals we should acquire self-esteem by accepting ourselves for what we are. There is much that is initially attractive about this view, but it will be my argument that when it is put into practice it creates the harmful social pathologies we witness in Western societies as the twenty-first century begins.

For some time, I have felt an increasingly urgent need for a national conversation – a moral debate – that we seem repeatedly on the point of having but never quite achieve. It would not arrive at complete consensus, nor would we wish it to. But it would begin a process that would reinforce many of the values we share but have lost the confidence publicly to express. It might point the way to a more effective interaction between schools and families, governments and local communities, state action and voluntary initiative – in short, between our highly institutionalised political structures and our highly local sources of moral energy. It might enable us to see more clearly than we do at present the connections between morality and politics, between 'civil society' (a phrase I will later explain) and the state. Not least, it might let us see what has been there all along but has somehow been masked from view: that we are and remain moral beings despite all evidence and argument to the contrary. What has been eroded is not our moral sense but the institutions which sustain it and the language in which it is expressed.

2

Losing Confidence

A person caught in a philosophical confusion is like a man in a room who wants to get out but doesn't know how. He tries the window but it is too high. He tries the chimney but it is too narrow. And if he would only *turn around*, he would see that the door has been open all the time.

A *picture* held us captive. And we could not get outside it, for it lay in our language and language seemed to repeat it to us inexorably.

Ludwig Wittgenstein[1]

IN THE SUMMER of 1994 I visited Sherborne House, the centre for young offenders so vividly described in Roger Graeff's book *Living Dangerously*. I was making a television documentary about the family and I wanted to meet people with varied experiences of childhood, to try and understand how those early years had affected their later lives. The young men I met with were in their late teens. Most had been living a life of crime – theft, robbery, occasional violence – for several years. The centre was their last chance of avoiding a custodial sentence. It gave them the opportunity to learn practical skills in the hope that they would be able to find jobs and avoid the bleak prospect of a future of prison and hopelessness.

Once the initial suspicions had abated they spoke freely and with deep feeling. The moment that unlocked the floodgates came when I asked them what kind of fathers they would like eventually to be. They spoke of how they wanted to be there for their children, supportive, available, teaching them how not

[1] Norman Malcolm, *Ludwig Wittgenstein: A Memoir*, London, Oxford University Press, 1966, 51; Ludwig Wittgenstein, *Philosophical Investigations*, Oxford, Blackwell, 1963, para. 115.

to go down the road they had travelled. All of them came from broken homes. Talking about their dreams for the future reminded them of what they had experienced in the past: fathers who were absent, or who left suddenly, or were violent. None of them made excuses for the crimes they had committed, nor did they express remorse. Instead they expressed an air of sad inevitability about the unfolding of their stories, as if they felt that what had happened to them was simply what occurs when you leave children alone without structure, stability and guidance. They knew that what they had done was wrong, perhaps not intrinsically wrong but the kind of behaviour that ends badly one way or another. Their view of parenthood was intensely moralistic. Most of them said that they would be strict disciplinarians with their children. As they spoke about the life they wanted to build and thought about the one they had experienced, several of them broke down in tears.

I thought about that occasion many times in the months that followed. I came away from it with powerfully mixed feelings. The young offenders were likeable people. They had plans for the future. They had a strong moral sense. They wanted to get jobs, get married, build homes, have children, and be attentive, if strict, parents. But they were trapped in a moral maze from which it was difficult to see a way out. They had no childhood experience on which to build. None had strong homes or communities to which they could return. Out in the world after their time at the centre, they would find themselves facing an arduous journey with little help from others. The director told me, as I was leaving, that she saw only the most remote chance of their being able to change. They had too few networks of support.

Two years later I found myself in an encounter at the opposite end of the social spectrum. At a formal dinner I was seated next to the wife of a peer, a sincerely committed Christian, who together with her husband had led a distinguished life of voluntary public service. As the conversation unfolded it became clear that she had deep anxieties about her role as a parent. Was she right, she wondered, to say prayers every evening with her ten-year-old son, or to insist that her fifteen-year-old daughter should be home before midnight? It was immediately clear that she was a marvellous parent. She loved her children, spent a great deal of time with them, and understood the importance of giving them a framework of rules, clear, consistent, explained, and gradually relaxed as they grew older. Their home was everything the Sherborne young offenders wished they had had in their childhood. How different their lives might have been had they had it.

What she conveyed, though, was an overwhelming lack of self-confidence as a parent. This had nothing to do with her personality, which in every other respect was assured and poised. It had everything to do with the cultural environment. Her idea of parenthood was at odds with what was happening around her and her children. Was she wrong not to leave them free to do their own thing, make their own mistakes, find their own religious faith?

I told her what I believed, namely that they would do this anyway. Children explore. But what she was doing was the most important thing any parent can do for a child. She was giving them a map so that if they got lost they could find their way back. She was giving them habits – of discipline, structure, consideration for others, respect for rules and the capacity to defer the gratification of instinct – that would serve them well whatever path they chose. She was teaching them how to be a child and how to be a parent, how to handle relationships and negotiate a recalcitrant world. She was passing on a tradition, her own Christianity, which, though they might one day and for a while reject, they would at least know from within.

She was giving them the rules and virtues, the grammar and semantics, of the language of morality. Far from inhibiting their development she was giving them the preconditions of maturity: civility, self-control, due but not uncritical deference to authority, the capacity to argue your case and if need be accept defeat, above all a coherent frame of reference within which to build a life. I thought: how inspiring to meet so superb a parent, but how tragic to find one who is doing almost everything right half-convinced that she is doing everything wrong.

One of the guests at the dinner was the Archbishop of Canterbury. Two days later he introduced a debate in the House of Lords 'to call attention to the importance of society's moral and spiritual well-being'. No sooner had it been heralded than it was denounced by a fellow peer. 'This will be just one boring sermon from the Archbishop, but there is nothing we can do if he wants to navel-gaze. Then we will get all the right-wing peers ranting about bringing back hanging and sex education in schools. It will be a self-indulgent farce. Morality should be left to individuals' consciences.'

In the event the Archbishop's words were careful and constructive. His intention, he said, was not to lament the loss of a mythical 'golden age'. Young people today had a 'strong moral concern'. Nor was he talking of matters that concerned only the religious. What we teach children affects us all. His target was the view that morality is a purely relative or private affair, and therefore not something that can be taught. This, he argued, was simply not true. There are values we share and which bind us together as a society. There are rules we need to learn if we are to sustain relationships. They can be taught by families, schools and the wider community. They are part of our cultural tradition and for many people an aspect of their religious faith. Admittedly there can be difficult and highly personal decisions, but this is not because we have no shared sense of what is right, but rather because two rights can sometimes conflict. The Archbishop's concern was to 'support those who are seeking to explore in dialogue the shared values and beliefs which we hold dear and which as a society we expect schools to transmit to our children'.

The response was an explosion of righteous indignation. Several newspapers accused the Church of England of hypocrisy. It was, they said, not part of the solution but part of the problem. The church had failed in the past to give a moral lead. How dare it now instruct the nation in how to behave? The self-contradiction in the charge – here after all was a leader with the courage to lead – was lost amidst the sound and fury.

One paper led with the headline 'School Anger at Carey's Lesson in Moral Duty' and spoke of a 'scornful attack from teaching unions'. The reflex indignation on the part of educators overlooked the Archbishop's insistence that teachers could not be expected to bear the burden of moral guidance alone. They needed support from families and other role models. 'I want to emphasise most strongly,' he said, 'how wrong it would be to load all our anxieties about the spiritual and moral state of society onto schools.'

Some of the attacks were little short of apoplectic. Under the headline 'No More Feel-Smug Factor', a respected journalist responded the next day in *The Times*. He described the Archbishop's speech in the following terms: 'a fit of morality', 'waffle', 'bland', 'platitudes', 'vacuities', 'a total mish-mash'. Dr Carey, he said, 'presumes to hurl down moral absolutes on the teenagers, parents and teachers of Britain . . . Since the dawn of time, the old have decried the young as degenerate and summoned a crusade to lift them from moral squalor. It is the hoariest cliché in the book and those who utter it always find someone else to blame.' What then did he propose in its place? 'Moral choices, to be made by free citizens after due debate.' But this was precisely what the Archbishop was proposing. The attack bore no relation to the speech, which explicitly disavowed the language of 'degeneracy' or 'crusade'. This was journalism untainted by accuracy. It was contempt elevated to a form of art.

Most attention focused upon a moment that occurred shortly before the debate began. The Archbishop had been invited to express his views on a radio programme that morning. The interviewer, allowing him to relax through a series of predictable challenges, then bowled his fast delivery. Wasn't it a strange coincidence, he said, that on the very day the Archbishop was calling for higher national standards of morality, terms had just been announced for the divorce between the Prince and Princess of Wales? Would the Archbishop care to comment on the relationship between the church's moral values and the behaviour of the royal couple? It was a trap, seen and taken as such. If he uttered a condemnation, the next day's papers would be full of headlines like 'Archbishop Attacks Royal Family', and 'Royal Rebuke from Lambeth'. If he did not, he would be accused of equivocating, vacillating and failing to give guidance.

Like any practised interviewee, the Archbishop changed the subject, and like any seasoned interviewer, the presenter came back a second and third time, eventually provoking the reply from Dr Carey that he 'did not want to get involved in that particular question'. This was the moral response. There is a world of difference between advocacy of a moral code and an *ad hominem* condemnation of named individuals. There is a time to teach ideals and a time to comfort, or at least be silent about, those whose lives have been derailed. But such nuances are lost in the world of soundbites and aggressive interviewing. One could almost picture the scene: the interviewer leaping in the air and turning towards the umpire to see the Archbishop given out, leg before wicket. The newspapers, the next day, could hardly contain their *Schadenfreude*. The church had been defeated. Cynicism was triumphant. The one note of sanity was provided by a leader in one of the Sunday papers which asked what might have happened had Moses descended from Mount Sinai only to be confronted by a hostile radio journalist. The message of even the greatest of the prophets might have become muddled.

What is the connection between these three episodes? Reading them in the reverse order, they tell a story. When moral leaders cannot be heard above the noise of scepticism, good people begin to doubt their standards. Parents wonder whether they should not leave their children more alone. The principles on which the family is built lose public legitimacy. More marriages split apart. More children grow up without fathers. Some, hurt by the well-documented effects of broken families on children, turn to crime. A career that begins with minor theft can turn, in the natural course of events, to violence. And violence claims victims, especially the young, the old, the weak, the defenceless.

It is not that there is a causal link between these processes. Social science, aware of the complexity of almost all human behaviour, is rightfully reticent about attributing causes. But there is a moral environment, a public mood. It can be sensed at all times in all places. Can you walk safely down the street alone? Under stress, are people polite or abusive? When an assault takes place in a crowded square, do people watch or intervene? The answers would not be the same for London in the 1790s when there was street violence much like our own, as they would in the 1890s, when order was far more pronounced. They would not be the same in all parts of the country. When our son went on holiday in the north of Scotland recently, his rented bicycle developed a fault. The owner of the bicycle shop lent his car to our son's friend to go and collect him, and told him to leave the bicycle on the side of the road. No one would steal it, he said, and he himself would pick it up later. In that region there was a trust missing elsewhere, and trust, as in this case, can be part of the atmosphere, a public graciousness, not just a private relationship.

It is often assumed that we have moved beyond morality, that instead of thinking in terms of shared, objective values we now make choices on the basis of subjective inclination. The decisions we make have, and are meant to have, validity for us alone. We would not seek to impose them on others, and we resent it if others try to share their values with us. The old ideas, that there are moral rules and moral knowledge, that there are virtues we need to learn, have gone, never to return. That, at any rate, is the prevailing orthodoxy, reiterated daily in the media. Those like the Archbishop who attempt to challenge it are subjected to a trial by public humiliation not unlike the 'ordeals' of the Middle Ages. But this apparent consensus does not fit the reality I encounter every day.

The people I meet, from anxious parents to young offenders, have a strong and active moral sense. They know that violence, theft, and robbery are wrong. They know that drugs are an evasion, not an embrace, of reality. They know that children need stable homes and that they do better in families where both parents are present and stay together. They know we do best when we are given responsibility and guidance and are held accountable for what we do. They know that almost anything worthwhile – anything in which one can take pride – demands time, effort, willpower, discipline, persistence, self-restraint, the willingness to learn, the authority of teachers, the support of friends. They know the difference between unearned self-esteem and hard-won self-respect. They *know* these things, and all their experience confirms it. The problem is that too much of our culture disconfirms it and denies the fact that we can have moral knowledge at all.

What we can talk about, we can cure. What we cannot talk about eventually takes a heavy toll. In an age in which the most private emotions are paraded in public and the most intimate confessions broadcast to millions, things that used to be public knowledge have become unsayable. Words like virtue, vice, sin, evil, righteousness, modesty, grace, humility and repentance have become the ultimate solecisms. They have taken on the role that was once occupied in our culture by blasphemy and obscenity. Utter them out loud in a crowded room and there is shocked silence and lingering disbelief. The barriers we have erected against moral debate are formidable. Judgement, a quality we once prized, has become judgementalism, 'blaming the victim'. Moral statements are dismissed as moralising. Concern about the weakening of our social framework is described as moral panic. Morality has been exiled from polite conversation.

There is an air of unreality about this situation. For several months Britain was seized by a wave of panic about the infection of cattle with BSE, which had a possible, not yet proven, connection with the death of twelve people from the condition known as Creutzfeldt-Jakob Disease. For several years acute concern has been expressed about an environmental phenomenon, global warming, whose existence is still being debated. These anxieties were justified. A risk however remote, a possible connection however speculative, is worth taking into consideration if we are to do all we can to ensure public safety. Yet the possibility that many of our social ills are related to the way we live and the principles we teach is resisted with a vehemence hard to understand, fateful in its consequences. The relationship between beef-eating and CJD is far more remote and speculative than that between promiscuity and AIDS, or divorce and depressive illness, or fragmented families and child dysfunction, but while we find it possible to debate the one, we find it difficult to talk about the others. Livy's words about ancient Rome are uncomfortably close to us: 'We have reached the point where we cannot bear either our vices or their cure.'

If we are to talk openly about our shared future, moral principles cannot be excluded. They are central to any conversation about what kind of society we seek to create, what kinds of people we aspire to be, and what ideals we wish to hand on to our children. Such conversations have been at the heart of democratic civilisation. In the first half of the nineteenth century they were joined by such figures as Coleridge, Southey and Carlyle; in the second half by Dickens, Ruskin, Matthew Arnold and William Morris. Earlier this century R. H. Tawney, T. S. Eliot, George Orwell and Archbishop William Temple set out their very different visions of ethics, politics and culture. None of these was a sermonic exhortation to virtue, but they were expressions of moral conviction none the less. Their assumption was that society is, at least in part, constituted by its image of itself, and that this must regularly be tested, probed, and if need be, criticised. The idea that moral language is essentially private and that a nation is no more than the arena in which individuals do their own thing would have struck them as absurd. That, they would have said, is not a society but the absence of a society, not a culture but the destruction of the possibility of culture. Surely they were right.

I need, therefore, to make one thing clear at the outset. As I understand it, moral judgement is about the future not the past, about the ideals to which we aspire, not about condemnation or accusation. Our abortive moral conversations – like those in the wake of the murder of James Bulger (1993) or during the International Year of the Family (1994) – fail because almost immediately they descend to the question of blame. Who is responsible? Politicians blame religious leaders. Religious leaders condemn the politicians. Parents accuse the schools. Teachers reproach the parents. Thinkers on the right indict the liberalism of the 1960s. Thinkers on the left point the finger to the free market philosophy of the 1980s. In the dock stand the usual suspects: affluence, poverty, genetic programming, original sin, footballers, pop singers, and the media. The air is thick with mutual recrimination and there are only two things on which we can agree. Someone is to blame, and it isn't me.

I want to move away from the language of blame. It is not helpful. It produces defensiveness, self-justification and counter-accusation. It turns us into a finger-pointing society, which is not the place most of us would choose to live. It does not meet the standards of generosity and charity demanded by our great religious traditions, almost all of which teach that judgement in the sense of blame belongs to God alone. It confuses righteousness with self-righteousness (a great Jewish teacher once said: 'I prefer a wicked man who knows he is wicked to a righteous man who knows he is righteous'). Above all, it is not true.

Most politicians I know struggle seriously with the dilemmas of power. Most religious leaders think deeply about the conflict between condemnation and compassion. Parents wrestle with the pressures of work or unemployment and try to do their best. Teachers are the unsung heroes of our society, under-recognised, underpaid, and often desperately unsupported. None of us is or should be immune to criticism, but we do not need to be told by those who neither know nor understand that we are not doing our job. It is demotivating and undeserved. More importantly, it misconceives the nature of the moral enterprise.

To build, it is not necessary to blame. The leader of a team knows that after losing a match the best way to prepare for the next encounter is not to make accusations about whose fault the defeat was. It is to build the morale of the players so that they can, honestly and together, face the fact of defeat, analyse why, and work out how to avoid repeating the same mistake a second time. It is no dishonour to lose. To play a game means being willing to take that risk. What is fatal, however, is the inability to learn. This can happen for two quite different reasons: because we are convinced we can never win, or because we are sure that losing was someone else's fault. That is the difference between, and the common outcome of, being de-moralised and being over-moralised.

The moral tradition most familiar to us, that of the Judaeo-Christian ethic, suggests that our failures are forgiven as soon as they are acknowledged. It says that risk is of the essence of the moral life, as it is of learning generally, and that it is often less important to be right than to be open: to wisdom, experience, the voice of tradition and the insights of the present. The true moral leader is the captain of the team, the one who has faith in us even when we have lost faith in ourselves, who is always there when we call on him but rarely when we do not; who never second-guesses us or steps in front of us when we are about to kick the ball; who allows us to make our own mistakes but who asks us to take time out for reflective moments in which we can recognise that they are mistakes. That is a religious vision, but you do not have to be religious to share its essential outlines.

The inability to talk about the public dimension of morality closes off to us one of our most important problem-solving resources. It separates the individual from society and suggests that whatever we do affects us alone, and therefore whatever can be done on a larger scale is beyond our direct participation. This induces a potentially tragic and quite unfounded sense of helplessness. For many centuries, the moral world view allowed people to feel connected to one another, joining their individual striving to a larger world of common purpose. That connectedness is part of the logical geography of hope. To reconnect we need to recover confidence in a way of speaking which we have never forgotten but which has become systematically undermined. That, as Ludwig Wittgenstein said in a memorable line in his *Philosophical Investigations*, is part of the task of thought and its greatest aspiration. 'What is your aim in philosophy?' he asked. 'To show the fly the way out of the fly bottle.'[2] The fly keeps banging its head against the glass in a vain attempt to find a way out. The one thing it forgets to do is to look up.

[2] Ludwig Wittgenstein, op. cit., para. 309.

3

Language and Violence

Vulgar relativism is an invisible gas, odourless, deadly, that is now polluting every free society on earth. It is a gas that attacks the central nervous system of moral striving. This most perilous threat to the free society today is neither political nor economic. It is the poisonous, corrupting culture of relativism. The people know this, while the intellectuals do not. If our intellectual betters knew this, they would be sounding the alarm.

Michael Novak[1]

IN AMERICA, PRO- and anti-abortion lobbies meet in head-on conflict between the 'right to choose' and the 'right to life'. Abortion clinics are fire-bombed. A doctor who performs abortions is shot. In Britain animal rights activists attack research stations, university laboratories, butcher's shops, meat delivery lorries and shops selling furs. Between 1990 and 1992 Scotland Yard recorded 3,073 crimes related to the animal liberation campaign,[2] the cost of a great collision between animal and human rights. From 1989 onwards the publication of Salman Rushdie's *The Satanic Verses* provoked a wave of confrontations throughout the world, resulting in several deaths. Once again rights were in conflict. Which is the more fundamental, the right to freedom of speech or the right to protection against blasphemy? As I write, in an Orthodox vicinity of Jerusalem each Sabbath there are violent confrontations between secular and religious Jews over the opening or closure of a main thoroughfare. Which takes priority, the right of free movement or the right to maintain the character of a neighbourhood?

To each of these questions, given the terms in which they

---

[1] Michael Novak, *Awakening from Nihilism*, 19.
[2] Anne Glyn-Jones, *Holding Up a Mirror*, 549–51.

are framed, there is no answer. Rights present themselves as absolute claims, 'trumps' as Ronald Dworkin calls them.[3] They cut a path through the complexities of moral deliberation – consideration of consequences, weighing of conflicting principles – and make a direct appeal to unconditional entitlement. When rights conflict, there is no language of resolution. Instead, all too often, there is violence, protest and direct action.

The way we think and speak affects the way we act, and our moral vocabulary is our most important resource for mediating between contending interests or desires. If that language is strong and wide, then we have an expansive public square in which to meet and talk about our differences and work out a way in which they can be equitably resolved. A rich repertoire of shared concepts allows us to develop the liberal virtues of mutual respect, toleration, and the kind of practical compromise that does not entail compromise of conviction. It encourages us 'to moderate our claims in the face of the reasonable claims of others, to balance, and split at least some of our differences'.[4] If our language becomes attenuated, conversation can come to seem like two cars meeting head-on in a narrow street when neither driver is willing to back up. 'Rights talk' – not the concept of human rights itself, but a moral discourse that becomes dominated by rights to the subordination of all else – can quickly develop this character. As Mary Ann Glendon of Harvard Law School puts it, 'Our stark, simple rights dialect puts a damper on the processes of public justification, communication and deliberation upon which the continuing vitality of a democratic regime depends.'[5]

It is not, however, talk of rights alone that erodes the public culture of reasoned conversation. Codes of civility, self-restraint

[3] Ronald Dworkin, 'Rights as Trumps', in Jeremy Waldron (ed.), *Theories of Rights*, 153–67.

[4] Steven Macedo, *Liberal Virtues*, 71.

[5] Mary Ann Glendon, *Rights Talk*, 171.

and politeness have broken down, giving rise to new forms of verbal and physical abuse. A doctor, appearing as part of a television discussion of an illness, is howled down by the audience who disagree with his suggestion that it may be of psychosomatic origin. Politicians confronted by a hostile interviewer storm out of the studio. Motorists break off arguments and engage in direct violence in a new syndrome described as 'road rage'. In an incident of a type becoming all too familiar, during May 1992, in Whiteville, North Carolina, a youth league baseball teacher, aged forty-five, cut the throat of the coach of an opposing team in front of the assembled eight- and nine-year-old players, during an argument about the rules.[6] Increasingly street attacks are justified in terms of the affront given by 'staring' or 'dissing' (behaving disrespectfully). There is no comparison between linguistic and physical violence, but they are ends of a common spectrum, part of a general fraying of the civic bond which allows strangers to meet and differ without either assaulting the integrity or the person of the other.

One of the insights of the Hebrew Bible is that we build worlds with words. 'And God said . . . and there was.' To speak is to bring something into being, in the case of God a physical universe, in the case of humanity, a social universe. When language fails, much else is exposed to danger. Churchill was not the first to prefer 'jaw, jaw' to 'war, war'. In an echoing verse, whose force is often lost in translation, the Bible describes the first murder. 'Cain said to his brother Abel. Then, when they happened to be in the field, Cain rose up against his brother Abel and killed him' (Genesis 4:8). The Hebrew original is deliberately structured to convey the sense of something missing from the sentence. 'Cain said', but we do not hear what he said. The words break off in mid-sentence. When conversation falters, brutality may not be far away. 'Violence,' said Alan Brien, 'is the repartee of the illiterate.' What, in recent years, has happened to our language?

[6] Cited in David Selbourne, *The Spirit of the Age*, 301.

In 1936 A. J. Ayer published a justly famous book, *Language, Truth and Logic*. In it he argued the case for logical positivism in its most extreme form, namely that a sentence can only be meaningful if it can be verified, tested and checked for its truth or falsehood. For the positivists, following a long tradition that goes back to Francis Bacon, there were only two forms of knowledge: observation and reason, the methods of science and logic. Moral language, argued Ayer, fails to pass this test. Two people can differ over whether something is good or not, but logic alone may not resolve the argument, nor may scientific experiment. It follows that moral sentences only seem to say something, whereas in fact they are meaningless. That is not to say that they are pointless. In fact, he suggested, it is quite simple to understand their point. They communicate the feelings of the speaker. They are expressions of emotion. If, for example, I say: 'You were wrong to steal that money', it is merely as if I had said: 'You stole that money' in a peculiar tone of horror.[7] This theory, later known as emotivism, meant that moral language is to be systematically deconstructed. The moral wisdom of the ages turns out to be no more than the feelings of a series of individuals, and feelings are notoriously subjective.

What would the world be like if emotivism were true? A. J. Ayer did not raise the question, since he believed that emotivism was true, and the world was as it was. However, in 1936 very few people thought likewise. Sixty years later, now that his view is more widely held, we are in a better position to judge. If moral arguments are no more than the clash of rival emotions, then the loudest, most intensely felt and forcibly expressed voice wins – not by convincing its opponents, since that is by definition ruled out, but merely by silencing them.[8] A emotivist world is one in which the connection has been broken between moral assertion and reasoned argument. And where reason, shared concepts and commonly held traditions falter, there is no way to secure victory

[7] A. J. Ayer, *Language, Truth and Logic*, 102–20.
[8] See Alasdair MacIntyre, *After Virtue*, 68–9.

other than by the use of force. Hence Alasdair MacIntyre's dire conclusion that 'Modern politics is civil war carried on by other means.'[9]

It was MacIntyre himself who told the most chilling parable about the contemporary state of moral language.[10] Imagine, he says, that at some time in the future there is a widespread revolution against science. There is a series of ecological disasters. Science and technology are blamed. There is public panic. Riots break out. Laboratories are burned down. A new political party comes to power on a wave of anti-scientific feeling and eliminates all science teaching and scientific activity. A century later, the mood subsides. People begin to try to reconstruct what was destroyed. But all they have is fragments of what was once a coherent scientific culture: odd pages from old books, scientific instruments whose use has been forgotten, bits and pieces of information about theories and experiments without the background of knowledge of their context. These pieces are reassembled into a discipline called science. Its terminology and some of its practices resemble science. But the systematic corpus of beliefs which once underlay them has gone. There would be no unitary conception of what science was about, what its practices were for, or what its key terms signified. The illusion would persist that science had been recovered; but it would have been lost, and there would be no way of discovering that it had been lost.

What is conjectured in this parable, MacIntyre argues, is what has actually happened to moral thinking. The Enlightenment and the social processes which accompanied it succeeded in destroying the traditions to which the key terms of morality belonged and within which they had lucidity and coherence. The words survived – good, right, duty, obligation, virtue – but they were now severed from the context which gave them sense. For they had belonged to coherent social orders in which people were shaped by a collective vision, in which there were

[9] Ibid., 236.
[10] Ibid., 1–5.

social roles not chosen but given by birth and tradition, and in which there was a narrative continuity between generations and within individual lives. Those socially given shared meanings have now gone, to be replaced by a world of autonomous choices and individual wills. 'What we possess', says MacIntyre, 'are the fragments of a conceptual scheme, parts of which now lack those contexts from which their significance derived. We possess indeed simulacra of morality, we continue to use many of the key expressions. But we have – very largely, if not entirely – lost our comprehension, both theoretical and practical, of morality.'

According to MacIntyre, then, emotivism or 'vulgar relativism' is the result of a long history of social and intellectual change, including the rise of science and the decline of religion. I agree with this assessment, and tell part of the story later on in the second section of the book. But this is not the whole story, and if it were, we would have more reason to be pessimistic about our future than is the case. It is, I believe, impossible to understand the spread of relativism – the belief that no one moral stance is better than any other – without also realising that it is driven by a profound and altogether moral conviction, namely a belief in the supreme importance of a free society.

To understand how, we have to go back to one of the most influential essays of modern times. Written by Isaiah Berlin, and entitled 'Two Concepts of Liberty', it argued that 'positive' liberty – freedom built on a concrete vision of the good life – had been immensely harmful. It had led, in fact, to the loss of liberty (we recall Rousseau's notorious remark about forcing people to be free). 'One belief, more than any other, is responsible for the slaughter of individuals on the altars of the great historical ideals,' he wrote. 'This is the belief that somewhere, in the past or in the future, in divine revelation or in the mind of an individual thinker, in the pronouncements of history or science, or in the simple heart of an uncorrupted good man, there is a final solution.' Against this our greatest safeguard lies in the recognition that there is no one ultimate truth. Instead there are many ways of living a good life, and they are not necessarily compatible with one another. The fundamental liberty which we should strive to secure is a 'negative' one, namely the ability of each of us, so long as we do not harm others, to pursue our own ends without interference. Berlin quotes with admiration the remark of Joseph Schumpeter: 'To realize the relative validity of one's convictions and yet stand for them unflinchingly, is what distinguishes the civilized man from a barbarian.'[11]

The essay was published in 1958 at the very beginning of what I will later call the second liberal revolution, and it had a widespread impact on the generation of academics and teachers who came to prominence in the 1960s. For many years its thesis was virtually unquestioned and it led to a vast spread of relativism, not so much as a form of scepticism or agnosticism, but as a moral imperative. Allan Bloom opens his famous lament on the intellectual failure of American universities, *The Closing of the American Mind*, with the words: 'There is one thing a professor can be virtually certain of: almost every student entering the university believes, or says he believes, that truth is relative.' He goes on to make it clear that this is a morally held position. Only openness guarantees freedom, and only one who believes in the relativity of truth can be genuinely open. The true believer is a threat to liberty. 'The study of history and of culture teaches that all the world was mad in the past; men always thought they were right, and that led to wars, persecutions, slavery, xenophobia, racism and chauvinism.'[12] In crude terms this is not a bad paraphrase of Berlin's argument, at least as it appeared on the surface. The new dogma of relativism, then, was due less to logical positivism or the breakdown of moral language than to the sincere determination of a post-war, post-Holocaust generation to avoid the possibility of any future 'final solution'.

The irony was that, despite the quotation from Schumpeter,

---

[11] Isaiah Berlin, 'Two Concepts of Liberty', in *Four Essays on Liberty*, 118–72.

[12] Allan Bloom, *The Closing of the American Mind*, 25–6.

Isaiah Berlin was not in any simple sense a relativist.[13] He believed in the integrity of different cultures and their traditions, and wrote eloquently about them. He would certainly have rejected the propositions that all moral convictions are equally valid, or that morality is a subjective affair, or that moralities are simply invented by our choices. But the idea had spread and taken hold. Tragically so, for of all defences of liberty, relativism is probably the worst. If all values are relative, so too is liberty. Toleration and fairness 'can hardly be defended by the claim that no values can be defended'.[14] Belief in relativism plays havoc with our ability to discriminate between good and evil, to justify our beliefs, or to say why one way of life is better than another. James Q. Wilson, a professor at Harvard, reports on his sense of shock when, during a class he was giving on courage during the Holocaust years, 'I found that there was no general agreement that those guilty of the Holocaust itself were guilty of a moral horror. "It all depends on your perspective," one said. "I'd first have to see those events through the eyes of people affected by them," another remarked.' What disturbed Wilson was not that the students were prepared to accept excuses for those who committed acts of mass extermination of innocent human beings, 'but that they began their moral reasoning on the subject by searching for excuses'.[15]

Like Sir Karl Popper, who did much to articulate a similar view of freedom,[16] Berlin was a Jew deeply conscious of the Holocaust and of the immense bloodshed within Stalinist Russia. For both writers, the great enemy of liberty in the twentieth century was totalitarianism. That, perhaps, is why they gave an account so different from previous writers on the subject, and in retrospect so much more vulnerable. The long history of freedom, from the days of Milton – or much earlier, from the biblical story of

[13] See the discussion in John Gray, *Isaiah Berlin*.

[14] See Michael Sandel, Introduction to *Liberalism and its Critics*.

[15] James Q. Wilson, *The Moral Sense*, 8.

[16] In works such as *The Open Society* and *The Poverty of Historicism*. See also his contribution to Susan Mendus and David Edwards (eds), *On Toleration*.

the Exodus[17] – was not vested in the relativity of truth but in the absoluteness of certain moral values: the sanctity of life, the dignity of the individual 'in the image of God', the primacy of right over might, and the accountability of all earthly power to a supreme moral authority. John Locke defended religious toleration on the religious grounds that faith brought about by coercion was not faith, since it was not a free act of the will. Abraham Lincoln, in his great Second Inaugural, denounced slavery by saying that it seemed strange 'that any men should dare to ask a just God's assistance in wringing their bread from the sweat of other men's faces'. As John Plamenatz writes, the development of freedom in the West was brought about as a result of religious ideals. 'Liberty of conscience was born, not of indifference, not of scepticism, not of mere open-mindedness, but of faith.'[18] The relativist defence of freedom is no defence at all.

It is not merely that relativism makes it difficult for us to say why we value liberty. It is that it makes it virtually impossible for us to make public judgements of any kind, or to sustain a coherent moral conversation. That is why our moral language is today dominated by two concepts, autonomy (our right to make our own choices without having to give reasons) and rights (the claims we make against others without having to give reasons). This affects more than the way we speak. It affects the way we live, and not just privately but collectively as well. In particular, it has made a profound difference to *institutions*, the way we structure relationships in society.

Traditionally our institutions have been constructed in terms of moral ideas: rules and virtues, praise and blame, reward and punishment, action and responsibility. However, during the post-war period a whole series of developments has taken place which, in effect, virtually eliminated moral concepts from our major social practices. Among them have been the replacement of punishment as justice and retribution by punishment as treatment;

[17] For the influence of this story on political thought since the seventeenth century, see Michael Walzer, *Exodus and Revolution*.

[18] John Plamenatz, *Man and Society*, vol. 1, 50.

the abandonment in schools of an ethic of achievement in favour of the cultivation of self-esteem;[19] the spread of non-directive counselling and therapies of self-acceptance; the abolition, in welfare, of the connection between benefit and desert; in medical ethics, the loss of absolute standards such as the sanctity of life in favour of utilitarian calculations;[20] the abandonment of marriage as a social norm and its reconceptualisation as 'just another lifestyle choice'; and the replacement of the classic term 'virtues' (socially prized dispositions) by the more modern and quite different word 'values' (individually selected preferences).

These changes have happened gradually, so that we can easily fail to notice their revolutionary character. Collectively they amount to an unprecedented experiment throughout Western liberal democracies to create a society outside a Judaeo-Christian frame of reference or, to put it another way, without morality as traditionally conceived. The classic view was that some ways of life are better than others. The task of society is to protect those ways of life, as far as possible without coercion or recourse to law. Hence, its most important institutions are the family and education, the twin vehicles through which society passes on its accumulated wisdom to the next generation. Through these and other experiences of childhood, the individual achieves maturity by acquiring a conscience – by internalising rules and habits of behaviour that at first have been imposed from the outside, by parents, teachers, and other childhood influences. He or she, we say, becomes socialised. This is not a mysterious process. It is akin to the way we learn a language. We enter a universe of sounds which at first seem random, but with remarkable speed we discover a system of meanings which allow us to communicate with others so long as we obey certain rules. We take a practice – the English language – which has been formed by countless speakers over many centuries, and make it our own. Write deeds in place of words, moral rules and virtues in place of syntax and semantics, and we

---

[19] See Charles J. Sykes, *Dumbing Down Our Kids*; Melanie Phillips, *All Must Have Prizes*.
[20] See Anne Maclean, *The Elimination of Morality*.

have the traditional view of how we become citizens of a free society. We learn to speak its language.

The more recent view, though, is that matters are, or should be, different. It is false to suppose that some ways of life are better than others. This aspires to a certainty we cannot reach. Worse, it inhibits the individual from making his or her own choices: it restricts the scope of freedom. Therefore institutions should be value-free. They should be neutral between different lifestyles. They should abandon their traditional role of embodying a set of virtues, and instead act simply to enhance the role of choice without making judgements between choices.

It will be my argument that this cannot be done. Trying to create a society without socialisation is like trying to have communication without a language. As soon as we attempt it, we encounter all the problems I have documented. When we lose the language of shared rules and understandings we resort to ways of settling our differences that are violent and damaging to human dignity. But this cannot be proven by mere assertion. We must assemble the evidence and think deeply about it. All I have done thus far is to raise a doubt as to whether it is possible to have praise without blame, law without guilt, reward without responsibility, and a free society without moral institutions. These are not new doubts, though they have only recently resurfaced in the mainstream of debate.

The classic defenders of liberty, though they feared totalitarianism (they called it tyranny), also knew that freedom was at risk from another direction as well: the collapse of a moral order. They contrasted liberty with 'licence' – the freedom to do what you like – and pointed out that a free society is only as secure as the disciplines of self-restraint among its citizens. It was no less a radical defender of freedom than John Stuart Mill who made the point: 'Whenever and in proportion as the strictness of the restraining discipline was relaxed, the natural tendency of mankind to anarchy reasserted itself; the state became disorganized from within; mutual conflict for selfish ends neutralized the energies which were required to keep up the contest against natural causes of evil; and the nation, after a longer or briefer interval of progressive decline, became either the slave of a despotism or the prey of a foreign invader.'[21]

The same argument was made by another equally distinguished liberal, Bertrand Russell. In his *History of Western Philosophy* he noted that the great ages of freedom and creativity had planted the seeds of their own destruction by failing to maintain moral standards. 'What had happened in the great age of Greece happened again in Renaissance Italy,' he writes. 'Traditional moral restraints disappeared, because they were seen to be associated with superstition; the liberation from fetters made individuals energetic and creative, producing a rare florescence of genius; but the anarchy and treachery which inevitably resulted from the decay of morals made Italians collectively impotent, and they fell, like the Greeks, under the domination of nations less civilized than themselves but not so destitute of social cohesion.'[22]

That last phrase, 'destitute of social cohesion', is surely one that resonates with us and with the picture I have been drawing in these chapters. The breakdown it describes has become a real and present danger in the liberal democracies of the West. But this does not leave us powerless. There is an alternative embodied in our great classic traditions, British and American, Judaeo-Christian and republican, religious and humanist. It offers an altogether more expansive and humane conception of liberty, and it is this for which I want to argue. Liberty is not achieved by relativism, value-free practices, and the devastation of our rain-forests of moral language until all that stands are autonomy and rights. That is not the creation of a free society but the beginning of its destruction.

Freedom is a moral accomplishment. It needs strong families, cohesive institutions, habits of civility and law-abidingness, and a widely diffused sense of fellow-feeling. It needs virtues: self-control, decency, politeness, rational reflection and conversation, courage and persistence in the pursuit of ideals, the capacity to work with others, to win untriumphantly and to lose graciously, the ability to admire and sometimes to revere. It needs the carefully

[21] John Stuart Mill, *Essays on Politics and Culture*, ed. Gertrude Himmelfarb, 137.
[22] Bertrand Russell, *History of Western Philosophy*, 18–19.

cultivated disciplines of dialogue and mutual respect for those with whom we disagree. It needs principles, held not with relative but absolute conviction: the sanctity of human life, the dignity of the individual as moral agent, and the moral claims made on us by the afflicted, the vulnerable and those without power. It needs belief in the centrality of responsibility, and hence choice, and hence of a society that respects choice. It needs institutions which teach these principles and inculcate these virtues, and it needs role models who exemplify them and inspire our own efforts. It needs a language in which these things can be said, and shared, and respected, and owned. When moral language breaks down – as it has broken down – much else is at risk, including freedom itself. That is why we must learn again how to speak together of such things.

4

Public Spaces

If the institutions of democracy and capitalism are to work properly, they must coexist with certain premodern cultural habits that ensure their proper functioning. Law, contract, and economic rationality provide a necessary but not sufficient basis for both the stability and prosperity of postindustrial societies; they must as well be leavened with reciprocity, moral obligation, duty toward community, and trust, which are based in habit rather than rational calculation. The latter are not anachronisms in a modern society but rather the sine qua non of the latter's success.

Francis Fukuyama[1]

NOT FAR FROM where we live, in north-west London, is Regent's Park. Completed in 1827 and opened to the public in 1838, it is one of John Nash's finest achievements. Stretching across some five hundred acres – originally a hunting ground of King Henry VIII – it is a glorious mixture of lakes, tree-lined avenues, open spaces for games, and flower-beds that for half the year are an impressionist masterpiece of blazing colour. There are coffee shops and restaurants, a zoo and an open-air theatre and a magnificent rose garden. There are places for children to play and for people to have picnics or row boats on the lake or simply stroll and enjoy the view. Around it are the great Nash terraces, originally villas, now luxury apartments, with their Corinthian columns, domed towers and decorated façades. I don't know enough about landscape gardening or domestic architecture to appreciate the finer points of this complex creation, but it is varied and very beautiful, and like millions of others, I am glad it's there.

When the French historian Hippolyte Taine visited it in 1864,

[1] Francies Fukuyama, *Trust: The Social Virtues and the Creation of Prosperity*, 11.

41

he was struck by its quiet. Coming into it from the bustle of the Victorian streets, he found it 'a solitary place with no noise of traffic; London is forgotten and you are quite alone'. I don't have the chance to go there often, but when I do, that is not the impression I get. At most times of the day it is full of people, relaxing, talking, drinking coffee, reading the papers, jogging, walking, exercising the dog, meeting friends, or just enjoying the sight of other people enjoying themselves. The point about it is that it is a public place. It is somewhere where we can all go, on equal terms. It is surrounded by private homes, places where I and most of the people who love the park know we could never afford to live however much we would like to do so. But that regret is tempered by the fact that something far more magnificent, the park itself, is ours. In it we are equal citizens. And because we enjoy it and want it to be there, we keep to the rules, usually without having to be told. We keep radios quiet, dogs on a lead, put our litter in the baskets, return a passing stranger's smile and otherwise respect people's privacy. That is part of what makes it a gracious place.

For me the park is a metaphor for a concept I have been inching towards without yet spelling it out, namely *society*. Society is a vague and complicated idea, and it is easier to say what it isn't than what it is. It isn't the state, it isn't the market, and it isn't a mere aggregation of private individuals. Walk around London and you can more or less locate these other ideas. Around Westminster are the great institutions of government, the Houses of Parliament, Downing Street, the Home and Foreign Office, the residences and arenas of power. Around the City and in every high street are offices and shops where exchanges take place, where money passes hands and goods and services are bought and sold. Away from these buzzing centres of activity are the streets of private houses or apartment blocks where people lead private lives whose content we will never know. So we can identify the state, the market, and the private domain. But where is society?

The simple answer is that it is everywhere in general and nowhere in particular. It is an abstract concept, but we encounter its presence wherever we go, from the 'Good morning' we share with neighbours to the television programmes we watch at night.

But should someone say that is still too vague to understand, I would show them the park. That is a public place, accessible to all, where we go not as voters or consumers but simply to enjoy the sights and sounds of a fine landscape which no one in particular owns. We go there because not everything in life is politics or business, and because not everything else is private, however splendid our own home or garden may be. We didn't create the park, but in a certain sense we maintain it by what we do, or are careful not to do, when we are there. So there are things we own collectively and maintain informally, even though we enjoy them as individuals, each in our own way. Whatever we share, without transactions of power or exchange, is society.

The issues I have been talking about – rising crime, the breakdown of the family, loss of civility, the erosion of moral language – are *social* problems, and that is what makes them easier to recognise than to cure. On the one hand they cannot be solved by my acting alone as an individual. If I am polite, it does not stop other people being rude. If I am law-abiding, that does not end crime; it merely makes one less criminal. On the other, these problems cannot be solved, in and of themselves, by governments. There can be laws, and police to enforce them. But laws touch only the surface of social life, checking its most harmful manifestations. As Martin Luther King said, laws can 'restrain the heartless'; they cannot 'change the heart'. They can prevent us from doing harm, but they cannot teach us to do good. An American justice, Judge Learned Hand, once put this very powerfully. He said: 'I often wonder whether we do not rest our hopes too much on constitutions, upon laws and upon courts. These are false hopes; believe me, these are false hopes. Liberty lies in the hearts of men and women; when it dies there, no constitution, no law, no court can save it; no constitution, no law, no court can even do much to help it.'[2]

Order, then, needs not only law but the widespread habit of law-abidingness. Society needs social virtues, much as our

---

[2] Judge Learned Hand, 'The Spirit of Liberty', in Irving Dilliard (ed.), *The Spirit of Liberty*, New York, Knopf, 1960, 189–90.

enjoyment of the park depends upon its users respecting it and the other people who use it. When these habits break down, we need not just law but collective resolve – many people deciding together to save something they love. So social problems are of their essence matters that lie somewhere *between* the individual and the state, between the individual who makes choices and the state which makes laws. That is why social problems are intimately related to moral institutions, because it is these which have traditionally mediated between the individual and the state.

Consider a family: father, mother and children. They live, eat and relax together, though each wants times and spaces where they can be alone. There are certain rules which bind them together, without which they would find it difficult to get along. Let us suppose that they include such things as this: that on at least some nights of the week they eat together, that not everyone talks at once, that there is a roughly equitable sharing of responsibilities for cutting the grass, doing the dishes, feeding the cat and making the beds, and that when mum or dad say that it's time to go to bed, there are rituals of protest followed by reluctant obedience. Sometimes the rules break down, as they do in every family. There are arguments, 'scenes', minor rebellions. These are followed by the routines of reconciliation – someone says 'Sorry', he or she is forgiven, order is restored, and love reaffirmed. In this sequence of everyday transactions we witness, in miniature, the making and sustaining of the moral life.

The family is made up of individuals. But it exists because each is willing to place limits on the pursuit of his or her own desires. This can range from Paul being quiet for a moment, even though he has something to say, in order to give Susan a chance to speak, to Simon giving up an evening watching his favourite television serial to go and collect Jane who has been stranded at the office because public transport services are on strike. These rules of self-restraint and concern for others are often informal and unarticulated, like a language we learn to speak before we even know that there are such things as grammar. They are followed not because the members of the family do not value individuality or privacy. On the contrary, it is precisely the family that gives them the confidence to be who they are as individuals, knowing that they are loved by others who will be around if they need help or encouragement or sympathy or advice.

Deep beneath the surface of this family are certain fundamental concepts: fidelity, loyalty, responsibility, authority, obedience, justice and compassion. Together they define the relationships of the parents and children to one another. They frame a series of expectations: that neither husband nor wife will commit adultery, that when the children are young they will do what they are told, sometimes (though as rarely as possible) without fully understanding why, that parental requests will be consistent, fair and in the long-term interests of the children, and that the members of the family will not walk out on one another or ignore a cry for help. Except in extreme situations, these things do not need to be spelled out, because the family is a social institution. It is not something its members have invented, any more than they have made the language they speak. It is something they have inherited from the culture – from habit or custom, or the example of their parents, or possibly religious teaching. But when one of the basic rules is broken, there is a breach in the wall of trust, and unless it is mended the family will not be the same again.

The family is often thought of as belonging to the sphere of private life, but it is easy to see how it is the birthplace of the social virtues. It teaches us that the space we seek to create for ourselves is dependent on our being able to rely on other people with whom we have to establish relationships of predictability and mutuality. These relationships do not rest on the basis of power or exchange. A family in which getting along together was secured only by bullying and the threat of violence on the one hand, or by putting a monetary value on services rendered on the other, would not be a family. It would not be held together by the unspoken bonds of habit and reciprocity. It would not, to put it at its simplest, be a place of trust. Society, like its smallest component, the family, is a moral institution built on and sustained by trust. How does this relate to the argument I have begun to unfold in the previous chapters?

In chapter 2 I spoke about our reluctance to discuss morality in public, and in chapter 3 about our commitment to relativism as the basis of freedom. These phenomena are connected – they are a strong defence of privacy. When the subject of morality is raised in the public domain we suspect that someone is trying to impose his or her own standards in an area where we wish, and feel entitled, to be left alone. The conversational barriers we build around such conversations are like the walls we build around our homes. They are fences against the intrusion of strangers. We have homes because we want private spaces. We make choices because we want private lives. Moral talk about things-in-general has come to seem to us like a form of trespass into territory where it has no right to be.

This intuition is surely right as far as it goes. But a city is more than private houses. It is made up of parks, streets, shops, pubs, restaurants, libraries and museums, places we can enter although they don't belong to us. Some we own collectively because they belong to the nation or town of which we are a part. Some we do not own at all but we go there to get the things we need. A city is made up of this great mix of private and public places, and the quality of our lives is affected by the kind of environment they constitute.

The same applies to our moral world. Some of our ideals and aspirations are intensely private. They are ours and no one else's. But we have relationships with colleagues and friends. We have encounters with strangers. We are influenced by the way others behave. To a considerable degree our lives are shaped by institutions – families, schools, businesses – whose character has been moulded as much by custom and convention as by the conscious choice of specific individuals. The public media we watch, read and listen to every day embody values no less than they inform or entertain. Even our most private ideals are shaped by a public culture, by the books we read, the films we watch, the music we hear, the role models we adopt, the friends we make. A morality without public dimensions is as inconceivable as a city without pavements or roads, and it makes a difference whether they are straight and safe. The things we share, and for whose maintenance we bear collective responsibility, we must be able to talk about, and for this we need a public language of shared values rather than private claims, the claims of autonomy and rights. We need, in short, to be able to talk about the goods we hold in common – the conceptual equivalents of Regent's Park – and not just the things we privately own.

Every age has its characteristic preoccupations. For the past century and a half, one of the leading concerns of thinkers in the West has been to preserve for individuals the space to be themselves without interference from others. When that case was first made, in 1859 by John Stuart Mill, it had a mild and limited objective. Mill felt himself surrounded by the suffocating proprieties of Victorian England and felt that human creativity – what he called 'experiments in living' – needed more room in which to develop. A century later, when Isaiah Berlin and Karl Popper came to formulate their views, the subject had become more grave. The enemy was now no longer Victorian busybodies peering into other people's windows, but the totalitarian state and its crushing sacrifice of liberty and lives. As the twentieth century draws to its close, however, it would be fairer to say that we stand in the opposite situation. In today's liberal democracies, it is not that we are too much together but that we are too much alone and seek to learn again how to connect with others in lasting and rewarding ways. If thoughtful individuals a generation ago suffered from claustrophobia, today they are more likely to experience agoraphobia, the fear of the wasteland of our shared domain, the 'naked public square'.

It is not merely that we face problems. It is, rather, the feeling that we have run out of solutions, that we have reached an impasse in our public life. From the mid-1940s to the mid-1970s governments relied on public ownership and control to improve the workings of society. From the mid-1970s to the mid-1990s a different model emerged. Its driving force would be individual initiative. State-owned utilities were privatised. The government would concentrate on managing the economy, reducing inflation and leaving as much as possible to the free market. So a period of individualism replaced an era of collectivism. Each addressed a different problem: collectivism, that of social justice and equality, individualism, that of economic growth and prosperity. But now that our attention has shifted to the social bond itself we are faced with a set of problems to which neither government action nor individual initiative seems adequate.

Crime, violence, family breakdown and depressive illness have risen since the early 1960s under both collectivist and individualist regimes. Neither the one nor the other seemed to help. State action and market forces have both damaged our social institutions in different ways, and neither offers a promising way forward. Further retreat by the state will leave many already vulnerable individuals still more exposed. Greater intervention by the state – more police, draconian punishments, more authoritarian methods – will restrict liberty rather than enhance it. Already we are in danger of a collision between rising expectations of the state and a diminishing willingness to pay for them, and between growing dependence on government action and a reduced belief in its effectiveness.

Ages can be defined by their anxieties. Michael Sandel, Professor of Government at Harvard University, has recently written of what he calls the 'two concerns at the heart of our discontent'. The first is 'the fear that, individually and collectively, we are losing control of the forces that govern our lives'. The second is 'the sense that, from family to neighbourhood to nation, the moral fabric of community is unravelling around us'.[3] These are problems less of governments and economics than of social institutions and relationships. When I first raised these concerns, in my 1990 Reith Lectures,[4] I sensed that mine was a lonely voice. The subjects about which I chose to speak – family, community, morality, and the fragmentation of culture – seemed eccentric at the time. Since then they have come to dominate our thoughts about the future. A new political language is in the making. If the dominant ideology in the 1960s was collectivism, and in the 1980s individualism, the key word as we approach the millennium is *communitarianism*.

It is a broad term, perhaps too broad. Some of the figures widely regarded as its protagonists – Alasdair MacIntyre for example – have explicitly disavowed the label. It covers a wide variety of

[3] Michael Sandel, *Democracy's Discontent*, 3.
[4] Jonathan Sacks, *The Persistence of Faith*.

concerns and emphases. Some speak of community, others of civil society, some of virtue, others of the 'principle of duty'. Those associated with the new thinking come from both sides of the political spectrum. In the United States they include figures on the right such as Gertrude Himmelfarb, Michael Novak and James Q. Wilson, and representatives of the left like Amitai Etzioni, Robert Bellah and Michael Walzer. In Britain they include cultural conservatives like Roger Scruton, civic conservatives like David Willetts, ethical socialists like A. H. Halsey, Norman Dennis and Melanie Phillips, the 'communitarian liberal' John Gray, and David Selbourne, advocate of what he calls 'civic social-ism'. If there is a common strand to their thought it is the conviction that the health of a society depends not only on its political and economic structures but also on its moral resources and the institutions that give them vitality. The fact that such diverse individuals have converged on this set of concerns is the clearest indication that we are witnessing the birth of a new style of politics.

Such climate changes take place only rarely, and when they do they force us to raise again many of the fundamental questions that at other times are taken as settled. Ages of reflection roughly coincide with ages of transition. So it was with Plato, Aristotle and the travails of the Greek city state, Hobbes and the English civil war, Rousseau, Burke and the French Revolution, Alexis de Tocqueville and the birth of American democracy. Ours is another. Old forms, from the nation-state to the traditional family, are losing their power to generate allegiance, and it is unclear what will take their place. At such times we ask one of the most basic questions of all: what is it that binds us together and enables us to form lasting associations? It is at this, the basement level of our common life, that politics and morality most closely come together.

There is a reason why morality has not been on the public agenda for the past fifty years, other than for periodic laments for the loss of the old order. Quite simply, it was deemed to be irrelevant. Morality, relativised, was seen as the private choices of individuals. The task of the state was to be neutral between such choices, to give everyone as far as possible the resources with which to pursue their vision of the good life, and to mediate impartially when conflict arose. The public conversation was a dialogue scripted for two *dramatis personae*, the individual and the state, or more precisely the *abstract* individual and the *procedural* state. The individual, insofar as he or she entered the civic arena, was the bearer of rights regardless of class, colour, race, religion, birth or background. The state provided services and arbitrated between conflicting claims, but it was not the architect of a way of life or the promoter of a set of virtues among its citizens. In such a dialogue talk about morality is *ultra vires*, against the rules, out of place.

In such a conversation, though, one thing is missing, *society*, and the complex of institutions, habits and shared understandings by which it is sustained. Society, I have argued, is something other than political and market institutions on the one hand, and the disconnected, self-interested decisions of individuals on the other. At the height of the economic liberalism of the 1980s, Margaret Thatcher made the famous remark that 'There is no such thing as society'. But there is, and when it begins to disintegrate, we all feel the effects. At times of stability we take it for granted. Like the air we breathe, we are barely conscious of it. But ages of transition are different. It is then that morality rejoins the public conversation.

It is one thing to redecorate a private room, another to plan a new town. It is precisely when new towns are envisaged that architects and planners come together to discuss large questions about the environment they want to create: its parks, shops, businesses, streets, transport systems, its civic amenities, its look and feel, the kind of life it will sustain. It is not enough to think about individuals in the abstract and planning regulations in general. Instead they have to think about *this* place, *these* people, *this* landscape, *these* opportunities. Together they frame a question about *character* – the character of the proposed town – and it is a public question, since it will affect how people will live and work together. The words *political* and *civic* derive respectively from the Greek and Latin words for city and they remind us that from time to time our collective life raises questions not unlike those involved in designing a new town.

After the Second World War, under the influence of architects like Le Corbusier, many older neighbourhoods in Britain and the United States were replaced by tower blocks, surrounded by great open spaces of greenery and grass. It seemed the perfect solution, a planned environment, a rational division between private dwellings and shared amenities without the messy complexity of older urban streets. The experiment failed. With astonishing speed the new developments became, in Jane Jacobs' words, 'worse centres of delinquency, vandalism, and general social hopelessness than the slums they were supposed to replace'.[5] Planned neighbourhoods uprooted people, rode roughshod over old loyalties and institutions – the corner shop, the local business – and destroyed the sense of place and belonging. Those blocks are a powerful metaphor for the social order that is now in crisis: the sharp division between individuals pursuing private choices and the state neutral between them, the faceless rectangular architecture of the abstract individual and the procedural state.

These matters require debate, and the strength of a democracy can be measured by the extent to which we are able to deliberate reasonably together, without anger or vituperation, about the kind of society we wish to create and hand on to our children. No one can claim infallible expertise on such matters. The great virtue of democratic debate is that it asks us to reason together rather than have our opinions accepted on the basis of authority or stridency. There are many who have a stake in this debate and whose life experiences qualify them to speak and to be listened to: parents, teachers, employers, employees, police, judges, politicians, civil servants, academics, those who work for charities and other voluntary organisations, indeed all of us as citizens, for we are joint owners of the *polis*, and we have a stake in its future.

A plural society surely means just this: that without any of us sacrificing our privacy on the one hand, our several faiths and ways of life on the other, once in a while we meet and talk about our hopes for the future. Yes, our new town will have private homes. It will also have space for a synagogue, a mosque, a temple and several churches. We will pass each other in the street and exchange festive

---

[5] Jane Jacobs, *The Death and Life of Great American Cities*, 14.

greetings, worshipping separately but not unmoved by the fact that in our different ways we still have something to worship. But we will also have parks, streets, shopping arcades, coffee bars, and it will matter to us that they are places where we can go safely, enjoy one another's company, and let our children play without fear of danger. It will matter too that our children understand what we have made and why, so that they can continue it into the future, changing this, adapting that, but respecting its purposes and conserving its essential features. This will require education, virtues, internalised rules, habits of self-restraint. Civic amenities presuppose collective virtues. Societies do not merely happen; they are, in part, moral achievements.

This brings us to a fundamental question. How are societies formed, and how are they sustained? What institutions do they require? To the history of answers to this question, the most fundamental of all in our common life, I now want to turn.

II

Social
Covenant

5

Political Society, Civil Society

> Whereby it is plainly to be seen, the societies of men among
> themselves, to have been at first sought out for the leading of
> their lives in more safety and quiet: and them first of all to have
> sprung from the love which was betwixt man and wife: from them
> to have flowed the mutual love betwixt parents and their children:
> then the love of brothers and sisters one towards another: and after
> them the friendship between cousins and other kinsmen: and last
> of all the love and good will which is betwixt men joined in
> alliance: which had all at length grown cold, and been utterly
> extinguished, had it not been nourished, maintained and kept
> by societies, communities, corporations and colleges: the union
> of whom hath for a long time maintained many people, without
> any commonwealth, or sovereign power over them.
>
> Jean Bodin[1]

FROM TIME TO time, in their more reflective moments, people
have asked the fundamental question common to both morality
and politics: what is it that leads individuals to form associations
and sustain them over an extended period? Not every thinker has
given the same answer, nor has every society formed the same kinds
of institutions. In fact any complex society is a confusing mixture
of reasons and associations which emerge, like a great river from
its countless streams and tributaries, out of a vast range of histories
and traditions. None the less, sometimes it is helpful to simplify,
to draw a diagram rather than a map, in order to understand what
may be at stake in a social transition. In this chapter I want to tell
two stories that, between them, provide us with a framework for

---

[1] Jean Bodin, *The Six Bookes of a Commonweale*, trans. Richard Knolles, London,
1606; quoted in Robert Nisbet, *The Quest for Community*, 127.

THE POLITICS OF HOPE

understanding much of what has happened in our social landscape over the past few centuries, and with increasing speed for the past thirty years.

Western society was largely formed from two primary influences, ancient Greece and ancient Israel, and it owes their combination and dominance to Christianity, formed in the encounter between these two civilisations. At the height of the Victorian age Matthew Arnold, in *Culture and Anarchy*, made much of the distinction between these two sources: he called them Hellenism and Hebraism. To Hebraism, he said, we owed morality, to Hellenism, culture (I would also add, politics). The one emphasised proper conduct, the other, great flights of the imagination. For Arnold, Victorian society had erred on the side of Hebraism and now needed a greater injection of Hellenism. *Culture and Anarchy* was published in 1869. It is this contrast, though in a different and more modest way, I want to re-explore.

Both Greek and Jewish civilisations have a philosophical tradition. The most distinguished representative of the first is Aristotle, of the second, Moses Maimonides. There are profound similarities between them, not surprisingly since Maimonides was a neo-Aristotelian. But there are differences too, and these are no less telling. Each used a phrase to describe our tendency to form groups. Aristotle described man as a *political* animal.[2] Maimonides described man as a *social* animal.[3] There is a distinction between these two ways of seeing things, and it may help us understand certain tensions in contemporary life. My concern here is not to discuss Aristotle and Maimonides,[4] but simply to meditate on those two phrases, taken out of context and used as metaphors of human association.

I want to suggest that behind them lie two different stories of how individuals move beyond their isolation to form communities. Both are true, but they describe different aspects of our collective

[2] Aristotle, *Politics*, 1253a3.

[3] Maimonides, *Guide for the Perplexed*, II, 40.

[4] Aristotle also in some places called man a social animal, and Maimonides wrote extensively about politics. I am interested in the phrases, and the different emphases that are given to them in different cultures at different times.

life and give rise to different kinds of institution. Man as a political animal creates the institutions of *political society*: states, governments and political systems. Man as a social animal creates the institutions of *civil society*: families, friendships, voluntary associations, charities, congregations and moral traditions. There is a significant contrast between the two and the forms of life to which they give rise. Much of the history of our attempts to live together can be written in terms of their relationship, sometimes close, sometimes distant, with now one, now the other, in the ascendancy. But to understand each, we have to begin at the beginning, in this case with the most famous of all starting-points: 'In the beginning God created heaven and earth.'

The opening chapters of Genesis form one of the great meta-narratives of Western civilisation, and their literary form is designed to draw attention to certain fundamental features of our sense of location within the world. They open with a repeated construction: 'And God said, "Let there be . . ." And there was . . . And God saw that it was good.' The repetition induces a certain mood. The universe unfolds according to a plan and it is good. What breaks the mood is the sudden appearance, in the second chapter, of the phrase 'not good'. Nothing has prepared us for this expression. Thus far we have encountered only God, the natural world and its highest life-form, *Homo sapiens*, the one being on whom the Creator has set His own image. Almost by definition there is no resistance or drama, since there is only one personality, the artist who is not merely fashioning a work of art but also bringing into being the materials out of which it is made. What, in such a universe, can be 'not good'? In a single sentence – five words in the Hebrew – the origin of all love and conflict is set forth. 'It is not good for man to be alone.'

In its initial verses, therefore, the Bible sets out two propositions that will frame its entire vision of mankind. The first affirms the sanctity of the human individual as individual. Every person is in 'the image of God'. The second asserts the incompleteness of the individual as individual. 'It is not good for man to be alone.' Hence the human need for relationship, association, and for stable structures within which these can grow and be sustained. In fact much of the rest of the Hebrew Bible is the story of the unfolding of these relationships, from the nuclear family of Adam and Eve, to the extended family of Abraham and Sarah and their children, to the confederation of tribes in the days of Moses and Joshua, to the sovereign state in the age of kings and prophets.

So the Bible begins with the recognition that it is difficult for human beings to live alone. Almost immediately, though, it recognises that it is also signally difficult for human beings to live together. With Adam and Eve comes conflict, with Cain and Abel, fratricide. By the sixth chapter, the generation of the Flood, 'the earth was full of violence' and a social order was nearing its end in disarray. The problem which has haunted humanity from its origins and which is rarely far from the surface has been posed in its full drama and starkness. How do we move from unbearable isolation to some form of tolerable association? By way of answer, I want to tell two stories, both implicit in the Bible, but quite different in their implications.

The first is told in its most influential form by Thomas Hobbes in the *Leviathan*. Hobbes takes as his starting-point the condition of humanity before any structured form of relationship. He calls it the 'state of nature', and it closely resembles the biblical description of the era of the Flood. As does the Bible, Hobbes pictures a situation of unmediated conflict. When human beings converge without rules or institutions there is an inevitable collision of purposes and desires. People find themselves 'in that condition which is called War; and such a war as is of every man, against every man'. The outcome is simple, and no one has described it more bluntly. In such an environment, said Hobbes, life would be 'solitary, poor, nasty, brutish, and short'.

How then do human beings create societies? Hobbes' answer is this. What drives individuals to form associations is fear of violence and death. Some of us are stronger than others, but none of us is so strong that we are invulnerable to attack. Indeed each of us has reason to fear the pre-emptive attacks of others. Therefore it is in the essential interests of each of us, as a minimal precondition of peace and security, to hand over some of our powers as individuals to a supreme authority which will make laws and enforce them.

This, the social contract, brings into being the 'great Leviathan' of the state, and thus is born *political society* – the central repository of power needed to bring about a social order.

Hobbes' story is a central narrative in the evolution of Western society over the past three centuries. *Leviathan* was published in 1651, but it has certain features that make it a more contemporary work than, say, Locke's treatises on government, or Rousseau's *The Social Contract*, and this will become clear during the course of the presentation. But for the time being, I want to step back from the story and think about the assumptions that lie behind it.

The central character in Hobbes' drama is the individual, the 'I'. Hobbes has a certain amount to say about institutions like the family, but his primary concern is with the individual as such, pursuing his or her own interests, concerned for safety and the protection of life, an individual detached from any binding loyalties to family or friends, community or traditions. This became an extremely important feature of political thought as it has evolved to recent times. In an important modern work, John Rawls' *A Theory of Justice* (1971), a different kind of social contract is envisaged, under different starting conditions, but with this same feature: that it is about an agreement formed by persons for their several interests, regardless of their ties or backgrounds. They are 'abstract' individuals, and their histories, loyalties and loves are regarded as irrelevant to the political contract they make. The hero of Hobbes' story, then, is that peculiarly modern figure, the individual seeking self-preservation.

What motivates the individual? Hobbes' answer is *interests,* not moral commitments. This is not accidental but essential to his way of thinking, because for Hobbes there is no motivation beyond the pursuit of interest. Morality, he claims, is simply a dignified way of talking about desire: 'But whatsoever is the object of any man's Appetite or Desire; that is it which he for his part calleth *Good*; and the object of his Hate, and Aversion, *Evil* . . . There being nothing simply and absolutely so; nor any common Rule of Good and Evil.' This too is a strikingly modern way of speaking: there are no moral absolutes. What we call good is no more than what we as individuals choose or seek or desire. Hobbes, of course, is not saying we are incapable of conferring benefits on others. He would understand the argument that we should give up part of our income to be redistributed by government for the sake of peace and social stability. But that is always because we gain more than we lose thereby. Man as a political animal is driven by calculation of rational self-interest.

It follows that the political arena will be one of conflict. My interests are not yours, and there is no objective moral standard by which we are bound. One of the central issues of politics is the distribution of finite goods – wealth, power or honour – whose short-term character is such that if I have more, you have less. The political domain is therefore peopled by contending claimants, historically institutionalised in the form of classes, interest groups and political parties. That conflict is contained by the use of external power, by legislation or taxation backed up, *in extremis*, by the threat of coercive force – an army or police force. Power, for Hobbes, is the essence of the Leviathan. There therefore arise the perennial questions of politics, namely the forms and legitimation of power. To the first, our answer (not Hobbes') is representative democracy; to the latter, it is that without power, conflicting interests would result in chaos and a return to the state of nature.

Thus is born political society. I have told the story according to Hobbes, but with variations it could have been told according to many other thinkers. Among them I have mentioned John Rawls, and I would add another great modern thinker, Robert Nozick, whose *Anarchy, State and Utopia* (1974) is another modern political classic. The common theme running through this, the single most influential story about our common life for the past three hundred years, is of humanity as an aggregate of rational self-seeking individuals; of society as an arena of conflicting interests; and of the resolution of conflict by a central power given legitimacy by a social contract. In and through this contract, individuals recognise that it is in their interests to yield up part of their freedom to governments, which then become the sole or dominant source of power through which violence is prevented, order maintained, obligations enforced, and conflicts mediated.

I now want to tell a quite different kind of story, beginning at the same starting-point, but using different concepts and evoking a distinct set of themes. The simplest way of proceeding is to ask what actually happens in the Hebrew Bible after the words: 'It is not good for man to be alone'? God creates woman. Man then responds with the first poem in the Bible:

> This is now
> bone of my bone,
> flesh of my flesh;
> she shall be called woman [*ishah*]
> because she was taken from man [*ish*]. (Genesis 2:23)

I have included two Hebrew words, because the Hebrew text contains a nuance often missed in translation. Until this point man has been called *adam*, man-as-part-of-nature (the word *adam* signifies 'that which is taken from the earth'). Now for the first time man is called – indeed calls himself – *ish*, which means man-as-person. Significantly, he does this only after he has named woman. The Bible is suggesting, with great subtlety, that the human person must first pronounce the name of the other before he can know his own name. He or she must say 'Thou' before he can say 'I'. Relationship precedes identity.

In this narrative the primary social bond is not the state, but marriage ('Therefore a man will leave his father and mother and be united to his wife, and they will become one flesh', Genesis 2:24). What kind of bond is this? Clearly, given the way the Hebrew Bible describes it, it is not a Hobbesian contract between two independent individuals, each seeking their own interests. It is instead – in a key word of Jewish thought – a *covenant* (*brit* in Hebrew), and this is neither an alliance of interests nor, strictly speaking, an emotional state. Instead it is a bond of identity, as if to say: 'This is part of *who I am*.'

This central concept is taken up in various ways in the Hebrew Bible. There is a covenant handed on by parents and children (the subject of much of Genesis) and another and more structured covenant at Mount Sinai, with the Israelites as a people. This affects the way the Bible understands certain obligations. Consider welfare.

The book of Leviticus defines the duties of citizens to one another with such phrases as 'If your brother becomes poor'. On this view, I owe help to others, not because it is in my long-term interest to do so, nor because a government has so decreed, but because the other is part of my extended family, and thus in a certain sense part of who I am. The members of a society are linked by a bond of kinship and fraternity.

Kinship, however broadly conceived, is an exclusive concept. In a world in which there are kin, there must also be non-kin. In one where there are neighbours, there must also be strangers. This creates a question (deeply troubling throughout much of human history) of the moral status of outsiders. The Bible therefore explicitly and repeatedly extends the domain of obligation to the 'stranger', the person who is not a member of the extended family. The book of Leviticus contains the famous command: 'You shall love your neighbour as yourself' (19:18), but the same chapter includes the far more significant and strenuous command: 'You shall not oppress the stranger . . . instead, you shall love him as yourself, for you were once strangers in the land of Egypt' (19:33–4). The historical reference is significant. Theologically, the obligation to love the stranger follows from the first chapter of Genesis. If God is parent, humanity is indeed a single extended family. But simple reflection on creation has not always sufficed to persuade people to love as themselves people who are manifestly unlike themselves. The Bible suggests that the Israelites underwent exile and slavery precisely to know what affliction feels like, and thus to learn the lesson that we must not inflict on others what we ourselves have suffered. Morality is sometimes taught by history.

How then does this narrative differ from that of Hobbes? Its central figure is not 'I' but the 'We' of which I am a part – marriage, the family, the nation understood as an extended family, and ultimately humanity itself, considered as a single family under the parenthood of God himself. On this account, our affiliations and attachments are not irrelevant, but essential, to the structure of obligations we form. We owe duties to others because they are a part of who we are. This insight will become important when, at a later stage in the book, we come to consider modern 'communitarian' critiques of liberal political theory.[5]

What then of motivation? The driving force of the biblical drama is not self-interest but something else, for which the Hebrew word is *hesed*, usually translated as 'compassion' (a key word of politics of a certain kind). More accurately, though, *hesed* should be translated as 'covenantal obligation'.[6] It means the duties and responsibilities that flow from identification and belonging, the kind of relationship that exists between husbands and wives, or parents and children.

What constitutes society, on this view, is not a contract but a *covenant* (*brit*). One difference between them is that those bound by a covenant are 'obligated to respond to one another beyond the letter of the law rather than to limit their obligations to the narrowest contractual requirements'.[7] Another is that covenants have a moral component that renders them more binding and open-ended than could be accounted for in terms of interest. As Daniel Elazar puts it, covenant 'expresses the idea that people can freely create communities and polities, peoples and publics, and civil society itself through such morally grounded and sustained compacts (whether religious or otherwise in impetus), establishing thereby enduring partnerships'.[8] To put it simply, parties can disengage from a contract when it is no longer to their mutual benefit to continue. A covenant binds them even – perhaps especially – in difficult times. This is because a covenant is not predicated on interest, but instead on loyalty, fidelity, holding together even when things seem to be driving you apart.

This helps us understand the significance of another key word in Judaism, *emunah*, often, and wrongly, translated as 'faith'. Faith is a cognitive or intellectual attribute. *Emunah* is a moral one. It signifies the willingness to enter into and to stand by a long-term, open-ended commitment. It is what is needed to sustain a covenant. It means 'faithfulness'.

[5] See chapter 14.
[6] Daniel Elazar and Stuart Cohen, *The Jewish Polity*, 4.
[7] Daniel Elazar, *People and Polity*, 19.
[8] Ibid.

THE POLITICS OF HOPE

One of the key differences between a society based on contract and one built around the idea of covenant is what holds it together. A social contract is maintained by an *external* force, the monopoly within the state of the justified use of coercive power. A covenant, by contrast, is maintained by an *internalised* sense of identity, kinship, loyalty, obligation, responsibility and reciprocity. These promptings cannot always be taken for granted and have to be carefully nurtured and sustained. Hence the centrality, within covenantal associations, of education, ritual, sacred narratives, and collective ceremony.

A social contract gives rise to the instrumentalities of the state – governments, nations, parties, the use of centralised power and the mediated resolution of conflict. It is the basis of political society. A covenant gives rise to quite different institutions – families, communities, peoples, traditions, and voluntary associations. It is the basis of civil society. This is one way of understanding the difference between man as a *political* animal and man as a *social* animal.

So there are two stories about human associations, one told in our political classics, the other in our great religious texts. Clearly they are not mutually exclusive. Civil society requires the institutions of politics for the resolution of its conflicts and the maintenance of peace and defence. Political society, according to most of its theorists, needs the undergirding of civil virtue. Both stories represent enduring truths about the human situation and both need to be told if people are to live together peaceably for any length of time. To some extent they represent a difference of emphasis within the Greek and Jewish traditions, which is why I mentioned Aristotle and Maimonides. The ancient Greeks emphasised political structures as the context of the good life. Jews, with their long history of dispersion, tended to locate it within the family, the community and the educational system.[9] But Western civilisation is the product of both influences, heir to both stories.

By telling these two deliberately simplified narratives, I have constructed a framework, a template, which will allow us to understand what happens, and what is at stake, when slow,

[9] See Michael Walzer, *Spheres of Justice*, 64–94.

imperceptible changes take place in the ecology of associations. For there is a third story to be told, about the relationship between the two other stories. Though they are both true, their relative force and authority, their salience within a culture, differs from one age to the next. For some time now, the Hobbesian narrative has increasingly displaced its alternative, and much in our current social environment flows from that fact. A fateful drama has been enacted which can be described in two movements: the domination of political society, and the progressive de-institutionalisation of civil society.

6

The Liberal Revolution

Liberty of conscience was not admitted in the Middle Ages, and even the Athenians, for all their passion for freedom, scarcely knew it. The Greeks were a highly critical and intellectual people; they discussed many problems quite freely, and were capable at times of remarkable tolerance. So, too, though in a lesser degree, were the Romans, especially after they had absorbed Greek influences . . . Scepticism and tolerance were at times as widespread among the educated classes in the ancient world as ever they have been in the West. Yet the ancients did not value liberty of conscience as we have learned to do.

John Plamenatz[1]

GREAT REVOLUTIONS DO not always signal the presence of new ideas. Sometimes they occur when an old idea is given a new form or is applied to a new domain. The concept of freedom is ancient. We can trace its history back to the development of Athenian democracy or earlier still, to the great biblical story of the exodus, the liberation of a people from slavery and its radical implication that God desires the free worship of free human beings. For the ancient Israelites and Greeks, freedom meant a number of things. It meant not being a slave. It meant being able to govern oneself, for the Israelites as a sovereign people in their own land, for the Greeks as a participant in the democratic process itself. And it meant protection against intimidation and corruption: the rule of law as a defence of order and justice. What it did not mean was the freedom to hold, and live by, convictions that went contrary to those of the majority of society while still remaining a full member of that society. We can identify, with some precision, the birth of

[1] John Plamenatz, *Man and Society*, vol. 1, 50.

this idea. It appeared in Western Europe, falteringly in the sixteenth, more confidently in the seventeenth century, and it created a form of society never before known in civilisation. This was the liberal revolution.

That a person might take a stand against prevailing opinion and be admired for it is not new. This, after all, was the role of the prophets of Israel, and in a different way, the fate of Socrates. But Socrates was put to death, and the prophets, though they too were sometimes persecuted, were appealing to an authority they shared with the rest of society, namely the voice of God and the Sinaitic covenant. There had also long existed the idea of tolerated minorities. There were the constituent peoples of the Greek and Roman empires during their more liberal ages. There was the *millet* system of the Ottoman empire, under which different religious groups were given significant powers of self-administration. Jews, throughout their long exile and dispersion, were often afforded a degree of autonomy. The liberal revolution was nevertheless a true revolution and its extent can be seen in this, that though Jews had been a (sometimes) tolerated minority since the days of the Babylonian exile, in the sixth century before the Common Era, it was not until the nineteenth century anywhere in the world that they were permitted to take part in the processes of government. Until then they had been subjects not citizens. This was the birth of the open society.

Liberalism arises directly from the question raised in the previous chapter. There is political society, institutionalised in the form of government, and there is civil society, the institutions built around families, communities and traditions bound by a common faith, or at least the shared pursuit of the good. What is the relation between them? For much of human history they have gone hand in hand. Indeed the first users of the phrase 'civil society' meant by it 'political society'. Not until the nineteenth century could anyone have understood that these were fundamentally different and counter-balancing ideas. The reason is this. At most times, society and its institutions were seen as a single entity with various manifestations. The 'vice', writes Lord Acton, 'of the classic State was that it was Church and State in one'.[2] Religion, politics and morality belonged together, taught by the one, enforced by the other, and shared or at least professed by all. To stand outside this single truth – Christian or Islamic, Catholic or Protestant – was to stand outside society itself, its rights, liberties, and privileges of membership.

We sometimes forget how close in time we are to this idea even in a country like England with its long tradition of individualism. As late as 1838, Gladstone published a book, *The State in its Relations with the Church*, in which he argued that no one who was not a member of the Church of England should be allowed to hold public office of any kind, elected or appointed. His argument was simple. 'National will and agency are indisputably one, binding either a dissentient minority or the subject body, in a manner that nothing but the recognition of the doctrine of national personality can justify.' The collective action of the nation implies the existence of a collective personality. The state is an individual writ large. Gladstone goes on to draw the conclusion: 'A nation, then, having a personality, lies under the obligation, like the individuals comprising its governing body, of sanctifying the acts of that personality by the offices of religion.'[3] Just as an individual ought to go to church, Gladstone contended, so in effect ought the state. The idea that a non-Anglican might hold public office was as absurd as that he might officiate at a Church of England service. Church and state were one and the same under different guises.

When and why was this idea first challenged? In a sense, it was inevitable, part of the development of the idea of the nation-state itself. The medieval political domain, whether it took the form of republics, kingdoms or empires, was less cohesive than its modern counterpart. There were towns, guilds, estates, religious minorities, each of which had its own culture and inner life, and which were

[2] Lord Acton, *Essays in the History of Liberty*, 17.

[3] These quotations are taken from Lord Macaulay's 1839 review of the book, republished in his *Critical and Historical Essays*, London, Longmans, 1874, 474–5.

to some degree self-governing. These were not voluntary bodies. To be deprived of entry to a guild, or to be excommunicated by a faith, was a significant exile into no-man's-land. In such a society there were few neutral spaces unruled by such associations. The state itself managed – or was the arena of conflict between – these various corporations, but its direct power of action, other than at times of war, was limited. Its presence was not felt as part of daily life. At its highest reaches, society needed a sovereign power to prevent civil war. But at a more intimate, day-to-day level, matters lay in the hands of more local authorities.

What changed this was the industrial revolution. By the end of the eighteenth century, populations were on the move. Industrialisation meant mines and factories, Blake's 'dark, satanic mills'. Old habits of work were being displaced. Traditional crafts, learned by long apprenticeship and often handed down from father to son, were giving way to mechanised modes of production. Workers were moving from the countryside to towns. Long-standing villages and townships and the habits and hierarchies that went with them were gradually ceasing to be the backbone of England. People were becoming more mobile, productive processes more complex, and the division of labour more elaborate and specialised.

All of this called for organisation on a larger scale and led to the emergence of what Max Weber saw as the most distinctive feature of modern consciousness – bureaucratic rationality. In it people were no longer defined by their past but by their function, not by their history but by their role. If the organising principle of the medieval community was religion – an ordained hierarchy, endorsed by a church that was at the same time at the centre of local life – its modern replacement would have to be something altogether more neutral and managerial. The marriage of religion and state, which had once seemed part of the inevitable order of society, now began to look implausible and counter-productive. In the new urban dispensation people of different faiths worked together, lived together, and participated equally in the economic process. Why should they not have equal access to the political domain? By 1838, the ideas of the young Gladstone, that 'rising hope' of the 'stern and unbending Tories', as Macaulay called him, already seemed outmoded and absurd and the book was laid quietly to rest.

But the idea of liberty of conscience as such – the forerunner of the separation of church and state – lay in an earlier crisis, the Reformation and the wars of religion which dominated Europe in the sixteenth and seventeenth centuries. In their wake, wars bring tolerances which, had they existed before, would have prevented the outbreak of war. The growth of toleration, always precarious, is nevertheless a sign of humanity's capacity to learn by its mistakes so long as it remembers them. John Plamenatz points out the striking fact that it was not ancient Greece or Rome, with their eclectic, sceptical and tolerant cultures, but seventeenth-century Europe with its intense religiosity, which gave birth to the modern idea of liberty. It did so for many reasons, but one at least was simple. If people of profound convictions find themselves at war with one another because of those convictions, how can they learn to live peaceably together? Short of the victory of one side and the conversion of the other, the alternative is to find a framework of coexistence, which means in effect a society in which religious truth is not enforced. For the first time a fateful separation is made between private and public. Religious truth belongs within the mind of the believer, not within the conscience of the state.

Not the first, but certainly the most influential, thinker to give voice to this idea was John Locke. In his *Letter Concerning Toleration* (1685) Locke argued for toleration of religious dissent on two quite distinct grounds. The first was religious. Belief is a free act of the will. By definition it cannot be compelled. Those who persecute others in order to save their souls are guilty of a self-contradictory ambition. What they achieve is not worth having: forced assent rather than genuine conviction. It is impossible 'to make other people Christians who have not really embraced the Christian religion in their hearts'.[4] This, though, was not a new argument. The Babylonian Talmud in the fifth century already contains a similar line of thought, more daringly applied to God Himself. Had the offer of the covenant to the

[4] John Locke, *Political Writings*, 390.

Israelites at Sinai not been genuinely free (had 'God suspended the mountain over their heads' as the Talmud puts it) it would have been null and void, because coerced agreement is not consent.[5]

Locke, however, adds a further and secular proposition. To understand what governments may do, we have to ask what governments are for. They are not, as Gladstone thought, the corporate personality of the nation, nor as many then believed, the church in its secular guise. Instead they are bodies brought into being by a contract with strictly limited aims. The state (Locke called it the commonwealth) is 'a society of men constituted only for the procuring, preserving, and advancing of their own civil interests', which for Locke meant life, liberty and property.[6] Toleration followed from the premiss of limited government.

Fifteen years before Locke, another philosopher, Spinoza, had published another and somewhat more far-reaching defence of liberty. Spinoza was descended from a Jewish family that had been exiled during the Spanish expulsion and eventually found a home, a century and a half later, in the tolerant climate of Amsterdam. Though in direct impact his work had less influence than Locke's, it was a precursor of a much more radical line of thought developed in 1859 by John Stuart Mill, and taken up in the second half of the twentieth century. For Spinoza, freedom of opinion is a natural and inalienable right. No person can hand over to any other 'his natural right of free reason and judgement'. More than this: the role of the state is not for Spinoza the mere defence of person and property against assault. It is to enable people 'to develop their minds and bodies in security, and to employ their reason unshackled'.[7] Spinoza did not push this thought very far. In practice he still conceded that rulers had, and were entitled to have, draconian powers. But for the first time we hear of negative liberty (freedom

[5] Bablyonian Talmud, *Shabbat*, 88a.
[6] Locke, op. cit., 393.
[7] Spinoza, *Tractatus Theologico–Politicus*, 257–9.

from interference) as a positive ideal flowing from the concept of the person as defined by a capacity to seek truth for himself. It was not that in persecuting the dissenting conscience, governments were acting beyond their powers. It was that they were betraying the ideal of a society of autonomous agents. If Locke defended the free church, Spinoza defended the free individual.

So the first stage of the liberal revolution was the battle for *toleration*, the right of individuals to profess opinions on matters of religion at odds with the established church and to form associations for the purpose of collective worship. It was slow, and halting,[8] but it was won. By the early nineteenth century the battleground had shifted. It was one thing to have the freedom to meet with others of one's faith, but this was not yet equal citizenship in the full sense of the word. By 1800, Catholics, dissenters, Jews and atheists were still unable to take part in Parliament, to hold ministerial or administrative office, to obtain commissions in the armed services, or to attend universities. As the role of the state and the value of higher education grew, these disabilities became ever more painful. As the principle of toleration became accepted, they also seemed ever more arbitrary. The great battle of the nineteenth century was the struggle for *emancipation*.

This was a political rather than an intellectual development. The arguments for the one were essentially the same as for the other: the nineteenth century merely had to apply seventeenth-century ideas. Thus, for example, Lord Macaulay, arguing the case for removing the civil disabilities of Jews in 1831, put the proposition straightforwardly. Governments exist 'for the purpose of keeping the peace, for the purpose of compelling us to settle our disputes by arbitration instead of settling them by blows, for the purpose of compelling us to supply our wants by industry, instead of supplying them by rapine'. Why a person should be less fit to exercise these powers because he goes to a synagogue instead of a church 'we

---

[8] Locke, for example, did not go so far as to extend toleration to Catholics or atheists.

cannot conceive'.[9] The argument comes straight from Locke. The case was won for Catholics in 1829, and during the course of the century the same rights were secured by Jews, members of the Free Churches and atheists. The two-stage revolution was complete.

By now the connection should be clear between this history and the two stories I told in the previous chapter. The liberal revolution meant, in effect, the separation of political and civil society, the uncoupling of the two narratives of Hobbes and the Hebrew Bible. Political society – the domain of states, governments, legislation and coercion – was to practise self-limitation when it came to matters of religion and belief. Despite the fact that England still had an established church, non-membership carried no abridgement of citizenship rights. Meanwhile the institutions of civil society – families, communities, and non-establishment religions – were seen as voluntary bodies. To put it somewhat differently, a distinction was opened up between society and state. The state was singular, society (religiously) plural. The state was the domain of coercion, society of free association.

It would not be an exaggeration to say that these developments were one of the great achievements of human civilisation. They created the open society. They institutionalised tolerance. They made individuals less dependent on fortunes of birth or fate. They made possible the free exchange of goods, services and ideas on which depended the vast growth of wealth, power and knowledge which has transformed the scope of human possibility. They gave new substance to the ideals of liberty and equality, human dignity and the free exercise of conscience. They emerged from the collision of two circumstances: the growth of the state, and the fact that modern societies are composed of a multiplicity of groups. The great problem was how to secure the unity of the former without denying the integrity of the latter. Many other solutions have been tried, and they have ended in tragedy, from the forced conversions of the Middle Ages to the totalitarian states and 'ethnic cleansing' of the twentieth century. There are societies which do not encounter the call of liberalism: those that are closed

---

[9] Macaulay, op. cit., 135.

or homogeneous or the result of a voluntary gathering of those who share a common faith. But when society is organised on a large scale and encompasses diverse populations, there is no morally acceptable alternative.

What, then, does the liberal universe look like? It is populated by the state on the one hand, and on the other by associations held together voluntarily by bonds of tradition, habit, virtue, loyalty and affection. These two domains institutionalise the primary aspects of the human situation: conflict and kinship. Political liberalism separates them without compromising either. It restrains political society from exclusivity, which anyway it should not have. It divorces civil society from power, which anyway it does not need. Each now has its own rightful territory, complementing one another without intruding into the other's domain. An equilibrium is reached between man the political animal and man the social animal.

To a considerable degree this was the situation that prevailed in mid-Victorian England. In his masterpiece of social observation, *Democracy in America*, Alexis de Tocqueville painted a similar portrait of the United States in the early 1830s. In both countries, family life was strong. Attendance at places of worship was increasing. There was a prevailing public ethic of self-help and help-to-others. It was an age of what Shirley Robin Letwin describes as the 'vigorous virtues'. The key terms of approbation were upright, self-sufficient, energetic, adventurous, independent-minded, loyal to friends, and robust against enemies.[10] No age is perfect, and the Victorian era had many failings, but the liberal century was one which valued independence and strong character, respect for one another's beliefs and heeding the call of social responsibility.

Voluntary organisations and charities proliferated. The social upheavals of the industrial revolution, though they had uprooted old associations, led also to the growth of new ones. By the 1860s most towns and cities in England had their own charitable hospitals, infirmaries, friendly societies, temperance groups, maternity societies, reading rooms, church schools and missions. By 1895

[10] Shirley Robin Letwin, *The Anatomy of Thatcherism*, 33.

the Charity Commissioners could look back and report that 'the latter half of the 19th century will stand second in respect of the greatness and variety of the Charities created within its duration, to no other half-century since the Reformation'. As Frank Prochaska notes, 'In an era in which the government had little interest in social policy . . . the needs of the community bound the citizenry together in a web of kindness, obligation and expectation.[11]

That phrase 'bound the citizenry together' answers a key question about liberalism. On traditional assumptions, an open society should be an impossibility. Throughout history, what has held societies together has usually been a common faith, a shared religion. The word 'religion' itself comes from the Latin verb meaning 'to bind'. When the profession of a faith is no longer needed for citizenship, what else weaves the strands of private lives into the fabric of a shared existence? Nineteenth-century thinkers, with few exceptions, had no doubt. It was the existence of a shared morality.

Classical liberalism distinguished between the moral life and its sources of authority. People might do their duty and keep their promises because of belief in revelation, or habit, or custom, through the 'moral sense' or an educated conscience, because it flowed from the dictates of reason or because it secured the greatest happiness of the greatest number. The origin of obligation might be of surpassing interest to the individual, but it was of no concern to society. What mattered was what people did and could be relied on to do, not why. So long as there is a generally accepted morality, society can survive religious diversity. As Lord Devlin was to put it in 1964, at the very turning-point from liberalism to a second transformation far more profound, 'the removal of religion from the structure of society does not mean that a society can exist without faith. There is faith in moral belief as well as in religious belief. Though it is less precise and less demanding, it is not necessarily less intense.' So long as people could agree on this, they could coexist. 'A band of travellers can go forward together without knowing what they will find at the end of the journey

---

[11] Frank Prochaska, *Royal Bounty: The Making of a Welfare Monarchy*, 67.

but they cannot keep in company if they do not journey in the same direction.'[12] There is a certain poignancy to this sentiment and its date. It was probably the last time it could be publicly expressed with conviction by a prominent lay authority. For what lay in store during the 1960s was a revolution *against* liberalism in favour of a more radical alternative, libertarianism, which would carry the battle for emancipation from the sphere of religion to that of morality itself. And with this we come to the heart of what will be my case over the next few chapters.

Social processes are not stories. They do not have a beginning, a middle and an end. They are set in motion by forces of which some of the key participants may be only dimly aware. Those forces continue to operate long after the conscious goals of architects of change have been achieved. Stories have endings, history does not. Between the seventeenth and nineteenth centuries liberalism achieved a remarkable separation and equilibrium. Political society was disentangled from civil society, state from church, government from the myriad networks of faith and belonging. Each now had its own domain and distinctive character, the one operating through law and force, the other through voluntary association. But the process did not stop there. It continued, with outcomes liberals had not anticipated. Two things happened, one largely in the twentieth century as the result of two world wars, the other which had been in the making a century or more before. The first was the immense growth in the activity and presence of the state. The second, chronologically prior, was the appearance of the uniquely modern phenomenon – the individual.

---

[12] Lord Devlin, *The Enforcement of Morals*, 119–20.

7

The Birth of the Individual

[A]t a certain point in history men became individuals.

Taken in isolation, the statement is absurd. How was a man different from an individual? A person born before a certain date, a man – had he not eyes? had he not hands, organs, dimensions, senses, affections, passions? If you pricked him, he bled and if you tickled him, he laughed. But certain things he did not have or do until he became an individual. He did not have an awareness of what one historian, Georges Gusdorf, calls internal space. He did not, as Delany puts it, imagine himself in more than one role, standing outside or above his own personality; he did not suppose that he might be an object of interest to his fellow man not for the reason that he had achieved something notable or been witness to great events but simply because as an individual he was of consequence.

Lionel Trilling[1]

IN HIS TRAVELS in the United States in 1831 Alexis de Tocqueville noted a phenomenon which gave him considerable perplexity and for which he felt the need for a new name. He called it *individualism,* and was later to say that 'Our fathers did not have the word "individualism", which we have coined for our own use, because in their time there was indeed no individual who did not belong to a group and who could be considered as absolutely alone.'[2] Tocqueville had no doubt that he was in the presence of something original, a mutation in human character brought about by the profound social changes of the nineteenth century. Before then there had been individuality but not individualism. What was this new disposition?

[1] Lionel Trilling, *Sincerity and Authenticity*, 24.
[2] Alexis de Tocqueville, *L'Ancien Régime et la Révolution* (1856), quoted in Steven Lukes, *Individualism*, 14.

It was, he said, something quite distinct from egoism or selfishness. That was a vice which could be found in all times and places. Individualism was less a vice, a failing of individuals, than an entirely new type of personality whose emergence he attributed to the mobile, democratic and egalitarian society he saw in the making in the United States. It was, he said, the 'mature and calm feeling, which disposes each member of the community to sever himself from the mass of his fellows and to draw apart with his family and his friends, so that after he has thus formed a little circle of his own, he willingly leaves society at large to itself.'[3]

Tocqueville's insight was to see that social change has an effect on human character. Different environments give rise to different kinds of people. When patterns of life change, so too do our personalities. Virtues, dispositions, 'habits of the heart', are not timeless and universal. They have a context; they grow and flourish under particular circumstances. Military ages yield different kinds of heroes from periods of peace. Times of affluence produce different ideals of behaviour than do ages of famine and poverty. Societies do more than bring people together; they have a part in shaping the individuals who make them up. We make society, but society also makes us. In this respect there is a connection between politics and personality. Democracy, Tocqueville thought, was creating a new type of human being. What did it replace?

In the relatively fixed, hierarchical order of traditional societies, people were defined by roles largely determined by birth. Their choices, though real, were limited. They were born into a class, a country, a region, a culture, a faith, and often an occupation. Their chance of movement across these boundaries was limited. They were part of a way of life which preceded their birth and would continue long after their death. Change was imperceptible and unselfconscious. To grow to adulthood was not, first and foremost, to make choices, but rather to make oneself at home in the landscape of the social world, to internalise its values, become part of it and make it one's own.

[3] Alexis de Tocqueville, *Democracy in America*, 395.

In such societies – Tocqueville called them 'aristocratic' – the individual had a strong sense of kinship between past and future, and an equally strong feeling of identification with the local community of which he or she was a part:

> Among aristocratic nations, as families remain for centuries in the same condition, often on the same spot, all generations become, as it were, contemporaneous. A man almost always knows his forefathers and respects them; he thinks he already sees his remote descendants and he loves them. He willingly imposes duties on himself towards the former and the latter, and he will frequently sacrifice his personal gratifications to those who went before and to those who will come after him. Aristocratic institutions, moreover, have the effect of closely binding every man to several of his fellow citizens. As the classes of an aristocratic people are strongly marked and permanent, each of them is regarded by its own members as a sort of lesser country, more tangible and more cherished than the country at large ... Men living in aristocratic ages are therefore almost always closely attached to something outside their own sphere, and they are often disposed to forget themselves.[4]

It was this forgetfulness-of-self that had now been destroyed by the new kind of society taking shape in America. Tocqueville, as a Frenchman in the early part of the nineteenth century, was no stranger to political turmoil. But he was entirely unprepared for the sheer pace of change he found in the United States and speaks of it often with amazement. In place of permanence, he found a society caught up in a vortex of transformation. People made fortunes, lost them and made them again. No sooner had they built a house than they were ready to sell it and move on. Nothing in America was constant: not class, nor wealth, nor power, nor place: 'the woof of time is every instant broken and the track of generations effaced'.

This new, unsettling environment was producing a distinctive character type, capable of surviving and flourishing under conditions of constant change. It was mobile, rootless, pioneering,

[4] Ibid., 395–6.

independent. Americans owed far less than Europeans to a sense of past, or place, or belonging. They were nomadic and relentlessly self-sufficient. 'They owe nothing to any man, they expect nothing from any man; they acquire the habit of always considering themselves as standing alone, and they are apt to imagine that their whole destiny is in their own hands.' This created its own form of forgetfulness, quite different from that to be found in a traditional society. There, people were inclined to forget themselves. In America they were more likely to forget others. Not only does individualism make 'every man forget his ancestors, but it hides his descendants and separates his contemporaries from him; it throws him back forever upon himself alone and threatens in the end to confine him entirely within the solitude of his own heart.'

Tocqueville was writing about America. But by the end of the eighteenth and the beginning of the nineteenth century observers in Europe were noting something similar, closer to home. What prompted them were the upheavals following the French Revolution. While the revolutionaries saw a new and more enlightened world in the making, conservatives were alarmed at the destruction of everything that connected the present with the past. Edmund Burke voiced his fear that constant change would 'separate and tear asunder' the bonds of community, dissolving it into 'an unsocial, uncivil, unconnected chaos of elementary principles'. Under such repeated assaults, he argued, the commonwealth itself would, in a few generations, 'crumble away, be disconnected into the dust and powder of individuality, and at length dispersed to the winds of heaven'.[5]

In France itself, opponents of the revolution argued that exaltation of the individual was devastating the stabilising force of custom and authority. In 1829 Lamennais protested against '*Individualism* which destroys the very idea of obedience and of duty, thereby destroying both power and law; and what then remains but a terrifying confusion of interests, passions and diverse

[5] Edmund Burke, *Reflections on the Revolution in France*, 96.

opinions?'[6] Nine years earlier the Catholic conservative, Joseph de Maistre, had seen the new politics as a secular counterpart to the Reformation. Just as Luther had substituted individual salvation for the collective discipline of the church, so revolution was enthroning individual judgement in place of obedience to established constitutional authority. He wrote witheringly of 'this deep and frightening division of minds, this infinite fragmentation of all doctrines, *political protestantism* carried to the most absolute individualism.'[7]

It was Karl Marx, however, who noted that another kind of individualism had been in the making in Britain in the course of the seventeenth and eighteenth centuries in the work of political philosophers like Hobbes and Locke and economists such as Adam Smith and David Ricardo. The starting-point of their theories was the abstract individual whose desires, interests, advantages and rights are to be secured by the institutional arrangements of government and the economy. Such systems assume the priority of the individual to society in a double sense: the individual precedes society, and is served by it rather than the other way round. Marx himself made a pointed observation about these thinkers, namely their curious blindness to history. They took it for granted that the 'individual' of whom they spoke was a product of 'nature', existing before and outside society. In fact, though, the very concept of the individual emerged at a particular time in response to specific historical developments, the dissolution of the feudal economy and the new forces of production which had been developing since the sixteenth century. 'It is but in the eighteenth century, in "bourgeois society", that the different forms of social union confront the individual as a mere means to his private ends, as an outward necessity.'[8]

Clearly, even in this limited range of contexts, individualism could mean several different things. For Tocqueville it meant

[6] F. de Lamennais, *Des Progrès de la révolution et de la guerre contre l'église* (1829), quoted in Lukes, *Individualism*, 6.

[7] Quoted, ibid., 4.

[8] Karl Marx, *A Contribution to the Critque of Political Economy*, translated N. I. Stone, Chicago, 1913, 266–8.

withdrawal from public life and the valuing of privacy. For opponents of the French Revolution it meant the willingness to overturn existing institutions in the name of freedom and equality. For Locke and Adam Smith it simply meant that institutional structures were justified if they protected the private ownership and accumulation of property. For some, individualism was the original sin of the modern age; for others its glorious virtue. The mid-nineteenth-century historian John William Draper could write glowingly about North America, its cities, canals, railroads, factories, banks, churches, hospitals and schools, that: 'This wonderful spectacle of social development was the result of *Individualism*; operating in an unbounded theatre of action. Everyone was seeking to do all that he could for himself.'[9]

The very fact, though, that such different developments could be observed in different countries at about the same time and be described by the same word suggests that Tocqueville was right. A transformation was taking place in the relationship between individual and society, as revolutionary as Copernicus' discovery that the earth travelled round the sun. In a variety of ways people were discovering that society revolved around the individual rather than the individual around society. It is impossible to date the beginning of this long and complex process, but we can identify significant moments: when Shakespeare has Polonius say to Laertes: 'This above all: to thine own self be true'; when Descartes sits down to discover certainty on the basis of personal reflection alone; when Rembrandt starts painting his long series of self-portraits; when authors embark on the new literary genre of autobiography; when couples begin to marry because of personal affection rather than social or parental expectation. Each of these testifies to a new and liberating sense of self-awareness. The world within has begun to resonate no less powerfully than the world outside. Reality's centre of gravity has begun its long journey inward to the self.

How and why did it happen? Some historians trace it to rising standards of living in the sixteenth and seventeenth centuries. Christopher Hill points to new domestic arrangements such as

[9] J. W. Draper, *History of the American Civil War*, vol. 1, New York, 1868, 208.

the spread of private bedrooms and the replacement of benches by chairs. In a similar vein, Philippe Ariès remarks that: 'The historians taught us long ago that the King was never left alone. But in fact, until the end of the seventeenth century, nobody was ever left alone. The density of social life made isolation virtually impossible, and people who managed to shut themselves up in a room for some time were regarded as exceptional characters.'[10] Jacques Lacan once offered the fascinating speculation that the increasing use of the first person singular came about as the result of Venetian techniques of plate-glass manufacture which resulted in the more extensive use of mirrors. Each of these developments meant that, at least in the upper and middle strata of society, individuals had more opportunity to be on their own, to contemplate their thoughts and feelings, keep diaries and journals, and cultivate private space.

Others are inclined to attribute a decisive influence to the Reformation. By contrast with Catholicism, the Protestant ethic places a far greater emphasis on the individual and his or her salvation. Alasdair MacIntyre notes that for Luther, 'the community and its life' are no longer the area in which the moral life is lived out. In his theology 'the events that matter all occur in the psychological transformation of the faithful individual'.[11] Max Weber famously attributed the rise of capitalism to the spread of Calvinist doctrine with its tendency to 'tear the individual away from the closed ties with which he is bound to this world'.[12] Werner Stark contrasts the role of individual and church in Catholic and Calvinist teachings. Catholicism 'is an incarnation of the principle which Tönnies called community: the whole is before the parts. Calvinism, on the other hand, is a product of the principle of association: the parts are before the whole. Catholicism thinks in terms of organic unity; it is collectivistic. Calvinism for its part thinks in terms of contractualism; it is individualistic.'[13] Whether as cause or consequence, there can be no doubt that the new doctrines

[10] Philippe Ariès, *Centuries of Childhood*, Harmondsworth, Penguin, 1973, 385.
[11] Alasdair MacIntyre, *A Short History of Ethics*, 121–3.
[12] Max Weber, *The Protestant Ethic and the Spirit of Capitalism*, 108.
[13] Quoted in Lukes, *Individualism*, 95.

of the sixteenth century played a significant role in placing the self at the centre of the religious drama, giving new dignity to introspection.

Alongside these changes and lending them momentum was the huge cumulative impact of social change, the breakdown of long-established ways of doing things. Virtually all commentators on the 'birth of the modern' have attempted to convey the fundamental transformation involved in the shift from a static society to one in continual motion. They have used terms such as the transition from 'fate' to 'choice', from 'status' to 'contract', or from 'community' to 'society', *Gemeinschaft* to *Gessellschaft*. Peter Berger speaks of the demise of moral systems built on the concept of honour, the respect that accrues to an individual in virtue of his or her role, and their replacement by an ethic of dignity, the respect due to the person as such. In a world of honour, 'identity is firmly linked to the past through the reiterated performance of prototypical acts'. By contrast, in a world of dignity, 'history is the succession of mystifications from which the individual must free himself to attain "authenticity".'[14]

Each of these categorisations is a way of signalling the radical change that takes place in the idea of selfhood when society is transformed from an order received from and sanctioned by the past to one consciously made in pursuit of a desired future. The individual is no longer born into and subordinate to a set of defining roles established by custom and community. Instead roles must be chosen, and the self that chooses is defined precisely by its independence from all non-voluntary ties. Alasdair MacIntyre describes the 'specifically modern self' as one that 'finds no limits set to that on which it may pass judgement'. To be a moral agent in this new dispensation is 'precisely to be able to stand back from any and every situation in which one is involved, from any and every characteristic that one may possess, and to pass judgement on it from a purely universal and

[14] Peter Berger, 'On the Obsolescence of the Concept of Honour', in Michael Sandel (ed.), *Liberalism and its Critics*, 149–58.

84

abstract point of view that is detached from all social particularity'.[15]

This, surely, is the heart of the revolution. It is not that before a certain date there were no such things as individuals who were conscious of themselves as such. Throughout history there have been heroic or tragic figures who set themselves against the idols of their age. But at a certain point, what had once been exceptional became the norm. The individual is no longer defined in and through society, but over and against it. Roles become masks, hiding rather than revealing the true self beneath. Conventions become inhibitions, no longer the precondition of individuality but rather of its suppression. Slowly – the process takes several centuries – the biblical narrative becomes reversed. Instead of its being 'not good for man to be alone' it becomes his essential dignity.

In place of Adam and Eve, conscious and ashamed of their nakedness, the modern self glories in self-disclosure, for clothes, concealments, reticences – the multiple constraints of self within society – have come to stand for an unwarranted intrusion of public standards into private space. Where Cain once saw the fate of becoming 'a restless wanderer on the earth' as an unbearable curse, we have come to see it as a challenge, a destiny, the essence of autonomy. As Gail Sheehy put it in the mid-1970s, 'You can't take everything with you when you leave on the midlife journey. You are moving away. Away from institutional claims and other people's agenda. Away from external valuations and accreditations, in search of an inner validation. You are moving out of roles and into the self. If I could give everyone a gift for the send-off on this journey, it would be a tent. A tent for tentativeness. The gift of portable roots.'[16]

In this long, at times imperceptible, metamorphosis we see what Nietzsche called a 'transvaluation of values'. What for the Hebrew Bible was the beginning of the human story becomes,

---

[15] Alasdair MacIntyre, *After Virtue*, 30.
[16] Gail Sheehy, *Passages: Predictable Crises of Adult Life*, New York, Bantam, 1976, 30.

in its post-modernist expression, its triumphal conclusion. Society is no longer the redemption of the individual but a threat to his or her individuality. The lonely self, the reflexive subject, the autonomous agent, reigns supreme. It was Karl Marx who noted the irony of this development. The period in which 'this view of the isolated individual becomes prevalent' – he is referring to the eighteenth century – 'is the very one in which the inter-relations of society . . . have reached the highest stage of development'. The self conceived of as something independent of the social order is precisely the outcome of a social order of unprecedented complexity and sophistication. 'Production by isolated individuals outside of society . . . is as great an absurdity as the idea of the development of language without individuals living together and talking together.'[17]

Marx's closing analogy raises an obvious question. Identity, the knowledge that I am and who I am, is intimately related to language. In biological terms, it is only because man is a talking animal that he is (not merely a conscious, but also) a self-conscious animal. In biblical terms, it is only when Adam attaches names to things that he discovers that he is alone. What, then, had been happening to language during this same period, in particular the language of morals, the vocabulary within which we have traditionally sought to express the connectedness between the self and others?

[17] Marx, op. cit., 268.

8

Languages of Morals

No home, no tea. Insouciant carelessness. Eternal indifference.
Perhaps it is only the great pause between carings. But it is only
in this pause that one finds the meaninglessness of meanings – like
old husks which speak dust. Only in this pause that one finds
the meaninglessness of meanings, and the other dimension. The
reality of timelessness and nowhere ... nothing is so meaningless
as meanings.

D. H. Lawrence[1]

IN 1357 A CERTAIN Eleazar, living in Mainz, sat down to write
a letter to his children. It was a will, not a conventional kind of
will, disposing of this or that item of property. It was what came
to be known as an 'ethical will', a custom, indeed a literary genre,
through which Jewish parents handed on to their children advice
and instruction in how to behave. The existence of the genre recognises that parents bequeath their children more than possessions.
They leave them ideals, sometimes large, sometimes quite specific.
The letter covers several pages. This is how it began:

These are the things which my sons and daughters shall do at my request.
They shall go to the house of prayer morning and evening ... As soon as
the service is over, they shall occupy themselves a little with the Torah,
the Psalms, or with works of charity.

Their business shall be conducted honestly, in their dealing both with
Jew and gentile. They must be gentle in their manners, and prompt
to accede to every honourable request. They must not talk more than
is necessary, and by this will they be saved from slander, falsehood
and frivolity.

They shall give an exact tithe of their possessions; they shall never turn
away a poor man empty-handed, but must give him what they can, be

[1] D. H. Lawrence, *Kangaroo*, London, Martin Secker, 1923, 374.

it much or little. If he beg a lodging overnight, and they know him not, let them provide him with the wherewithal to pay an innkeeper. Thus they shall satisfy the needs of the poor in every possible way.

My daughters must obey scrupulously the rules applying to women; modesty, sanctity, reverence, should mark their married lives. Marital intercourse must be modest and holy, with a spirit of restraint and delicacy, in reverence and silence. They shall be very punctilious and careful with their ritual bathing. They must respect their husbands, and must be invariably amiable to them. Husbands, on their part, must honour their wives more than themselves, and treat them with tender consideration. If they can by any means contrive it, my sons and daughters should live in communities, and not isolated from other Jews, so that their sons and daughters may learn the ways of Judaism. Even if compelled to solicit from others the money to pay a teacher, they must not let the young, of both sexes, go without instruction in the Torah. Marry your children, O my sons and daughters, as soon as their age is ripe, to members of respectable families . . .[2]

There is nothing remarkable about this letter. Israel Abrahams, from whose work this translation is taken, calls the author 'an average Jew'. He was doing what parents did. Nevertheless, from this distance of time, the letter, like a medieval woodcut, evokes a world of simplicity and not a little dignity. Eleazar, of whom we know little, was not a rabbi. He simply belongs to a tradition which, having received it from his parents, he now prepares to entrust to his children. Its values are not personal. They are those of rabbinic Judaism from the first to the nineteenth century, and which may still be found in orthodox circles today. He speaks of a life of prayer, study and good deeds, laying special emphasis on honesty, civility and charity. Relations between husband and wife are formalised and charged with religious meaning. Marriages in such a world are arranged. The concept of romantic love, though it has existed since biblical times, has not yet developed the power to override such considerations, though the medieval sages did recognise the right of children to marry the partners of their choice.

Eleazar, like most Jews at most times, is aware of the vulnerability of his way of life. In the Middle Ages, Jews were everywhere a minority, surrounded by a religious culture different from,

[2] Israel Abrahams, *Hebrew Ethical Wills*, Philadelphia, Jewish Publication Society, 1976, 208–10.

sometimes hostile to, their own. Hence his concern that his children stay attached to a Jewish community rather than live in isolation. He knows that a family alone is not sufficient to sustain a tradition. It needs the support of fellow believers. And hence his insistence, again utterly characteristic, that his children do all they can to ensure that their children are educated in the texts and ways of Judaism, which they must do even if they have to borrow money to do so.

The conceptual world from which this letter is drawn is what is sometimes described as a 'thick morality'. In it, obligations flow from facts. This is a poor person, *therefore* you must give him charity. This is your wife, *therefore* you must give her honour. This is your child, *therefore* you must give her an education. Between the premiss and the conclusion there is no intervening act of choice. This is a morality received, not made. It is embedded in and reinforced by a total way of life, articulated in texts, transmitted across the generations, enacted in rituals, exemplified by the members of the community, and underwritten by revelation and tradition. It has no pretensions to universality. It represents what a Jew must do, in the full knowledge that his Christian neighbours in Mainz are bound by a different code. But it is not voluntaristic. Jews received their identity, and thus their obligations, by birth not personal decision. What separates his world from ours?

One key difference can be traced to a justly famous sentence in David Hume's *Treatise of Human Nature* (1740). Hume notes that: 'In every system of morality, which I have hitherto met with, I have always remark'd, that the author proceeds for some time in the ordinary way of reasoning, and establishes the being of a God, or makes observations concerning human affairs; when of a sudden I am surpriz'd to find, that instead of the usual copulations of propositions, *is*, and *is not*, I meet with no proposition that is not connected with an *ought*, or an *ought not*.' This, Hume observes, breaks one of the rules of syllogistic reasoning, namely that there should be nothing in the conclusion that was not already contained in the premisses. 'This small attention', he writes, 'cou'd subvert all the vulgar systems of morality.'

The significance of this discovery was hardly apparent at the time. Hume himself said about his book that 'it fell dead-born from the

Press'. What he had done, though, was to open up a fateful gap between 'facts' and 'values', description and prescription. There was no way of reading off values from an external world, from the objective properties of things. The hairline fracture which Hume had noticed would eventually grow into an abyss. Where there had been one world, there were now two. There was the world of *is*, charted and explained by science. And there was the realm of *ought*, whose foundations would become increasingly problematic as the centuries passed.

A second, no less momentous, transformation occurred later in the eighteenth century, in the work of Immanuel Kant. For Kant, goodness is to be found not in acts but motives. The good will, the only thing that is unconditionally good, is that which seeks to do its duty for the sake of duty. All other inclinations yield hypothetical imperatives ('You ought to do this if you want that'). Only the good will yields categorical imperatives, absolute commands. But this means that if I am to act morally, I must issue these commands to myself. I must be self-legislating or 'autonomous'. If I do something because someone else has commanded me to do so, my obedience will be based on some extraneous consideration. I act because I want to win favour or avoid punishment. But that means I am pursuing inclination rather than duty, acting prudentially rather than morally, and this applies even if the person whose commands I am obeying is God. To put it another way, if I act morally by doing what God commands, this can only be because I have independently arrived at the conclusion that what I am doing is right. Any other consideration is inappropriate. With this single argument, authority has been transposed from revelation to personal reflection, from 'the starry heavens above me' to the 'moral law within me'. If Hume had released morality from its moorings in the physical world, Kant had liberated it from the Divine will.

Neither man was a revolutionary. Hume described himself as 'a man of Mild Disposition, of Government of Temper, of an open social and cheerful Humour, capable of Attachment, but little susceptible of Enmity, and of great Moderation in all my Passions'. Bertrand Russell paints a charming picture of Kant as 'a man of such regular habits that people used to set their watches by him as he passed their doors on his constitutional'. Neither envisaged that what he was doing was paving the way for vast changes in our moral life. To the contrary, each took the content of morality as more or less given. The question was: what was its basis? The traditional answer, religion, would no longer do. Since the Reformation, Catholics and Protestants had argued over religious truth and, far from agreeing, their disputes had led to two centuries of conflict throughout Europe. There seemed to be two other alternatives: reason and emotion. Kant chose the first, Hume the second. For Kant emotion was too arbitrary to provide the basis for moral judgement. For Hume reason was too detached to provide a motive for action. It was too early for either to see that their answers cancelled one another out and that the search for a foundation of ethics might ultimately prove fruitless. If Hume or Kant were to be followed, however, one thing was clear. Moral certainty could not be found in the world outside. It was neither written into situations nor readable in sacred texts. Morality had travelled from 'out there' to 'in here'.

Perhaps because he wished to avoid such an outcome, Jeremy Bentham proposed an alternative. Morality could borrow the methods of science, especially the new science of economics. Hobbes had said that 'good' and 'evil' simply represented what people desired or had an aversion to. What was observable was that people desired pleasure and sought to avoid pain. These were the 'two sovereign masters' of human motivation. It should be possible, therefore, to construct a science of optimal behaviour. Its principle was simple. Borrowing a phrase from Adam Ferguson, he stated that an action was right if it promoted 'the greatest happiness of the greatest number', happiness defined in terms of pleasure and the absence of pain. The theory, which developed a number of internal variants, became known as 'utilitarianism'. As time proceeded, it became clear that it was open to a number of serious objections. Not least, as one of its disciples, John Stuart Mill, realised, it threatened individual liberty itself, for it meant that the sufferings of the few could be justified by the satisfactions (not always benevolent) of the many.

Long before its fatal flaws were exposed, utilitarianism became a most powerful means of overthrowing every kind of moral tradition. Within the utilitarian frame of mind itself is a transition from 'traditional' to 'modern' consciousness. Hitherto, behaviour had been justified by reference to the past. Now it was to be judged by reference to the future, to outcomes or consequences. The question was no longer: 'Is this sanctified by revelation or custom or age?' but: 'Is it effective, does it yield the best results?' With the confidence of his age, Bentham assumed that these could be counted, aggregated and quantified. They could be known. One of the insights of traditional systems was lost in the translation to modernity, namely that consequences of change can sometimes be very distant indeed and impossible to know in advance. But this was out of tune with the temper of the age, and so the scientific approach to human behaviour, later known as social engineering, was born. Bentham's theory was hardly practicable for individuals. It meant long chains of calculation before even the simplest decision. But it was to become vastly influential in the way governments viewed their purposes and procedures, and the theory had a certain symmetry with democracy, government by the greatest number for the greatest number.

As the nineteenth century progressed, however, more radical voices could be heard. Society was moving rapidly. The idea that morality, the established consensus of reasonable people, could be taken for granted came to seem more and more tenuous. Travellers had long noted that other cultures organised matters differently, but the increased speed of travel and the expanding field of anthropology now made people increasingly aware of the diversity of human cultures. Charles Darwin's theory of evolution opened up the possibility that a particular form of life might not be the result of a conscious process of design. If natural selection held true for human societies there might be a fundamental discrepancy between what happened and what people thought they were doing. As two of his modern commentators put it, 'In an important sense, ethics as we understand it is an illusion fobbed off on us by our genes to get us to cooperate.'[3] The idea, first mooted by Plato

---

[3] Michael Ruse and Edward O. Wilson, 'The Evolution of Ethics', *New Scientist*, October 1985, 51.

in *The Republic*, that a society might be maintained by a 'noble lie' – that our moral convictions might be no more than myths designed to mask quite different underlying realities – now began to seem more plausible. Three immensely influential figures took up the case: Marx, Nietzsche and Freud.

For Marx, the significant human realities were material ones. The superstructures of consciousness – morality, religion and philosophy – were by-products rather than the causes of what people did. They were 'phantoms formed in the human brain'. Moral and religious systems concealed rather than revealed the true nature of society: the division of labour, the exploitation of one class by another, money relationships, and the bourgeois interests of the capitalist system. As Engels put it, 'What is good for the ruling class is alleged to be good for the whole of society with which the ruling class identifies itself. The more civilization advances, the more it is found to cover with the cloak of charity the evils necessarily created by it, to excuse them or to deny their existence.'[4] The only way to address real problems was to proceed without illusions, to circumvent the 'false consciousness' by which people accept their situation, and directly to change the social and economic structure.

Nietzsche's aims were different, but his method was strikingly similar. Morality, by which he means primarily the Judaeo-Christian ethic, is an invention designed to further the interests of a particular class. Nietzsche's bold thesis is that the class in question was not the rulers but the slaves. The 'slave revolt in morals' taught people to value self-restraint, compassion, charity, the protection of the weak, the defence of the vulnerable. In so doing it inverted the values of life itself, of which the most important is the will to power. The slave, he wrote, 'is suspicious of the virtues of the powerful: he is sceptical and mistrustful, keenly mistrustful, of everything "good" that is honoured among them'. Instead he favours 'those qualities which serve to make easier the existence of suffering', namely 'pity, the kind and helping hand, the warm heart, patience, industriousness, humility, friendliness'. It is precisely these virtues, cherished in the West since the rise of Christianity,

[4] Frederick Engels, *The Origin of the Family*, Chicago, Charles Kerr, 1902, 216.

93

which Nietzsche sees as contemptible, false, at odds with nature itself. 'Wherever slave morality comes to predominate, language exhibits a tendency to bring the words "good" and "stupid" closer to each other.'[5] Like Marx, Nietzsche aims at the overthrow of conventional morality, a 'transvaluation of values'. For both, an essential prelude is the 'unmasking' of ordinary moral language to uncover the harsh reality beneath.

Freud's views on morality are difficult to summarise and underwent revision in the course of a long career. In their simplest outline, though, they are that in their primitive state people are driven by a set of aggressive and sexual instincts which have to be repressed for civilisation to be possible. In the individual this takes the form of an internalised restraint, the superego. In the case of cultures it takes the form of myths and rituals. In *Totem and Taboo*, Freud argued that their origin lay in an ancient memory of parricide. The sons of the tribe had risen against their father, envious of his monopoly of the tribe's women, and had killed him, only to be haunted by guilt which was then assuaged by rituals of atonement and reparation. All civilisation, whether of the individual or society, depends on the suppression of instinct, which generates internal conflict and neurosis. Religion was simply this conflict writ large and projected onto the universe; it is 'the universal neurosis of humanity'. Freud himself believed that discontents are an inevitable outcome of civilisation, but this did not prevent a number of his followers from arguing for a new and less repressive form of existence, in which instinctual gratification came to be seen not as a hazard to society but as a route to health. This was the origin of what Philip Rieff calls the 'therapeutic ethic'.

These three thinkers, quite different in their concerns and aspirations, nevertheless share important points of similarity. Unlike Hume and Kant, they no longer merely bypass religion. They take active pains to explain it away in the hope of overcoming it. Each is engaged in a massive revisionary enterprise, whose ultimate outcome will be to change the way we think and speak about

[5] Friedrich Nietzsche, *Beyond Good and Evil*, Harmondsworth, Penguin, 1973, 178.

ourselves, even the way we structure society. Their aim is not to vindicate morality but to offer a language from which morality, in the Judaeo-Christian sense, has been removed. Most significantly, each expresses (or in the case of Freud, makes possible) a new and adversarial relationship between the individual and society. The external order was, in Marx's key word, 'alienating'. It had come to seem something foreign and oppressive, hostile and falsifying. The very failing of morality was that it postulated a harmony between 'in here' and 'out there', a harmony that did not exist and which, in the striving to create it, divided man against himself. If Hume and Kant sought to justify morality, Marx, Nietzsche and the post-Freudians undertook to free him from it.

By the time the impact of these thinkers had been felt, the radical conclusions already implicit in Hume and Kant could finally be spelled out. In 1936, A. J. Ayer took Hume's argument to its logical conclusion. If there is no legitimate transition from *is* to *ought* then moral judgements can be nothing more than expressions of emotion. Unlike scientific statements, which can be tested and verified against experience, sentences containing 'good' or 'ought' are pseudo-propositions, apparently meaningful but actually not. They do not convey information. They merely express emotion. They are the communication of subjective states. If so, not only can there be no moral knowledge, there can be no meaningful moral discourse.

What Ayer did for Hume, Jean-Paul Sartre did for Kant. Autonomy, the self as sovereign over its own choices, might have meant, in the eighteenth century, no more than free assent to established custom. But after the Second World War, for Sartre, it meant radical, 'existential', choice, freedom without guidance or constraints, the courage to face a world without external meanings. As he puts it, 'Dostoevsky once wrote "If God did not exist, everything would be permitted"; and that, for existentialism, is the starting-point. Everything is indeed permitted if God does not exist, and man is in consequence forlorn, for he cannot find anything to depend upon either within or outside himself.' For Sartre, 'Man makes himself; he is not found ready made; he makes himself by his choice of morality, and he cannot but choose a morality, such is the pressure of circumstances upon him.' Kant believed that we could discover morality through reason. Sartre has no such illusions. All that remains is autonomy itself, in which the individual discovers 'that there is no legislator but himself; that he himself, thus abandoned, must decide for himself'.[6]

Let us now return to Eleazar in fourteenth-century Mainz. What is clear is that within our present frame of discourse we cannot make sense of much of his world. What interests us – private emotion, individual choice – does not overly concern him. He speaks not of the self and its dilemmas but of family and community, the relations between husbands and wives, parents and children, the importance of living and handing on a tradition. He does not believe that his is the way of all people. He knows only too well that it is the way of a minority. But it defines who he is, who his children are, where he belongs, and what he is dedicated to continue. He can speak easily to his children of duty because it is a language he and they share. There is a certain coherence to his world which we may have lost.

By contrast, Ayer's and Sartre's individual has many more choices, indeed they are almost open-ended. But he has no particular reason for choosing one thing over another. The language of objective justification of choice is in principle ruled out. He has been taught and has accepted that all choices are equally valid. Nor, if he has absorbed popular versions of Marxism or sociobiology, has he any reason to suppose that his decisions are particularly significant. The world is as it is because of inexorable forces of which we are only dimly and intermittently aware. Choice becomes simultaneously open-ended and inconsequential. The modern individual has no reason to enter into binding commitments such as marriage or membership in a community, for these will restrict his options in a way he has learned to find intolerable and unjustifiable.

He might as a result find it difficult to say who and what he is. It will not be surprising if his life consists in a series of temporary engagements – jobs, relationships, lifestyles – none of which, since

[6] Jean-Paul Sartre, *Existentialism and Humanism*, London, Methuen, 1989, 34, 55–6.

they come and go, gives shape and unity to a life. He may even have little relationship with his parents or his children. Perhaps the cruellest realisation will be that for no one does he hold unconditional worth. A world without moral bonds, of free-floating attachments, is one in which we are essentially replaceable – as employees, sexual partners, or members of a 'lifestyle enclave'. It is a world in which individuals are not characters in a shared drama but the temporary occupants of roles. The concept of loyalty becomes hard to understand. But we anticipate, for with Ayer and Sartre we have begun to move beyond liberalism to libertarianism, a stage in the story we have not yet reached.

What we have seen, though, is that language has tracked the movement of the self, from embeddedness in the structures of society, to detachment from, even hostility towards, them. The self of individualism speaks a radically purified language, purged of the complex attachments to family, tradition, custom and community that once allowed words to bridge the gap between 'is' and 'ought'. What was happening to these institutions meanwhile, the 'little platoons', the local birthplaces of belonging and identity, the contexts in which we become not abstract individuals but particular persons with specific histories and loves?

9

The Assault on the Particular

> Sceptreless, free, uncircumscribed, but man
> Equal, unclassed, tribeless, and nationless,
> Exempt from awe, worship, degree, the king
> Over himself; just, gentle, wise: but man
> Passionless? – no, yet free from guilt or pain
>
> Shelley[1]

ON 26 AUGUST 1789, in one of the framing moments of modern history, the French National Assembly issued its Declaration of the Rights of Man and of the Citizen. 'All men', it stated, 'are born, and remain, free and equal in rights.' It went on to assert that: 'No person shall be molested for his opinions, even such as are religious, provided that the manifestation of these opinions does not disturb the public order established by the law.' The question was, did this include Jews?

The question was of more than academic significance. No sooner had the Declaration been made than anti-Jewish riots broke out in Alsace, where there was a large Jewish population. In the wave of revolutionary fervour, anti-Jewish sentiment was running high. The assembly equivocated and delayed. Finally, on 23 December, the Count of Clermont-Tonnerre rose to make a speech. The Declaration, he said, was entirely clear. No one should be persecuted for his religious beliefs. There should be separation of church and state. The law has no concern with a person's beliefs. It is interested only in his actions. Jews therefore were entitled to equal rights within the state. But he made one proviso. If Jews were to be part of the French nation, they could not at the same time be

[1] P. B. Shelley, *Prometheus Unbound*, III, iv, 194–8.

part of the Jewish 'nation'. In ringing tones he declared: 'The Jews should be denied everything as a nation, but granted everything as individuals . . . It is intolerable that the Jews should become a separate political formation or class in the country. Every one of them must individually become a citizen; if they do not want this, they must inform us and we shall then be compelled to expel them.'[2] It was the first sign that liberty, equality and fraternity had their limits. As Martin Buber was later to say, in the year that Hitler came to power, the tragedy of emancipation was that Jews had been granted rights individually but not collectively.[3]

The case of Judaism is significant because it allows us to see, in a peculiarly heightened way, that a mode of thought designed to promote tolerance may have quite sharp intolerances of its own. It was, for example, no less a defender of liberty than Voltaire who wrote in the mid-eighteenth century that the Jews are an 'ignorant and barbarous people who have long united the most sordid avarice with the most detestable superstition and the most invincible hatred for every people by whom they are tolerated and enriched'. Still, he added, 'we ought not to burn them'.[4]

The point is not that such sentiments could be found here and there within the Europe of the Enlightenment. It is that they are to be found in its most profound thinkers.[5] Kant once wrote of the 'euthanasia' of Judaism and spoke privately of Jews as 'the vampires of society'. Hegel took Judaism as his model of a slave morality. Schopenhauer spoke of Jews as 'no better than cattle', as 'scum of the earth', as people eminently worthy of expulsion (his work was taken up enthusiastically by early Nazi writers). Nietzsche fulminated against Judaism as the 'falsification' of all natural values. In the twentieth century Martin Heidegger, the greatest German philosopher of his time, became an active Nazi, declaring on one occasion that:

[2] The speech is reprinted in Paul Mendes-Flohr and Jehuda Reinharz (eds.), *The Jew in the Modern World*, New York, Oxford University Press, 1980, 103–5.

[3] See F. E. Talmage (ed.), *Disputation and Dialogue*, New York, Ktav, 1975, 54.

[4] See Mendes-Flohr and Reinharz (eds.), op. cit., 252–3.

[5] See my *Crisis and Covenant*, Manchester, Manchester University Press, 1992, 247–9; Nathan Rotenstreich, *Jews and German Philosophy*, New York, Schocken, 1984.

'The Führer himself and alone is the present and future German reality and law.' Even Jean-Paul Sartre in his sustained attack on prejudice, *Anti-Semite and Jew*, published after the Holocaust in 1946, argued that it was not Jews who created anti-Semitism but rather anti-Semitism which created Jews. The conclusion, hinted at and inevitable, was that in a tolerant world there would be no Jews since their sole source of identity lay in the hatred others had for them. These philosophers had little else in common. Nor were they people of unreflective prejudice. How then did anti-Semitism or anti-Judaism form so pronounced a feature of their work?

Jews were and are a particular people, a religious community bound by a covenant to be faithful to God. In this they were not unusual. Many nations and faiths have seen themselves in this light, not least Christianity (the 'new Israel') on the one hand, Jefferson's America (that 'almost chosen land') on the other. In the context of eighteenth- and nineteenth-century Europe, however, Jews represented differentness. But it was just *differentness* which the Enlightenment proposed to overcome. Its solution, brilliant in its simplicity, was that people would be regarded as individuals, regardless of birth, class or faith. But Jewish identity is precisely *not* regardless of birth. It is usually conferred by it. Jewishness therefore represented a problem for the Enlightenment, an anomaly within the terms it had constructed for itself.

In the previous chapter I described the evolution of modern moral thought. The norms of human behaviour were to be found in emotion (Hume), reason (Kant), social contract (Hobbes), the consequences of action (Bentham), the structure of history (Marx), human will (Nietzsche) or existential decision (Sartre). Not all of these were rationalist approaches, but what they have in common is that their subject-matter is man-as-such, not particular human beings set in specific traditions, each with its own integrity. There is a vast chasm separating those like Kant and Bentham who believed that there are universal principles of ethics, and those like Nietzsche and Sartre who argued that there is nothing beyond individual choice. But despite this they share the same fundamental Either/Or: either there is ethical truth, in which case it applies to all people equally, or there are only the private decisions of individuals, in which case there is no objective ethical truth. Moral principle is universal or it is private: such is the axiom of the Enlightenment's heirs.

It had one fateful consequence. It excluded Judaism. For Judaism is predicated on the conviction that there can be a commitment – a covenant – that is binding and yet particular. It is a faith which is neither private nor universal, and this was ruled out *a priori* by Enlightenment assumptions. One by one the key principles of Judaism were excluded by modern philosophy. Hume's dichotomy between 'is' and 'ought', together with Sartre's idea that 'existence precedes essence', made it impossible to understand that religious obligations might be conferred by birth. Bentham's utilitarianism opposed the idea that there might be absolute moral rules, that certain acts might be wrong regardless of the consequences. Kantian autonomy ruled out the idea of revealed command. Kantian universality vitiated the concept of a divine covenant with a particular people. Hegel's history condemned Judaism to a primitive past. Nietzsche's philosophy of will made obedience inconceivable as a virtue and saw morality, in the Judaic sense, as the original sin.

Let me now make clear why I have pursued this line of thought. My concern is not with anti-Semitism but with something else altogether, namely the deep hostility of modern thought to the *particular*: the local, the communal, the less-than-universal or at least (in the case of Hegel) the less-than-national. Judaism served many of these writers – some of whom, Schopenhauer and Nietzsche for example, were hostile to Christianity as well – as a kind of paradigm for what had to be overcome if mankind were to move to a new stage. It was less the fact that Jews were different than that they were *collectively* different that made them so ready a target. They had allegiances to one another as well as to the state, and this opened them up time and again, in one country after another, to charges of dual loyalties, despite their endlessly repeated acts of patriotism and despite the tragic fact that they had nowhere else to go.

The point – and it is crucial – is that we *all* have multiple allegiances, to family, friends, neighbours, colleagues, 'significant others', to interests, vocations, institutions, groups and teams. These play an important, sometimes definitive, part in making us the person we are. Relationships are often bounded by rules, codes, customs and conventions. Marriage, parenthood and collegiality each have their own ethic, one element of which is that we do *not* treat people who stand in this relation to us as persons-in-general. To make no distinction between strangers and friends is to lack the virtue, perhaps even the concept, of friendship. The assault on Judaism was therefore symptomatic of a far larger blind spot in Enlightenment thought. It was ultimately a failure to understand a significant dimension of what makes us human.

Consider the following remark of Montesquieu:

> If I knew something useful to me, but prejudicial to my family, I would reject it from my soul. If I knew something useful to my family but not to my country, I would try to forget it. If I knew something useful to my country, but prejudicial to Europe, or useful to Europe but prejudicial to humankind, I would regard it as a crime . . . [For] I am a man before I am a Frenchman, or rather . . . I am necessarily a man, while I am a Frenchman only by chance.

This is Enlightenment universalism at its purest. All local attachments are inferior to more general ones. To be truly human is to treat all alike. Montesquieu did not shrink from drawing the inevitable conclusion. 'If men were perfectly virtuous,' he wrote, 'they wouldn't have friends.'[6]

The English utilitarian William Godwin mounted a similar argument against the idea that bonds of kinship impose any obligations. Suppose, he said, I had the choice of saving one person from a fire, my father or Fénelon 'at the moment he conceived the project of his immortal Telemachus'. Justice (by which he means benefit to society) would dictate that I save Fénelon and allow my father to die. What consequence is it, he asks, that my father is *mine*? It surely cannot 'conduce to the benefit of mankind, that each man should have a different standard of moral judgement and preference'.[7] To be moral involves strict impartiality between the

---

[6] Montesquieu, *Mes Pensées*, quoted in Michael Sandel, *Democracy's Discontent*, 342.

[7] William Godwin, 'The Immorality of Filial Affection', in D. H. Munro, *A Guide to the British Moralists*, London, Fontana, 1972, 187–92.

claims of different individuals, regardless of their relationship to us. The family is an irrelevance to morality.

Godwin was inclined to extremes. Not all the philosophers of the seventeenth and eighteenth centuries were utilitarians and not all were revolutionaries. But it is striking, nevertheless, how subordinate a place the family holds in their systems. Hobbes, for example, writes that parental authority 'is not so derived from the Generation, as if therefore the Parent had dominion over his Child because he begat him; but from the Child's Consent, either expresse, or by other sufficient arguments declared'. Parenthood has thus become a mere contract between consenting parties. Rousseau, arguing for the transfer of authority from the family to the state, makes the astonishing statement that: 'Should the public authority, in assuming the place of father and charging itself with this important function, acquire his rights in the discharge of his duties, he should have little cause to protest; for he would only be altering his title, and would have in common, under the name *citizen*, the same authority over his children, that he was exercising separately under the name *father*.' The complete abolition of the family and its takeover by the government should, in other words, make no difference since 'citizen' and 'parent' are merely communal and private forms of the same thing.[8] Immanuel Kant once notoriously defined marriage as 'the union of two persons of the opposite sex for the lifelong, mutual possession of each other's sexual characteristics'.[9]

What these examples have in common is a deep tendency to reduce all relationships to contractual associations between atomic individuals. To be sure, there were dissenting voices. There was the English conservative, Edmund Burke, who argued that: 'We begin our public affections in our families'[10] and: 'To be attached to the subdivision, to love the little platoon we belong to in society, is the first principle . . . of public affections.'[11] There was the German Romantic, Johann Gottfried Herder, who suggested that: 'The

[8] See Robert Nisbet, *The Quest for Community*, 121–52.

[9] *Metaphysik der Sitten*, Rechtslehre, 24, 107; cited in Charles Larmore, *Patterns of Moral Complexity*, 168.

[10] Edmund Burke, *Reflections on the Revolution in France*, 198.

[11] Ibid., 46–7.

savage who loves himself, his wife and child, with quiet joy, and in his modest way works for the good of the tribe' may be 'a truer human being than that shadow of a man, the refined citizen of the world, who, enraptured with the love of all his fellow-shadows, loves but a chimera.' But these were isolated protests, minority presences. For the most part, in the philosophical literature from Hobbes onward, there is little sense that families, friendships or loyalties might play an autonomous role within the moral life and that they might, in fact, be constitutive of human individuality. Still less is there an appreciation of their role in forming character, in moral education, in transmitting wisdom and traditions across the generations.

Thus the moral legitimacy of the family had been eroded long before the massive onslaught of the past century and a half. What was new in what followed was the thesis that the family was not merely irrelevant but positively harmful, in a bewildering variety of ways. For Marx and Engels it was an institution of capitalism and bourgeois exploitation. For the post-Freudians it was the matrix of repression and psychic dysfunction. For radical feminists it was the perpetuation of patriarchy. By 1967 Sir Edmund Leach could say, in his Reith Lectures, that: 'Far from being the basis of the good society, the family, with its narrow privacy and tawdry secrets, is the source of all discontents.'[12] My concern here is not to evaluate these claims, but simply to show how they flowed almost inevitably from the terms of discourse previously established by Enlightenment thought.

The great thrust of eighteenth-century philosophy, with its relentless focus of the unique and the universal, was to marginalise the significance of all the institutions in which *belonging* was expressed, and in which moral habits and principles had traditionally been taught. It had little patience for the family or the community, for custom or the wisdom of the generations, for local associations and loyalties, or for religion itself except in the most abstract and deistic forms. Necessarily so, for these were and are *particular*

[12] E. R. Leach, *A Runaway World*, London, BBC, 1968, 44. See my *The Persistence of Faith*, 48–58; Ferdinand Mount, *The Subversive Family*.

institutions, larger than the individual but smaller than humanity as a whole. It was not only Jews, but *people*, who were to be given rights only as individuals but not in any other form. As Steven Lukes has pointed out, the idea of the abstract individual, without ties or allegiances other than those contractually entered into, 'runs like a connecting thread through the various forms of political individualism, from Locke to the present day'.[13]

That is not to say that the Enlightenment was systematically hostile to particular institutions, but it was systematically incapable of understanding them. At best they were tolerated and misinterpreted. Religion, together with all other particular loyalties, was moved to the private domain. Enlightenment morality had direct political consequences. The unique and the universal meant, for the nineteenth century, the individual and the (imperial) state. Everything else was a relic of an earlier and more primitive age. Particularist loyalties had neither right nor reason to exist other than as private agreements between individuals. Thus the stage was set for the assault on the family and the community. Their conceptual integrity, their metaphysical space, had been destroyed. They continued to exist, but within the terms set by the prevailing mode of thought no one could say with any cogency why they should exist. The philosophical obituary for intermediate institutions had already been written in the eighteenth century, when Hume first separated 'is' and 'ought' and Kant rejected all moral authority outside the self.

All this was understandable. It was, in its way, part of the long-term reaction to the wars of religion of the sixteenth century and the parallel rise of science. While religious belief led only to interminable dispute, science offered a universal language of experimentation and the testing of hypotheses. It became the new paradigm of human knowledge. Nothing that could not be tested could be known. Again it was Hume and Kant who set the terms for all subsequent development. Morality was a matter of either private emotion or universal reason. These formed the conceptual basis of the abstract individual and the (universal) state.

[13] Steven Lukes, *Individualism*, 138.

These developments, then, proceeded from deep reflection on a dismal past and they were conducted with high integrity and moral purpose. But with hindsight we can say that they ignored a central feature of the human situation. Morality cannot be assimilated to science. Human beings are not atoms; neither, for that matter, are animals. Our pathos and our glory lie in the fact that we cannot live alone, but only with the greatest difficulty can we live together. We form groups. In the case of human beings, we do so self-consciously. We form associations to give our collective purposes continuity and strength. These are more than a mere coming-together which can be observed and described from the outside. Associations have an inner life. They are systems of meaning, languages of self-understanding. They exist in the form of rules, codes, rituals and narratives which we learn and internalise as we enter and become part of them. Some of them – professional associations, for example, or guilds – are consciously made by and for people for purposes of regulation and protection. Others, most obviously religious communities, arise in response to a sensed external reality. They are, or are felt to be, revealed, summoned into being.

None of these associations is universal though some have universal aspirations. None is private: their very existence is an attempt to give structure to the social. Yet despite the fact that they lie in no-man's-land from an Enlightenment point of view, they form the very heart of humanity's attempt to give existence a collective purpose, an articulate meaning. Not until philosophy, sociology and anthropology began to study languages as forms of life would the human sciences have the resources to come to terms with the inherent particularity of our deepest commitments.

Enlightenment rationality failed to do justice to the way in which our attachments are born and grow. Love and loyalty are not universal. They are essentially particular – to this person, that place, this faith, that people. Shelley, in the quotation which heads this chapter, tried to envisage 'man equal, unclassed, tribeless, and nationless', free from 'guilt or pain', and yet with passions. But it is hard to understand what those passions might be, where they came from, what they are directed to or how they might be sustained. From the days of the Hebrew Bible, the effort of moral teachers was directed to extending the range of human attachment outward from the individual to the family to mankind as a whole – Pope's 'Self love thus pushed to social, to divine, gives thee to make thy neighbour's blessing thine'. The Enlightenment inverted this entire order. By loving people in general one would come to love people in particular. No less likely account of human emotion has ever been given. It is parodied savagely by Charles Dickens in *Bleak House*, in the figure of Mrs Jellyby, the lady of 'rapacious virtue' and 'telescopic philanthropy' who devotes her life in Holborn to the cause of the Borrioboola-Gha natives while shamelessly neglecting her own children.[14]

Over the Enlightenment lies a shadow. Clearly there is no connection between Kant's benign universe and the nightmare kingdom of the extermination camps, despite the fact that Adolf Eichmann declared himself a devotee of Kantian ethics.[15] Nor can we make connections between Hegel's absolute state and the Third Reich, or between Nietzsche's death-of-God, and the proposed death, seventy years later, of the people-of-God,[16] or between the anti-Judaic thrust of German moral philosophy and Hitler's remark that 'conscience was a Jewish invention'. The fact remains however that throughout much of continental Europe – where, more than in Britain, philosophical abstractions unleavened by common sense and a respect for history, tended to become political programmes – the Enlightenment failed in its stated objective. It did not create a rational, tolerant, unprejudiced society 'free from guilt or pain'. That is not to condemn it. It had immense achievements to its credit, of which the institutionalisation of the rights of the individual was the greatest. But its truths were partial, and there was much in human existence it failed to understand.

However our concern is with matters less weighty, more mundane. I have tried in the last four chapters to show how economic

14 Charles Dickens, *Bleak House*, chapter 4.

15 See Hannah Arendt, *Eichmann in Jerusalem*, Harmondsworth, Penguin, 1977, 135–7; and, especially, Emil Fackenheim, *To Mend The World*, New York, Schocken, 1982, 266–77.

16 See the discussion in George Steiner, *In Bluebeard's Castle*, London, Faber & Faber, 1971, 29–49.

and social forces, philosophical thought and political development combined over a long period to weaken the hold of 'civil' institutions, those intermediate groupings from the family to the community to religious and voluntary associations, leaving in their place a radically simplified landscape of the atomic individual and the encompassing state. They did more than render such institutions redundant. They made them inarticulate. They could not be justified because they were not universal. They spoke to human beings in the concrete particularity of their memories and histories, loyalties and loves. They addressed flesh-and-blood men and women, not man-as-such. It was precisely this that made the Enlightenment see them as the source of all conflict, and led some of the greatest of modern minds to search for a new and purified way of thinking about human life. This was a revolution of the highest consequence for, since the beginning of human civilisation, when we have sought meanings we have done so in the forms of narratives, traditions, codes and sacred texts through which one generation passed on its wisdom to the next, and individuals were socialised into the purposes of their shared world.

In Britain and America, though, throughout the nineteenth century, families and local institutions remained strong. They were not to lose their hold until the 1960s when, in one country after another throughout the West, a tidal wave of change hit traditional institutions and values. It was then that the second revolution took place.

10

The Libertarian Revolution

So it is only a matter of a 'detail': to recognize in time that fateful
first moment of deterioration, when an idea ceases to express the
transcendent dimension of being human and degenerates into a
substitute for it, the moment when the artefact, the project for a
better world, ceases to be an expression of man's responsible identity
and begins, on the contrary, to expropriate his responsibility and
identity, when the abstraction ceases to belong to him and he
instead begins to belong to it.

Vaclav Havel[1]

'TO THE BELOVED and deplored memory of her who was the
inspirer, and in part the author, of all that is best in my writings'.
So begins the dedication of one of the most influential works of
modern times, John Stuart Mill's *On Liberty*. Mill ends his tribute
with these words: 'Were I but capable of interpreting to the world
one half the great thoughts and noble feelings which are buried in
her grave, I should be the medium of a greater benefit to it, than
is ever likely to arise from anything I can write, unprompted and
unassisted by her all but unrivalled wisdom.'[2]

The person who inspired these powerful feelings was Mill's great
love and eventual wife, Harriet. They first met in 1830, when Mill
was twenty-four and Harriet was writing articles for a Unitarian
journal. At that time she was married to a Mr John Taylor. She and
Mill met regularly for many years, and this led to quarrels between
Mill and his family and close friends, who strongly disapproved of
the relationship. In 1849 John Taylor died, and in 1851 Mill and

---

[1] Vaclav Havel, *Living in Truth*, 175.
[2] John Stuart Mill, *Utilitarianism, On Liberty and Considerations on Representative Government*, 69.

Harriet were married. In 1857, the Divorce Act was passed, for the first time allowing divorce to take place without a special act of Parliament, thus placing it within the means of members of the middle class. A year later Harriet died, and in 1859 Mill published the essay *On Liberty*, with its powerful and striking dedication to her memory.

It is impossible to do more than guess at the connection between these events and the contents of the book itself.[3] This much, though, is clear. In it Mill departs from many of the views he expressed elsewhere, both before and after the book was published. In particular, the famous declaration of the purpose of the essay, 'to assert one very simple principle, as entitled to govern absolutely the dealings of society with the individual', stands at odds with his criticism of the French *philosophes* who attempted to reduce political science to simple principles. 'The united forces of society never were, nor can be, directed to one single end, nor is there, so far as I can perceive, any reason for desiring that they should,' he had earlier written.[4]

What was Mill's 'one very simple principle'? We know that he had been much struck by the observations of Alexis de Tocqueville in *Democracy in America*, in particular by Tocqueville's warning of the danger of the 'tyranny of the majority', a phrase Mill appropriates in his own book. Tocqueville's fear, however, was related to the growth of individualism. Its antidote, he believed, lay in the strength of family and community life that he observed in America. He was convinced that this 'art of association' was essential to maintaining democratic freedom. He ascribed particular importance to the influence of religion in 'directing the customs of the community', and held that the great defence of liberty in a democratic society lay in its 'habits of the heart', the 'moral and intellectual condition of a people'.[5]

Mill proceeded to turn this argument on its head. For him, it

[3] See, though, Gertrude Himmelfarb, *On Liberty and Liberalism: The Case of John Stuart Mill.*

[4] *The Earlier Letters of John Stuart Mill*, 1812–1848, ed. Francis E. Mineka, Toronto, University of Toronto Press, 1963, vol. 1, 36.

[5] Tocqueville, *Democracy in America*, 179–83.

was not individualism which was the danger, but the repression of individualism. 'Custom' was not a defence of freedom but a threat to it. For Mill, the individual needed protection from precisely the kind of social sanction and stigma which Tocqueville saw as what he called the 'apprenticeship of liberty'. Against this Mill argued that we need protection 'against the tendency of society to impose, by other means than civil penalties, its own ideas and practices as rules of conduct on those who dissent from them'.[6] Mill, in other words, sought not only limited government but the abolition of all social convention and judgement,[7] the things that had caused him such anguish within his intimate circle of acquaintances for nineteen years of his relationship with Harriet.

Mill's 'one very simple principle' was this, that 'the only purpose for which power can be rightfully exercised over any member of a civilized community, against his will, is to prevent harm to others. His own good, either physical or moral, is not a sufficient warrant.'[8] Leaving aside the difficulties in this and Mill's several paraphrases of the principle, the character of the project is clear. What Mill is in effect doing is to apply to morals what Locke had applied to religion. If freedom of thought, speech and association were imperative in the one case, so too in the other. If people should be

[6] Mill, *Utilitarianism, On Liberty and Considerations on Representative Government*, 73.

[7] To be sure, Mill is far from clear on this point. He notes that moral concern with someone else's behaviour may constitute good reason 'for remonstrating with him, or reasoning with him, or persuading him, or entreating him, but not for compelling him, or visiting him with any evil in case he do otherwise' (ibid., 78). He insists that his doctrine is not 'one of selfish indifference, which pretends that human beings should have no business with each other's conduct in life'. It is merely that 'disinterested benevolence can find other instruments to persuade people to their good than whips and scourges, either of the literal or the metaphorical sort' (ibid., 144). Mill was not arguing that we should be 'non-judgemental'. What is unclear is where he drew the line between coercive and non-coercive forms of public judgement. My reading of Mill has been influenced by the work of Friedrich Hayek and Gertrude Himmelfarb. For a somewhat different view, see Alan Ryan, *John Stuart Mill*, New York, Pantheon, 1970, 233–56.

[8] Ibid., 78.

free to worship their own deity, they should be free to choose their own lifestyle, what Mill called their 'experiments in living', without legal hindrance or reproach. If the earlier revolution had sought, first toleration, then emancipation, Mill now sought liberalisation of the enforcement, by law and opinion, of morality.

To distinguish this second stage of the revolution from the first, I will call its programme not liberalism but libertarianism. *Libertarianism is liberalism applied to the moral and civil domain.* The connection between them is clear, but so too is the fateful difference. Liberals believed that when a single religion no longer held society together, a common morality would. But when a common morality no longer holds society together, it is unclear where the bonds of cohesion lie. Doubtless, libertarians believed that just as society survived the first transition, so it would the second.[9]

Mill's 'one very simple principle' was a century ahead of its time. In 1957 the Wolfenden Committee on Homosexual Offences and Prostitution proposed the legalisation of homosexual acts between consenting adults in private. Its reason for doing so was precisely what Mill had suggested, namely that the task of the law was to prevent harm to others, and thus 'it is not, in our view, the function of the law to intervene in the private lives of citizens, or to seek to enforce any particular pattern of behaviour.' The Report concluded that: 'Unless a deliberate attempt is to be made by society, acting through the agency of the law, to equate the sphere of crime with that of sin, there must remain a realm of private morality which is, in brief and crude terms, not the law's business.'[10] With remarkable

[9] Mill himself believed that society *did* require a shared morality: 'All that makes existence valuable to any one, depends on the enforcement of restraints upon the actions of other people. Some rules of conduct, therefore, must be imposed, by law in the first place, and by opinion on many things which are not fit subjects for the operation of law' (ibid., 73–4). I do not want to read into the Mill of 1859, attitudes which came to the fore a century later. My argument in this chapter is that the libertarian revolution was a long one, the result of many factors, and that it gathered force in the late 1950s. Mill was not a libertarian in the modern sense. Nevertheless *On Liberty* was a seminal text in this development, not least because of its ambiguities, and its pervasive mood – noted by Mill's contemporaries – of chafing against social restraints.

[10] Quoted in Devlin, *The Enforcement of Morals*, 2–3.

speed, the principle was accepted not only in Britain but throughout most of the liberal democracies in Europe and America in the 1960s and was accompanied by the liberalisation of laws relating not only to homosexuality but also to abortion, censorship and divorce. Little over a hundred years after the publication of *On Liberty*, its views had become the new orthodoxy of the West.

In an earlier chapter, I suggested one possible explanation of why views expressed in the late 1850s gained ground in the late 1950s, namely the impact on the post-Holocaust generation of the dangers of a totalitarian state. When Tocqueville and Mill used the phrase 'tyranny of the majority' it was a remote theoretical possibility. After Hitler's Germany and Stalin's Russia it was a terrifying reality, and it was Isaiah Berlin's great essay, 'Two Concepts of Liberty', which connected the two. The pursuit of 'negative liberty', the right of individuals to freedom from interference, was, he argued, the best defence against a 'final solution'.

The libertarian revolution must, though, be set against another equally significant development which helped to transform the social contract between the individual and the state. In a famous passage, the historian A. J. P. Taylor once described the scope of government in Britain at the outbreak of the First World War. 'Until August 1914 a sensible, law-abiding Englishman could pass through life and hardly notice the existence of the state, beyond the post-office and the policeman. He could live where he liked and as he liked. He had no official number or identity card. He could travel abroad or leave his country for ever without a passport or any sort of official permission.' Taxation was less than 8 per cent of national income. In the second half of the nineteenth century the government had begun to impose health and safety regulations, and in 1870 it empowered local authorities to set up schools financed by the rates. But beyond this, 'the state acted only to help those who could not help themselves. It left the adult citizen alone.'[11]

War is one of the great agents of social change. While it lasts, rates of taxation rise to levels politically unsustainable at times of peace. There is a palpable sense of national identity, a common front

[11] A. J. P. Taylor, *English History 1914–1945*, Oxford, Clarendon Press, 1965, 1.

against a joint enemy. At no other time is the feeling of fraternity so strong. Strangers become neighbours, and neighbours friends. As the battles continue to take their terrible toll, a determination arises to make what amends can be made to those who have lost their lives, by building a better society in the wake of peace. Government revenues used to purchase arms will, once the battlefield grows silent, be used to ease suffering, ignorance and poverty. War is evil, but its after-effects are often profoundly benign. Thus, after both the first and second world wars, there was a massive rise in the activities of the state.

It took the form of greatly increased government participation in, and central control of, the economy, education, health and welfare and funding of the arts. One by one, areas of activity that had been dealt with by the family, local associations, voluntary and religious bodies, friendly societies and mutual assistance groups were taken over by direct government funding and administration, which offered greater expertise, efficiency and fairness; above all greater resources. The aim was to build a more equal and compassionate society. The conceptual justification, though, lay in a new political philosophy, a move from classical to welfare liberalism. This involved a new concept of rights.

In classical liberalism rights are things which the individual is deemed to have pre-politically, and which it is the state's duty to protect. For Hobbes this meant life, for Locke property. Edmund Burke summed up the traditional view when he wrote that people have 'a right to the fruits of their industry and to the means of making their industry fruitful. They have a right to the acquisitions of their parents, and to the nourishing and improving of their offspring ... Whatever each man can separately do, without trespassing on others, he has a right to do for himself; and he has a right to a fair proportion of all which society, with all its combinations of skill and force, can do in his favour. In this partnership all men have equal rights, but not to equal things.'[12]

Under welfare liberalism, the scope of rights vastly expands. They are now seen as those things which the individual does

---

[12] Edmund Burke, *Reflections on the Revolution in France*, 51.

not naturally have but which it is the state's duty to provide. In Roosevelt's famous 1944 agenda these were 'the right to a useful and remunerative job ... the right to earn enough to provide adequate food and clothing and recreation ... the right of every family to a decent home, the right to adequate medical care ... the right to adequate protection from the economic fears of old age, sickness, accident, and unemployment ... the right to a good education.' The counterpart in Britain was the Beveridge plan which set out the contours of the welfare state. The move from classical to welfare liberalism is, therefore, the change from minimalist to maximalist government.

So two things of great significance occurred around the middle of the twentieth century. By comparison with previous ages, the state *entered* the welfare arena and *exited* the domain of the enforcement of morality. Whether these two opposed and contrary movements are connected or not, they amount to a fundamental change in the terms of the social contract, from what Michael Sandel in an American context calls the 'republican politics' of the nineteenth century to the 'procedural republic' of the second half of the twentieth; or what we might more simply call a move from the politics of *character* to the politics of *interests*.

Liberalism had seen morality as the essential social bond. Though it was taught and cultivated informally, by families, religious groups, schools and social sanction, it was seen as the task of government, whether by law or fiscal means, to reinforce this moral consensus. By so doing, it gave support to the rules and virtues seen as necessary to a society of self-governing citizens. By contrast, the libertarianism which emerged by the 1960s saw the role of government quite differently. It was to provide citizens with the liberty and resources to pursue their own ends, consistent with a similar liberty for others.

Liberalism and libertarianism have different views of the nature of freedom and morality. For liberalism, freedom is collective self-government and morality consists at least in part in those virtues which support it. For libertarianism, by contrast, freedom is the protection of individual choice. Morality is not a matter of *virtue*, dispositions prized within a given society as necessary to its well-being, but of *value*, freely adopted personal preference.

Liberalism embodies a substantive idea of the common good. Libertarian politics rejects the idea that it is the business of the state to promote one vision of the good life at the cost of others. The good is a matter of private inclination. Instead the state focuses on fairness and impartiality. It is essentially *procedural*. So the nineteenth-century state legislated morality but had only a limited involvement in welfare, seeking as it did to develop independence. The modern state entered welfare and tended to retreat from morality because it sought to maximise choice.

These were political changes, but they coincided with a profound cultural transformation. Liberals had assumed that freedom was intrinsically associated with the classic virtue of self-control, the capacity to defer instinctual gratification. It was Burke who gave this view its classic expression. People, he wrote, 'are qualified for civil liberty in exact proportion to their disposition to put moral chains upon their own appetites'. There is a difference between liberty and 'licence', doing what you may and doing what you want. Where there is licence, there is conflict and violence, hence a greater need for external force, and thus an erosion of liberty. 'Society cannot exist unless a controlling power upon will and appetite be placed somewhere, and the less of it there is within, the more there must be without. It is ordained in the eternal constitution of things that men of intemperate minds cannot be free. Their passions forge their fetters.'[13]

As the 1960s unfolded, however, this came to seem less like the 'eternal constitution of things' than like a particular cultural artefact, that of bourgeois society. It was not the only, or even the most attractive, possibility. Popularisers of the ideas of Freud argued that far from enhancing freedom, the mechanisms of self-control and socialisation were repressive and psychologically harmful. The works of Marx and Nietzsche raised the suspicion that conventional morality was simply the imposition of a dominant class. Popular works of anthropology like Ruth Benedict's *Patterns of Culture* suggested that social structures were relative, and that we might choose to live differently, with fewer inhibitions. Rousseau's idea

[13] Burke, ibid., 289.

that the individual is born free and is placed under chains by society, began to enjoy a new vogue.

These ideas gained enormous currency in the fields of education, parenthood and therapy. In the classroom, teacher-centred methods were abandoned in favour of new child-centred approaches. Rote learning was gradually displaced by lessons which encouraged free expression on the part of the child. Formal examinations were supplanted by a desire to encourage 'self-esteem'. Widely read texts on parenthood undermined confidence in traditional forms of home discipline. Under the influence of Carl Rogers, the therapeutic process was seen to be essentially 'non-directive'. A new ethos was in the making, 'expressive individualism', in which the key to psychic well-being lay not in the internalisation of social norms but rather in liberation from them. The concept of socialisation – the induction of the individual into the shared norms of a wider world – was now seen not as the prime virtue of society but as the original sin of society against the individual.

All this coincided with a fundamental change in the economic environment. As Europe and America emerged from the austerities of the post-war years, high productivity and employment made not only possible, but also desirable, a new ethic of consumption. Older virtues like saving and frugality withered in the face of the credit card with its ethic of 'taking the waiting out of wanting', the precise opposite of the classic virtue of the deferral of gratification. The economist A. O. Hirschmann once argued that the birth of capitalism was accompanied by a cultural transition from 'passions' to 'interests'. By the same token, post-war capitalism involved an equally significant shift from 'interests' to 'desires'.

These forces converged like a tidal wave, sweeping away centuries of carefully cultivated habits. In the early twentieth century T. E. Hulme had contrasted romantic and classical views of human nature. The romantic idea was that 'man, the individual, is an infinite reservoir of possibilities; and if you can so rearrange society by the destruction of oppressive order then these possibilities will have a chance and you will get Progress'. The classical idea was that 'Man is an extraordinarily fixed and limited animal whose nature is absolutely constant. It is only by tradition and organization that anything decent can be got out of him.'[14] The 1960s were the high point of democratic romanticism.

This, in turn, had additional political consequences. Where liberalism had pursued virtue and the education of character, the new psychology took character as largely given. People were what they were, and their personalities were to be expressed, not cultivated or shaped. This was a far more deterministic view of personality than had ever been envisaged by morality. If Marxist, Darwinian or behaviourist theory were true, then the individual was subject to causal forces not under his or her control. The concepts of will, action and responsibility became more problematic than they had been under the Judaeo-Christian ethic. The result was an inversion of social causality. Previously people had believed that if you want to change society you have to change individuals. Now it was widely believed that if you wanted to change the individual you had to change society.

The most obvious impact was on judicial policy. From the Hebrew Bible to Kant the justification for punishment was retribution. Justice demanded that those who had wrongfully inflicted suffering on others should themselves be made to suffer. But if personality was causally determined by genetic endowment or psychological causation, by poverty or a damaged childhood, then the idea of responsibility for wrongdoing should be abandoned. The older jurisprudence had always made an exception in the case of *force majeure*, action under coercion, but the more social-scientific explanations of behaviour came to be accepted, the more this came to seem not the exception but the norm. Judicial policy gradually shifted from retribution to rehabilitation and reform.

This had wider implications. If punishment was no longer predicated on guilt, then reward should be made independent of desert. The nineteenth century, in Britain and America, had witnessed intense debates about welfare policy. Early on it was recognised that there was often a potential conflict between charity and human dignity. There is a moral imperative to help those in need, but help sometimes provides an incentive to remain in need.

[14] T. E. Hulme, *Speculations*, London, Routledge & Kegan Paul, 1924, 116.

On both sides of the Atlantic philanthropists wrestled with the problem of how to balance the alleviation of suffering with the encouragement of independence. There was no easy answer, but some rough-and-ready principles emerged: a distinction between the 'idle' and the 'deserving' poor (pauperism and poverty), a charitable effort that included education and character-formation, and a readiness to suspend benefits to those who seemed unwilling to help themselves, an approach that today would be called 'tough love'. These methods, pioneered by figures like Thomas Chalmers in Glasgow and by organisations like the Society for the Prevention of Pauperism in New York, became the model for thousands of philanthropic endeavours in the Victorian age.

The ethos they embodied could not survive the transfer of responsibility to the state. There is a conceptual difference between welfare as charity and as social justice. A privilege is distinct from a right. The relationship between beneficiary and benefactor changes when voluntary acts are replaced by a distributive system of taxation and benefits. Occurring when it did, however, the new welfare liberalism coincided with a changed view of human behaviour which made the idea of 'desert' seem an anachronism. Benefits should be given and received regardless of the merits of recipients, or their effects on character.

Despite this, attitudes took some time to change. During the great depression in the 1930s many people were reluctant to accept relief. Trained in habits of self-reliances they saw it as a source of shame, an acceptance of defeat. A noticeable change took place in the 1960s when for the first time benefits were seen as entitlements or quasi-property rights whose receipt carried no stigma. Increasingly, welfare came to be administered without preconditions. Any attempt to distinguish between, say, married and unmarried parents, or the unfortunate and the improvident, was an unwarrantable act of judgementalism on the part of government. The procedural state, having abandoned the project of character-formation, was bound to treat claimants equally.

So, by the end of the 1960s a new constellation of values had emerged in almost every sphere. Liberal society had been, above all, a moral order. The role of the state was limited, but it included

119

the inculcation of virtues – independence, law-abidingness and temperance – among its citizens. It was able to do so because of the supportive influence of families, churches, mutual aid societies and charities, groups which maintained a constant process of moral education, what Tocqueville called 'the slow and quiet action of society upon itself'. Legal sanctions, as Leslie Stephen put it, were no more than 'the seal on the wax of moral sentiment'.

Libertarianism was radically different. Its project was little short of the elimination of morality in its traditional forms. Punishment was no longer retributive. Benefits were not administered on the basis of merit. Neither the family nor the school were to be places where virtues were taught or customs passed on across the generations. The central concepts of morality – individual responsibility, the internalisation of restraint – had come to seem scientifically mis-guided and psychologically damaging. So the libertarian revolution was far more profound and far-reaching than its liberal precursor. The secular state had become the procedural state. The rights of the individual had multiplied and become the basis of an ethic of individualism and unfettered choice. Liberty itself was no longer an ideal of collective freedom, 'ordered liberty' as Justice Cardozo called it. It had become privatised: freedom as a personal possession, the right to do what one liked consistent with an equal freedom for others.

Not everyone saw the change as an improvement. Older liberals like Lionel Trilling and Daniel Bell warned of the corrosive effects of a culture of rising expectations and limitless demands. Philip Rieff, in his diagnosis of the new age, *The Triumph of the Therapeutic* (1966), prophesied that it would be radically unlike any previous civilisation. Cultures had always survived, he argued, because they had been able to instil in people habits of instinctual renunciation. For the first time in history this was being abandoned. He posed a stark challenge. 'The question is no longer as Dostoevski put it: "Can civilized men believe?" Rather [it is]: Can unbelieving men be civilized?'[15] Lionel Trilling uttered an equally dark prognosis.

[15] The argument is set out at length in Philip Rieff, *The Triumph of the Therapeutic*, 4.

The new 'adversary culture', he argued, was undertaking the 'socialization of the anti-social' and the 'legitimation of the subversive'.[16] But these were lonely voices. As I have indicated, the second revolution was a delayed but almost inevitable outcome of the first. Hume's emotivism and Kant's autonomy already contained within them the seeds of expressive individualism. Locke's liberalism, carried forward in Mill's *On Liberty,* was the germ of what was to take shape as the procedural state. These were possibilities, planted in the subsoil of the culture, slowly taking root, ready in time to emerge into the air.

The relationship between ideas and history is rarely immediate. A bridge can be weakened by a thousand crossings, though it breaks only on the thousand-and-first. Sometimes a new factor has to enter the equation before an idea finds its time. Historians have argued that the outline of the Reformation was already present in the mind of Wycliffe, who lived and taught in Oxford in the fourteenth century. But it took the invention of printing and the widespread ownership of Bibles before Luther could appeal successfully, two centuries later, to scriptural authority against that of the church. Often, ideas influence an elite long before they become democratised and are acted on by a large section of the population. So it was with libertarianism. It was the result of two histories of ideas – in ethics from Hume and Kant to Ayer and Sartre, in political philosophy from Locke to Mill to Isaiah Berlin. But it was not until a third factor was added – the growth of the state after the Second World War – that more than an elite could live by these ideas. As the state entered what had previously been the domain of civil society, the new thinking, carried by experts trained in its values, began to penetrate schools, families, and the administration of welfare. It was then that the procedural state met the abstract individual and the libertarian society was born.

It was a bloodless revolution of the most radical kind. The ground had been laid by two centuries of thought and social change. The result was that resistance was minimal, while support came from the

16 Lionel Trilling, *Beyond Culture*, New York, Viking, 1965, xiii, 26.

most widely respected sources. But the transformation was neither small nor gradual. Within a single generation, possibly the most profound climate change took place in the West since the days of the emperor Constantine. For centuries Western civilisation had been based on a Judaeo–Christian ethic. That was now being abandoned, systematically, ideologically, and with meticulous thoroughness. It was nothing short of a metamorphosis in the ecology of society. What was the result?

11

De-civilisation and Its Discontents

Liberals have always known that absolute power tends to corrupt . . .
[W]e are now discovering that absolute liberty tends to corrupt
absolutely. A liberty that is divorced from tradition and convention,
from morality and religion, that makes the individual the sole
repository and arbiter of all values and puts him in an adversarial
relationship to society and the state – such a liberty is a grave peril to
liberalism itself. For when that liberalism is found wanting, when it
violates the moral sense of the community or is incompatible with
the legitimate demands of society, there is no moderating principle
to take its place, no resting place between the wild gyrations of
libertarianism and paternalism.

Gertrude Himmelfarb[1]

IN RETROSPECT 1989 may come to seem as great a turning-
point in the history of the West as 1789, the year of the French
Revolution. In the East communism was crumbling throughout
Europe. The Cold War was over. It was the culmination of *glasnost*,
perestroika and the break-up of the Soviet Union. One of the great
confrontations of the twentieth century ended without a shot
having to be fired. As Ernest Gellner notes, it was the first war
to be fought not on the battlefield but in the arena of economic
competition, and it ended without the victors insisting on surrender,
and with the vanquished conceding defeat without being asked to
do so. 'Never before had an ideological contest ended with such
unanimity.'[2] European communism fell the way the Martians did
in H. G. Wells' *War of the Worlds*, not because of a victory by the
opposing side but simply through the collapse of its own internal

---

[1] Gertrude Himmelfarb, *On Looking into the Abyss*, 106.
[2] Ernest Gellner, *Conditions of Liberty*, 210.

systems. It failed to create prosperity. An American historian, Francis Fukuyama, promptly announced 'The End of History'. The consumer ethic would, he argued, prove to be the great solvent of ideological conflict. Supermarkets were more attractive than political creeds, and it is difficult to sustain a long war of attrition when shopping is your highest priority. The future would be dull but peaceful. Democratic capitalism and liberal individualism would prevail.

At the period of its greatest victory, though, the response of the West was significantly muted. It was not that it failed to sense the drama of what had happened in Eastern Europe. It was that certain profound doubts were beginning to be expressed about the future of liberal individualism itself. Those doubts came from West and East alike, from Alexander Solzhenitsyn and Vaclav Havel on the one hand, thoughtful American observers on the other. Mikhail Gorbachev himself, in 1987, said that while he admired the West, he feared for its future, conscious as he was 'that a deep, profoundly intelligent and inherently humane European culture is retreating to the background before the primitive revelry of violence and pornography'.

By 1995 Francis Fukuyama had published a new work, *Trust*, subtitled *The Social Virtues and the Creation of Prosperity*. Its tone was significantly different from that of his earlier work. He spoke of 'the rise of violent crime and civil litigation' in America, and of 'the breakdown of family structure; the decline of a wide range of intermediate social structures like neighbourhoods, churches, unions, clubs, and charities; and the general sense among Americans of a lack of shared values and community with those around them.' By then, the same concerns could be heard from almost every opinion poll and politician in Britain and America. Ours has become the new Age of Anxiety. What has gone wrong?

For the past forty years a social transformation has taken place whose cumulative impact has by now become immense. The most obvious symptom has been the rise of crime. Crime rates, which had fallen in the second half of the nineteenth century and been low throughout the first half of the twentieth, began to accelerate rapidly in the 1960s. The obvious explanations failed. Crime had been associated with poverty and unemployment, but when the new change began, unemployment was low and prosperity was high. By 1991 the incidence of crime had risen ten times since the mid-1950s. Violent crime had almost doubled with each decade.

This has had an effect on one institution after another. By the 1990s teachers were speaking openly about the danger of physical violence from pupils. The British Medical Association published a 'survival handbook' to guide doctors in defence against violent patients. Nurses, social workers, postmen and staff on the London underground all reported alarming increases in assault. Bank officials now sat behind bulletproof screens. Police officers started wearing protective vests. Commonplace activities a generation ago – going to a football match, walking in the street, strolling in the park – had become fraught with risk of hooliganism and mugging. There has been a palpable loss of security.

The second equally striking change has taken place within the family. The once traditional household has been replaced by an extraordinary variety of arrangements: single-parenthood, cohabitation, divorce, serial marriage, households with a succession of stepfathers, and growing numbers of people living alone. Divorce rose in Britain from 4,228 cases in 1931 to 173,000 in 1992. Rates of marriage have fallen consistently since the 1970s. The incidence of childbirth outside marriage, which had declined in the first half of the nineteenth century and stayed low throughout the first half of the twentieth, began to rise from 5 per cent in 1960 to 32 per cent by the end of 1992.

In tandem, there has been a rise of depressive illness among young people. In their monumental survey of psychosocial disorders, Sir Michael Rutter and David Smith traced a significant increase throughout the past fifty years in suicide and suicidal behaviour, depression, eating disorders and alcohol and drug abuse in the 12- to 28-year-old age group. As with the rise of crime, the growth of depressive illness coincided with the 'golden era' of economic growth, low unemployment and improved living conditions between the years 1950 and 1973. Their own conclusions are tentative, suggesting that family conflict, rising material expectations, the growth of a separate youth culture and the isolation of young people from adults may all have played their part. All European and North American countries show the same patterns, unlike Japan, where stronger social networks and an ethic of restraint had resulted in a more stable and secure psychological environment. A. H. Halsey has spoken powerfully of a 'moral wilderness filled with children seeking revenge against older generations who have seemed to turn their back on them'.

Changes in crime and the structure of the family have moved in exact tandem. Plot the rates of crime and illegitimacy from the 1860s to the 1990s, and you discover that their trajectories are identical. This is not to say that they are causally related. Even if there were a direct correlation between family structure and criminal behaviour we would expect a time-lag of at least ten years between the two developments. Nevertheless they point to the widespread effects of other changes taking place at the same time.

These have all interacted. One of the driving visions of Britain and America after the Second World War was of a new social order, the 'great society' or the welfare state, in which poverty, ill-health, malnutrition and gross inequality would be eliminated. By the end of the 1980s it had become clear that despite huge achievements, desperate social problems remained. Whole areas in both countries, often in inner cities, had become homes to a residual and self-reinforcing spiral of unemployment, crime, drug-addiction and broken families. In Washington or New York, Liverpool or Newcastle, the same stories could be heard: homes without fathers, mothers trying desperately to survive, children running riot, housing estates scarred and defaced by vandalism, shops boarded up, the elderly afraid to go out, and teachers and police wrestling with the breakdown of authority and order. Frank Field, a leading British politician of the left, called this the 'new barbarism'. It is, by any standards, an urban landscape of despair.

The coincidence of unemployment and family disintegration created a downward vortex from which, it seemed, there was no exit. The first person to diagnose the problem was Daniel Patrick Moynihan in the United States. In 1965, as assistant secretary of labour to Lyndon Johnson, he wrote a report arguing that the high rate of out-of-wedlock births in the black community was damaging its chances of economic and social progress. It was a view that went against the orthodoxy of the time and was widely criticised, but by the 1990s liberals in America and ethical socialists in Britain had arrived at a similar conclusion. Children from single-parent or broken families were more likely to suffer from emotional distress, behavioural problems and under-achievement at school. They faced significantly higher risks of unemployment, criminal behaviour, drug and alcohol addiction, and lasting trauma that made it difficult to sustain relationships in later life. These findings, initially challenged by libertarians, became clearer and more stark as the evidence accumulated. The loss of father-figures and stability within the home was creating a pattern of dysfunction among the affected children, offering them diminished hope in adult life.

Meanwhile, the hope of a more egalitarian world was in rapid retreat. If anything, Britain and America were becoming less equal societies, not more. It was not merely that higher income groups had benefited disproportionately from the tax-cutting programmes of Ronald Reagan and Margaret Thatcher in the 1980s. Structural as well as fiscal factors were at work. Post-industrial societies place a premium on high levels of education as technology displaces manual labour. There are fewer jobs in agriculture and manufacturing, more in computing and communication. Meritocracy claims casualties of its own, because equal opportunity ruthlessly exposes inequalities in natural aptitude. Not only the possession of wealth but the very access to work becomes polarised between those who have too much and those who have too little. As religion becomes less prominent and society's values become more material, there are fewer available consolations within the culture. It should not be forgotten that Karl Marx, religion's greatest critic in the nineteenth century, none the less described it as 'the feeling of a heartless world, the soul of soulless conditions'.

But the real inequality of post-industrial capitalism goes far deeper than this. In every earlier society, despite manifest differences in wealth, privilege and power, the various classes – lords and serfs, landowners and labourers, industrialists and workers – depended on one another and lived in close proximity. Their relationship was often one of subjection or exploitation, but those who held power had a vested interest in the welfare of those who did not. They were the labour force and to a large extent the consumers of the goods produced. Most traditional cultures mitigated their inequities by the virtues of benign paternalism and *noblesse oblige*.

Today, as Charles Handy points out, the new rich, the 'symbolic analysts', do not sell their services to, or work with, or live in the same vicinity as, the poor. Their field of action is international. There is no natural community in which the classes mix. The 'new class' do not use public transport or state education. They use private health and security provisions.[3] Robert Reich, secretary of Labour under Bill Clinton, has documented the gradual segregation of American society as affluent professionals move to 'homogeneous enclaves' or 'gated communities' and join private health and sports clubs. Social geography is gradually polarising between the urban ghetto and the gilded ghetto.[4]

The effect is not merely economic. Post-industrial democracies face the very real risk of a deterioration of the social bond – what I have called the covenant – that leads members of a society to see their destinies as interlinked. Two American writers from different ends of the political spectrum, John Kenneth Galbraith and Charles Murray, have both delivered warnings of this possibility. In their books, *The Culture of Contentment* and *The Bell Curve*, each envisages a situation in which, with wider diffusion of wealth and a narrower concentration of poverty, there may be an increasing reluctance on the part of the majority to pay for services and facilities for the new poor, already being stigmatised as 'the underclass'.

Murray asks the key question. 'In what direction does the social welfare system evolve when a coalition of the cognitive elite and the affluent continues to accept the main tenets of the welfare state but are increasingly frightened of and hostile toward the recipients of help?' His prediction is that welfare will increasingly be given in the form of services rather than money. Child care in the inner city will become the responsibility of the state. The homeless will be removed from the streets and placed in shelters. Policing and

[3] Charles Handy, *The Empty Raincoat*, 202.
[4] Robert Reich, *The Work of Nations*, New York, Knopf, 1991, 268–77.

surveillance will become more aggressive. What will emerge will be a 'custodial state', or what Galbraith describes as 'an increasingly oppressive authority in areas of urban desolation'.[5]

There are quite simply developments, benign in their early stages, which go too far. Unlimited consumption fuelled economic growth. It now threatens to despoil our natural resources. When the balance of effects in any process tilts radically to the negative the time arrives for a reconsideration, for moral reflection. We need to ask: was this what we sought when we began the journey? If the answer is no, we have to consider, not undoing the past nor necessarily regretting it, but at least making some change in course in the future. Our capacity to make adjustments in the light of unexpected circumstances is our greatest evolutionary advantage. It is what has allowed mankind – the environment-changing animal – to survive.

The libertarian revolution was a revolution too far. That is not to say that it is to be lamented, second-guessed, or edited out of history. We cannot go back to where we were. We cannot re-legislate morality or recover consensus in a society that is now highly – even constitutively – diverse. Nor may we overlook the fact that libertarianism brought significant gains in tolerance and the alleviation of suffering. It had high ideals and many of its effects were good. But it distorted the framework of human motivation. It gave people good reasons in the short run to do things that would be damaging to them and others in the long run. It undermined many virtues of character, virtues we need if we are to flourish in a difficult world which is often recalcitrant to our will. It weakened social structures. It harmed the institutions on which our growth as individuals and our cohesiveness as a society depend.

It flowed from the assumption – inevitable within the long history I have described, yet flawed none the less – that everything of significance could be contained within the concepts of the abstract individual and the procedural state. But as the 1980s progressed it grew evident that the very actions governments, courts, schools

[5] Charles Murray and Richard J. Herrnstein, *The Bell Curve*, 509–52; John Kenneth Galbraith, *The Culture of Contentment*, 172.

and social planners had taken to solve social problems in fact tended to exacerbate them. And as a decisive shift was taken in the 1980s away from state intervention to a laissez-faire regime of privatisation, deregulation and individual initiative, it became clear that the moral infrastructure which had sustained society in the earlier age of liberalism no longer existed. What happens to 'care in the community' when there is no community? How are we to rely on the family when stable, intact families are all too rare? What becomes of parental responsibility when fathers cannot be found?

The libertarian revolution broke a crucial set of connections: between action and consequence, virtue and reward, effort and achievement, outcome and self-restraint. It brought about a vast transformation in the understanding of rights, from an idea which limited the actions of government to one which called for its involvement in territories in which it had not previously been involved. Meanwhile the loss of a sense of society left only the state and the economy as entities beyond the individual. This affected the very structure of thought. Moral language was replaced in one area after another by political language as a means of expressing claims. Rights, a legal concept, replaced duties, a moral concept. Contract became the dominant mode of understanding human association. Morality – now, as never previously, a private language – could be expressed only in terms of autonomy, the right of the individual to make his or her own choices, pursue his or her own interests, minimally restricted by the need to have concern for others, whose interests instead would be dealt with by the government.

The result is manifest. Relationships become gender wars. Marriage is a contract, terminable at will and without fault on either side. Family life all too often turns into a battle-ground of contending rights, the rights of men, women and children, linked not by mutual belonging but by the mere accident of physical proximity. Compassion becomes a virtue of governments, not individuals. People are encouraged to learn assertiveness rather than the capacity to give, the better to receive. It becomes increasingly difficult to say, within the terms available within the culture, why anyone should go through the formalities of marriage, or have children, or at times sacrifice one's interests for the sake of others. A 1990 *Eurobarometer* survey asked respondents what was the most important role of the family in society. In Portugal, Greece and Spain, most people said it was about bringing up and educating children. Only 24 per cent in Britain gave this answer. The majority saw it in terms of personal adult fulfilment.[6] A fateful complaint first expressed by John Stuart Mill – that people often talked 'as if the interest of children was everything, and that of grown persons nothing'[7] – had taken on a monstrous life of its own.

In the libertarian world, communities become interest groups. Privileges are redefined as entitlements. The connection between rights and duties is broken. Interpersonal disputes are increasingly taken to courts for adjudication. Matters which have in all previous societies been governed by informal codes of civility, decency and honour now become the subject of written procedures. Moral issues like abortion and euthanasia, which had always been subject to an overriding sense of the sacredness, or otherness, or givenness of life, are now reduced to property rights: the right freely to dispose of what one owns, from a foetus to a life.

Relationships, whether at work or in private life, become a choice between manipulating and being manipulated, exploiting or being exploited. The idea that one might value another person or an institution sufficiently to make a long-term binding commitment to suspend strict calculations of self-interest begins to seem old-fashioned and naive. And when we lose the presence of those in whom we can confide, we turn instead to an anonymous public, to the point where there is no relationship so intimate, no secret so private, that it cannot be confessed in front of television cameras or sold for money to the press. It would be hard today to find a code of honour that cannot be broken for profit or under stress. Despite our insistence on privacy, no culture has been less private.

[6] Cited in Norman Dennis, *Who's Celebrating What*, London, Christian Institute, 1995.

[7] Mill, *Utilitarianism, On Liberty, and Reflections on Representative Government*, 173.

The gain in personal freedom has been purchased at the price of the systematic deconstruction of trust.

In my 1990 Reith Lectures I used a phrase which has since become widely used. I spoke about the privatisation of morality, and that is indeed one aspect of what has occurred. It might, though, be no less true to say that what has happened is the opposite, the *nationalisation of responsibility*. Good things – the provision of welfare, the protection and moral education of children, the arbitration of disputes, the maintenance of law and order – have been transferred to the state and its agents (police, courts, schools, social workers), leaving us free to pursue our own concerns, having delegated away concern for others.

Few cultural transformations have been more profound. It has moved us rapidly in the direction of becoming a society of claimants, interested in what we can get, not what we can give. The nationalisation of responsibility produces what Robert Hughes has called a 'culture of complaint' and Charles Sykes a 'nation of victims'. Too often, parents of children who have suffered or inflicted tragedy now blame teachers, the police, or social workers for failing to do their duty instead of accepting at least part of the responsibility.[8] The abdication of moral agency does not yield a guilt-free society. Instead it projects it outward, away from the self towards others. It produces a condition of systematic blame – when bad things happen it must be someone's fault, and it isn't mine. In ceasing to be a moral society we become in the full and worst sense of the word a moralising society.

The transfer of responsibility from the individual to the state is not just ugly in its consequences. It impoverishes our lives. At the core of the moral vision is the profoundly empowering idea that we have stature as human beings because we are moral agents. We do things for ourselves and others, by ourselves and with the help of others. Precisely because we face – as human beings have always faced – a threatening and potentially chaotic world and because we cannot survive alone, we join with others and create, in a hundred different ways, a garden of order out of the always encroaching

[8] Several examples are documented in Melanie Phillips, *All Must Have Prizes*.

wilderness. There is no greater satisfaction than to have brought a child into the world and to have nurtured it, or to have brought comfort to the afflicted and help to the needy, to have brought into the ceaseless discords of what Hobbes called the 'endless race for power after power' some other note, of kindness, decency, trust. In our most honest moments we know that such acts are among the greatest things we will ever achieve, however slight they may seem to be. They win us the respect of others; they give us self-respect. They tell us that individually and collectively we are creators of something that exists outside ourselves. To delegate away such sovereignty is, ultimately, an abandonment of human dignity itself.

The libertarian revolution which took shape between 1945 and the end of the 1960s enacted in the political domain what had long been contemplated in the cloistered rooms of philosophical reflection: the divorce between 'is' and 'ought', the world as we find it and the world we are called on, freely and collectively, to make. Philosophers had long taught that people could, even should, act as individuals, ignoring the claims of loyalty and unchosen commitment. But this was a possibility which, apart from a few persons of private means, was hardly a viable way of life. In the second half of the twentieth century, under state auspices, it became for the first time in history an economic and social possibility for large numbers of people. What John Stuart Mill had called 'experiments in living' were now not merely legal and uncensured. They were endorsed, encouraged and subsidised. Thus the subjectivisation of moral language became the de-moralisation, the de-civilisation, of society.

It was one of the great climatic changes of all time, and it transformed social ecology, producing an inevitable mutation in human character. Behaviours hitherto unsustainable now became practicable. In the short run they held immense allure. They promised a new dispensation, the doubly free pursuit of desire – free as in 'without restraints' and as in 'without a cost attached' – nothing less than Shelley's dream of a world 'free of guilt or pain'. The resultant universe, though, has turned out to have pains of its own: a loss of security, a measurable rise in depression and suicide, the widespread feeling that society has given rise to problems for which there is no cure and which have laid waste to wide tracts of life. The primary victims are children, whose distress, confusion and rapidly narrowing horizons of hope are the most painful, the most morally unacceptable, consequence of this entire transformation. We have gone too far, and in going too far we endanger hope itself.

But surely libertarianism was merely liberalism carried to its logical conclusion. If society could survive without religion, why not without morality? If faith could be privatised, why not virtue? How can a logical progression turn out, in the real world, to be a step into the abyss?

12

The Fatal Ambiguity

[A] society built entirely out of rational individuals who come together on the basis of a social contract for the satisfaction of their wants cannot form a society that would be viable over any length of time ... if individuals formed communities only on the basis of rational long-term self interest, there would be little in the way of public-spiritedness, self-sacrifice, pride, charity or any of the other virtues that make communities livable. Indeed one could hardly imagine a meaningful family life if families were essentially contracts between rational, self-interested individuals.

Francis Fukuyama[1]

THE TIME HAS come to summarise what has been a long argument. I began by telling two stories about how human beings come to form associations. One, taken from Hobbes, spoke about people as individuals, pursuing self-interest and forming contractual relationships for mutual advantage. The other, taken from the Hebrew Bible, spoke about people as members of groups, held together by identity, loyalty and shared commitment to the good they pursue together. Both are true and represent different aspects of the human situation. They give rise to two different types of social institutions, political and civil. The Hobbesian narrative explains how people form states and governments. The biblical narrative tells us how we form families and communities, Burke's 'little platoons', our complex networks of sociability.

One way of seeing why we need both narratives is this. The Hobbesian story tells what happens when we meet as strangers. The biblical story tells what happens when we meet as spouses, parents, neighbours, colleagues or friends. Society involves both

---

[1] Francis Fukuyama, *Trust*, 351.

135

kinds of encounter, therefore it needs structures of both types. We need families and communities to shape our identity. We need political structures to resolve our conflicts. It is precisely the balance between the two that humanises society, mediating between our particular loyalties and our wider sense of justice. There is always a tension between them, and this gives rise to the endless challenges of political and social life. But so long as there is a balance there is a healthy liberal society. The resolution between political and civil domains is always rough-and-ready, always provisional, always open to challenge. That is as it should be. Societies, like traditions, are 'continuities of conflict', to use Alasdair MacIntyre's penetrating phrase. But the existence of a balance lies in this: that we give due weight to both narratives, both aspects of our being.

My argument has been that, over the course of time and with recent dramatic acceleration, this balance has been fundamentally disturbed in favour of the Hobbesian narrative. A single story has prevailed: the one that sees us as individuals pursuing self-interest and self-expression, independent of any binding and definitive commitments, associating merely temporarily, provisionally and contractually. This has been the model of the political animal since the days of Hobbes and Locke. It has been the model of the economic animal since the days of Mandeville, Adam Smith and Ricardo. As theoretical constructs confined to their own disciplines there is nothing wrong with these accounts. Within limits they explain political and economic behaviour. But they do not explain behaviour of other kinds. They leave out of the equation the nature of our existence as social animals. And only social animals – *moral* animals – can sustain political and economic institutions.

The two stories have not always been distinct. In the seventeenth and eighteenth centuries the phrases 'political society' and 'civil society' were virtually synonymous. They were not contrasted with one another but with the idea of a 'state of nature', humanity before the emergence of social structures. The reason why the two concepts were closer than they are today is that political orders were identified with a particular religious outlook. States were the secular arm of the church. But this system, powerful in its time, does not work well in a society where there are many different faiths, cultures and moral traditions. Too strong an identification of the state with a specific religious community excludes too many people from the political process. That is why, though the phrase 'civil society' goes back to Adam Ferguson and the Scottish enlightenment, the first person to describe it in the form in which I have used the phrase – as the domain, distinct from governments, of families, neighbourhood groups, voluntary organisations and religious congregations – was Alexis de Tocqueville in the 1830s, commenting on America, the first society to be built on the principled separation of church and state.

This distinction between the practice of government and the pursuit of faith was at the very heart of liberalism, the nineteenth-century project of a free and open society. It meant that there would be a division between political and civil domains. There would be formal or substantive separation of religion and state. On the one hand there would be governments to secure defence, the rule of law and the mediation of conflict. On the other there would be families, churches and other local bodies. They would have a different character. One would act through law and taxation, the others through voluntary association, duty and moral education. The boundary between their respective domains might be permeable and constantly shifting. There was and is no general rule as to what should be done nationally, what locally, what through coercive and what through voluntary means. But the assumption of figures as diverse as Burke and Cobden, Tocqueville and Lord Shaftesbury, Disraeli and the Guild Socialists, was that a strong society is one in which both sectors flourish. A strong civil society protects liberty because it diffuses the centres of power.[2] It creates fraternity because it encourages people to work together as neighbours and friends. It promotes equality because it tempers self-help with help to others, and because the help given to others is such as to encourage their participation and eventually independence. Most importantly, civil

[2] This is the argument of Ernest Gellner in *Conditions of Liberty*. See also Simon Jenkins, *Accountable to None*.

society constitutes a moral domain, a world of covenants rather than contracts, in which duty, obligation, loyalty and integrity restrain the pursuit of self-interest, in which I learn to value others and win their trust because that is the only way families and communities can be maintained.

The nineteenth century created an equilibrium, but the second half of the twentieth has disturbed it in two ways. The first took place in the realm of facts. One by one, functions that had been performed at the level of civil society were transferred to government, increasingly to central government. Classical liberalism, which meant minimal government, became welfare liberalism, which meant maximal government. This was done from the highest motives, in the wave of collective sentiment and shared determination to build a more compassionate society after the terrible suffering of the Second World War, and this it achieved. But it had an unanticipated consequence, as do all large-scale efforts at social engineering.[3] It weakened all civil associations – families, communities and churches – which had hitherto mediated between the individual and the state. By the time the tide turned in the 1980s and welfare liberalism was succeeded by economic liberalism, the nineteenth-century environment which had supported a minimal state no longer existed. When families are fragile, communities tenuous and the state is in retreat, social problems become acute and can even seem insoluble.

The second no less fateful development took place at the level of language. Increasingly, as philosophers reflected on human institutions, they came to locate moral discourse at two and only two levels: private emotion and public reason, the unique and the universal, the precise counterparts of the abstract individual and the procedural state. This left the whole framework of traditional morality – families, friendships, loyalties and the codes of obligation that sustained them – inherently inarticulate, deprived of a discourse. These institutions are local rather than universal, but are also shared rather than private. To the individualists they could not

---

[3] This is the proposition advocated most forcibly in the twentieth century by Sir Karl Popper and Friedrich Hayek.

but seem repressive. To the universalists they could not but seem parochial. The entire thrust of moral philosophy since Hume and Kant has been to undermine the world of civil society, with its tangled cluster of fierce and conflicting loyalties, in favour of a world in which nothing coherent can be said except at the levels of the individual and the state.

The language that remains is acutely impoverished. It speaks of autonomy and rights, the former my protection against the state, the latter my claims upon it. What it does not speak about are the rich ties that bind me to other people. That is what I meant in the fifth chapter when I spoke about the de-institutionalisation of civil society. Mary Ann Glendon has accurately described the result:

> The lack of public discourse regarding responsibility, sociality and civil society, leaves us to work out our own vision of the kind of people we are and the kind of society we want to become, mainly in terms of the individual, the state, and the market. Our overblown rights rhetoric and our vision of the rights-bearer as an autonomous individual channel our thoughts away from what we have in common and focus them on what separates us. They draw us away from participation in public life and point us toward the maximization of private satisfactions.[4]

The politicisation of language destroys all attempts to render lucid the virtues on which civil institutions depend. If marriage and parenthood are no more than a contract, if the handing on of traditions and beliefs across the generations is ruled out as an assault on children's autonomy, if conflict is to be resolved by litigation rather than civility, if moral dilemmas are reduced to necessarily uncompromising wars of rights, then we will effectively have destroyed the basis on which civil society exists. We will have done so not by being immoral or amoral, but simply by translating virtues and institutions into a language in which they do not fit. Were families and communities to become no more than temporary and conditional alliances we would meet only as strangers, without love or loyalty or trust, and we would find ourselves dangerously close to that situation memorably described by Burke as 'the

[4] Mary Ann Glendon, *Rights Talk*, 143.

antagonist world of madness, discord, vice, confusion and unavailing sorrow'.[5]

How then was it possible to make the move from liberalism to libertarianism without being aware of the revolutionary nature of what was being proposed? The answer is that at the core of liberalism is a fatal ambiguity. This can be seen by asking a series of questions: Is liberalism a theory of the state or the individual? Is it about the scope of government, or does the liberal imagination embody a larger claim about the nature of human life? Is liberalism, to use John Rawls' terms, political or metaphysical?[6]

At its simplest, liberalism had a modest objective. It was a way of keeping politics and religion apart, a *modus vivendi* rather than an account of the moral life. It meant that Jews, Catholics, dissenters and atheists could all be part of the political process without facing a tragic conflict between citizenship and faith. It is worth recalling once more how this came about. It happened under the influence of John Locke, who argued not that faith is unimportant, but that faith is *too* important to be coerced. The state exercises a monopoly of force, but there are some commitments which lose all their value when they are forced.

On this version, liberalism is not neutral on matters of morality. To the contrary, it takes a strong and clear moral stand. A Christian country can come to the conclusion, for Christian reasons, that precisely because religious faith is of its essence a free act of the will, it should not be allowed to stand as a condition of political participation. In this respect it is not unlike the biblical command: 'You shall love the stranger because you were once strangers in the land of Egypt.' Jews did not cease to be Jews because they welcomed strangers, nor did Christians cease to be Christian because they allowed non-Christians to sit in Parliament.

[5] Burke, *Reflections on the Revolution in France*, 97.
[6] On this see John Rawls, 'Justice as Fairness: Political not Metaphysical', *Philosophy and Public Affairs* 14:3 (Summer 1985), 223–51, and his *Political Liberalism*; Charles Larmore, *Patterns of Moral Complexity*; Ronald Beiner, *What's the Matter with Liberalism?*; Stephen Mulhall and Adam Swift, *Liberals and Communitarians;* John Gray, *Enlightenment's Wake*.

They merely recognised that tolerance and coexistence are essential – even religious – virtues in a world in which not everyone is like us.

The same applies to the republican tradition in the United States. If the central values of the American constitution are 'life, liberty and the pursuit of happiness' then a government is not committed to moral indifference. To the contrary, it is committed to strengthening those institutions which in the long run protect life and liberty and make possible the pursuit of happiness, not all of which can be reduced to the rights of individuals to make their own choices. On both accounts, British and American, liberalism emerged out of the historic need to create a society in which a people of strong but conflicting commitments could live peaceably and justly together. To do this they had to share certain principles and agree to keep other matters off the agenda.

They had to share a commitment to reasoned debate, respect for others, the decision of the majority, and the art of compromise. They had to recognise that, despite certain passionately held positions, others might hold contrary views with no less passion, and therefore restraint was preferable to civil war. As Abraham Lincoln said in his Second Inaugural, both sides in the conflict over slavery 'read the same Bible, and pray to the same God'. Therefore, 'with malice toward none, with charity for all, with firmness in the right, as God gives us to see the right' let us 'bind up the nation's wounds'. This is the classic language of liberalism, and it is not abstract or procedural but moral and committed. Those who professed this view knew that certain institutions essential to a free society flourished only when left outside the political arena, and as a result they interfered as little as possible with the family, religious organisations and voluntary bodies while recognising their contribution to the well-being of the 'commonwealth'. The achievement of this balance was one of the high points of human civilisation, and it saved Britain and America from much of the bloodshed and revolution that marked other parts of the world as they struggled towards freedom.

In the minds of many thinkers, though, there was another dimension to liberalism. For them it was more than a *modus vivendi* between different ways of life. It was a new way of life in itself, based on the rejection of tradition. After all, if religions had produced war, would not peace be brought about by the abandonment of religion at least in its sectarian forms? Whether in Voltaire's '*écrasez l'infâme*', or Kant's donnish celebration of autonomy or John Stuart Mill's anti-Victorian hunger for 'experiments in living', a new voice enters the discussion. This is no longer liberalism as political coexistence but liberalism as a moral theory, a quasi-scientific scheme of salvation, based not on revelation or custom but on reason, experiment and choice.

This new form of the liberal imagination (the phrase is Lionel Trilling's) has a radically untraditional view of tolerance and freedom. It does not value the many older cultures and allow them to coexist. Instead it proposes an entirely new culture based on the rejection of people-in-their-particularity and their replacement by the individual-as-such. As John Gray puts it, 'The core project of the Enlightenment was the displacement of local, customary or traditional moralities, and of all forms of transcendental faith, by a critical or rational morality, which was projected as the basis of a universal civilization.'[7] Freedom in such a world is not the flourishing of many different cultures, sustained in community and passed on in families from one generation to the next. Rather it is the freedom of individuals to design their own life-project with minimal interference from others. Communality, for these thinkers, is not the precondition of individuality but one of its greatest threats.

There are many things wrong with this theory. It confuses the political and moral dimensions of society, two quite different things. It has, as I showed in the chapter on the 'assault on particularity', some quite dramatic intolerances of its own – liberalism as libertarianism can be as ruthlessly dismissive of alternatives as any other missionary faith.[8] But most simply, it makes no sense at all as a prescription for society. It is one thing to advocate a free-floating

[7] John Gray, *Enlightenment's Wake*, 123.
[8] See, for example, Bhikhu Parekh, 'Decolonizing Liberalism', in Alexsandras Shtromas (ed.), *The End of 'Isms'?*, 84–104.

life, the kind of existence once called bohemian or cosmopolitan, or to defend, as Bernard Williams has done, the decision of Gauguin to leave family and friends for the sake of art.[9] It is quite another thing to suppose that there could be a self-sustaining society of such individuals. They will always be dependent on others who do not live like them. In this respect, morality is like truth-telling or promise-keeping. We do sometimes tell lies and break promises, but if we did not generally tell the truth and keep our word there could be no communication or trust. There are individuals who live in Millian or Sartrean ways, and society is often enriched by those who break conventions. But that does not mean that we could exist without conventions, or that there should not be a price (preferably low) for breaking them. Libertarianism carries a terrible price for more traditional moralities – their dismissal as benighted, their enforced exile (often through ridicule) from the public domain, and their inevitable erosion and decline. This is not an enrichment of the social world but its devastation.

Liberalism works as a political theory, libertarianism fails as an account of the moral life. For if all commitments were contractual, no more than temporary convergences of mutual interest, I would lose a social world in which I hold a permanent place, in which I can be unconditionally valued, through which I can come to see my life as part of a larger story in which what I do and what I am makes a lasting difference to others. As an abstract individual I am substitutable, expendable, merely temporarily useful to others as they are to me. This may work for some individuals, some of the time, but if it were true of my entire social world I would have to learn to lower to the point of affectlessness my emotional investment in relationships. Lacking the capacity to love or be loved, I would have to learn to be satisfied with self-love alone. I would find myself in an environment in which there is virtually nothing I cannot choose to be, except what most people at most times have chosen to be, namely members of families, communities and traditions. This is not a dream but a nightmare, and it is what we have come close to creating for

[9] Bernard Williams, *Moral Luck*.

many of our children when we adopted metaphysical instead of *modus vivendi* liberalism, or what for clarity I have chosen to call libertarianism.

The Enlightenment error was to suppose that the whole of morality could be contained in a few simple ideas, chief among them universality, autonomy and freedom from interference by others. This is not the whole of morality but a very small part of it. The rest lies in what Gilbert Ryle calls 'thick description'. Moralities are particular ways of life, each of which has its own characteristic virtues, and within each 'ought' *does* follow from 'is': situations create obligations. Moralities are taught in narratives, enacted in rituals, celebrated in prayer and song, embodied in traditions, passed on in families. To understand morality is not to take the 'view from nowhere'[10] but to enter a concrete form of existence. Nor is morality ever an autonomous creation. Even a revolution is a development within a tradition, as Kant's was within Protestantism, Locke's within Socinianism, and Spinoza's within Judaism. Between different moralities there is no inevitable congruence. They conflict. They involve incommensurable values. There is no simple, painless way of combining the best in one with the best in another.[11] That is why, in any society of reasonable diversity, we have to learn new virtues – the true liberal virtues – over and above those of our particular tradition, namely tolerance, coexistence, civility, the give-and-take of the public square. But moralities are not relative. They make absolute claims on their adherents, and they are ultimately testable (as far as anything can be tested) against the history of man's moral imagination.[12]

Moralities have a home. In the Middle Ages they lived in states. In the nineteenth century they lived in society. Today, as society itself has grown more diverse, they live in intermediate associations, families, and communities of locality or calling or faith. These are not liberal institutions, mere associations of individuals pursuing

[10] The phrase is Thomas Nagel's; see his book of the same name.

[11] See Stuart Hampshire, *Morality and Conflict*; John Gray, *Isaiah Berlin*.

[12] Alasdair MacIntyre makes a helpful beginning in this direction in his *Whose Justice? Which Rationality?*

their own interest. They depend on concepts like tradition, authority, fellowship and honour (and in the case of religious groups, revelation). They involve loyalty and fidelity, duties and codes of self-restraint. Their very existence depends on our ability to suspend the choosing 'I' in favour of the 'We' of belonging and obligation. They are covenantal rather than contractual. They involve the investment of emotional identification. They affect not only what I do but also what I see myself as being. Moralities do not emphasise autonomy in the sense of 'making my own values'. They lay weight on the opposite virtues – humility, truthfulness, justice, selfless and unpossessive love, participation in and accountability to rules and truths I did not create.[13] They speak of giving rather than receiving, of duties rather than rights, and of the discovery rather than the invention of truth. They do not stand in opposition to liberty, because in a liberal society they are voluntary associations which we enter freely and are free to leave.[14] But neither are they separate from it, for they are where we learn habits essential to a free society itself. They form our 'apprenticeship in liberty'.

The cultural contradiction of libertarianism is simply this. *A liberal society depends on the existence of non-liberal institutions*. Without them we erode the ecology of civil society without which order can only be sustained by a Leviathan of the state. Liberal society and its economic counterpart, the market economy, are predicated on virtues that cannot be accounted for in terms of liberalism itself. They depend precisely on a willingness to forgo individual advantage for the sake of collective good. The political animal of Hobbes and the economic animal of David Ricardo were portraits of humanity operating within a society of strangers. It was their insight to realise that a transition might be made from the corporate

[13] See Iris Murdoch, *The Sovereignty of Good*, London, Routledge & Kegan Paul, 1970, and George Steiner, *Real Presences*, London, Faber & Faber, 1989, for suggestive discussions of aesthetic emotion and its relation to moral and religious experience. Central here is the concept of 'otherness'.

[14] This is the case argued, to my mind persuasively, by Chandran Kukathas, 'Are there any cultural rights?', in Will Kymlicka (ed.), *The Rights of Minority Cultures*, 228–55. See Leslie Green, 'Internal minorities and their rights', ibid., 256–72, for an opposing view.

society of the Middle Ages to the open society of the nineteenth and twentieth centuries, and to see that individuals unknown to each other might nevertheless frame political and economic structures in which the pursuit of individual gain brought collective benefit – law, economic growth and the exchange of ideas. However, there is something in human nature that requires us to seek more, or other, than a society of strangers – to seek friendship and trust, to bring stability and predictability into interpersonal relations, and to constitutionalise love in the form of marriage and parenthood.

Applied to politics and economics, the Hobbesian story yields order. Applied to morality it yields disorder and dehumanisation. Hobbes' immediate successors knew this. Locke, Rousseau and others realised that to maintain a Hobbesian contract, people would have to be different from Hobbesian individuals, ready at the drop of a hat to wage war. Somehow, though, their insight was lost to a later generation, and the great mistake was made, the transfer of a valid insight from the political to the moral domain. Liberalism became libertarianism, and we – or rather our children – live with the consequences. Liberalism, in short, cannot be the whole truth of our social situation. It is one story, and we need two.

Great truths bring good in their own domain and harm when they stray beyond it. Religion, the great truth about man's search for meaning, trespassed during the Middle Ages into two realms not its own: factual knowledge and political power. The result was ignorance and persecution. That was why the Enlightenment was necessary. Liberalism, the great truth about coexistence in diversity, trespassed during the twentieth century into a neighbouring field, morality, the great truth about living together in trust, and it too brought harm: broken families, abandoned children, the 'new barbarism' of post-modernity. Extending beyond its scope, it threatened to destroy its own foundations. That is the tale of the two stories. Now the question is: can we restore civility and begin to build the good society?

III

The Good Society

13

Surviving Catastrophe

Thus, the great *imitatio Dei* of the modern period has been not the Jews' endless capacity to suffer . . . or even their willingness to die for the sanctification of the Name [of God]. It has been their ability, in the midst and in the wake of the apocalypse, to know the apocalypse, express it, mourn it, and transcend it; for if catastrophe is the presumption of man acting as destroyer, then the fashioning of catastrophe into a new set of tablets is the primal act of creation carried out in the image of God.

David Roskies[1]

SOMETIMES, WHEN FACED with a perplexing and seemingly insoluble dilemma, it helps to move as far away as possible. How have other civilisations at other times overcome crisis? Many simply have not. They grew, reached a glittering climax, and simply faded from the pages of history. But others did succeed. They survived, sometimes under conditions that in retrospect seem little short of overwhelming. I want to consider one such example: Judaism between the first and fourth centuries CE. The way I will do so will be unusual, but its point will quickly become clear. I want to play back two fragments of conversation, one taken from the first century in Israel, the second, from the fourth century in Babylon. They are continuations of the same debate: the same subject, the same terms of reference. But we will notice that something has changed during the course of those three centuries. I want to understand what has changed, and how that is related to the fact that, despite facing its greatest catastrophe, the Jewish people survived.

[1] David Roskies, *Against the Apocalypse: Responses to Catastrophe in Modern Jewish Culture*, Cambridge, Harvard University Press, 1984, 310.

To understand the conversation we have to know certain things in advance. We are going to listen to a group of rabbis as they study Torah, a word which means 'the Hebrew Bible' (especially Genesis to Deuteronomy, the Mosaic books), or more generally 'instruction', that- which-is-studied-together-with-the-process-of-studying-it. The word 'rabbi' means 'my teacher' – in Judaism, the greatest term of respect. In this case the rabbis are discussing a detail in the laws of the Sabbath. The seventh day, in Judaism, is strictly observed and involves complete rest from any activity that might be considered laborious or manipulative of the physical universe. One of the prohibited activities is *carrying in a public place*. This might sound straightforward, but it is not. Clearly, carrying a burden is labour and therefore forbidden. Wearing a jacket is not. But what about carrying a weapon, a sword for example? Remember that we are in the first century, when wearing a sword or some other instrument of self-defence may have been normal, even a badge of honour. Is a weapon an item of clothing or a burden as far as the laws of Sabbath are concerned?

For the Jews of that time and place, the question is urgent and practical. May they, or may they not, wear a sword on the seventh day? It turns out that this is the kind of question in which we cannot separate facts and values. Whether a sword is an item of clothing or a burden will depend on how we evaluate weapons in general – much as Britons and Americans today hold markedly different opinions on the private ownership of handguns, one culture seeing them as a symbol of violence, another as an essential expression of the right to self-defence. Here, though, is the conversation between the rabbis as it takes place in Israel in the first century:

A man must not go out with a sword, bow, shield or spear, and if he does, he is liable to bring a sin offering. Rabbi Eliezer said, 'They are ornaments for him.' But the sages maintain that they are merely shameful, for it is said (Isaiah 2:4), 'And they shall beat their swords into ploughshares and their spears into pruning hooks; nation shall not lift up sword against nation, neither shall they learn war any more.'[2]

[2] Mishnah, *Shabbat*, 6:4.

The rabbis disagree (that is normal: they debate, then decide on the basis of majority opinion). For Rabbi Eliezer a weapon is a standard item of clothing, indeed an ornament. It belongs to an ancient and honourable tradition of self-defence. Israel had its poets and prophets but it also had its warriors and kings who carried the sword in battle. The other rabbis, however, dissent. A weapon cannot be considered an ornament since, in the messianic age as envisaged by Isaiah, there will be no weapons. And is not the Sabbath precisely an anticipation of that time, a day of rest and peace? From the standpoint of ultimate ideals, a sword is not an ornament but a burden, and wearing it in public on the Sabbath is therefore forbidden. It constitutes 'carrying'. These other sages are in a majority, so their view prevails.

However, in Judaism arguments rarely end, and this is no exception. Reviewing the conversation three centuries later, in Babylon, the rabbis note that the debate is incomplete. The (anonymous) sages state their view, Rabbi Eliezer states his. The sages then reply with a biblical proof-text, a verse from Isaiah, in support of their position. But surely Rabbi Eliezer could also quote Scripture in his own defence. Is there really no text in the Hebrew Bible which suggests that a weapon is an honourable thing to carry? There is, and the fourth-century rabbis find it for him. This is the exchange which ensues:

> What is Rabbi Eliezer's reason for maintaining that weapons are ornaments? Because it is written, 'Gird your sword upon your side, O mighty one, in your splendour and glory' (Psalm 45:4). However, Rav Kahana objected to Mar son of Rav Huna: 'But this refers to the words of Torah!' He replied: 'A verse cannot depart from its plain meaning.' Rav Kahana said: 'By the time I was eighteen I had studied all six orders of the Mishnah, yet I did not know until today that a verse cannot depart from its plain meaning.'[3]

According to the first opinion, Rabbi Eliezer, no less than the other sages, has logic and Scripture on his side. In the messianic age there will indeed be peace, but in the meanwhile we live

[3] Babylonian Talmud, *Shabbat* 63a.

in a world of war and violence and weapons. The proof is that the book of Psalms describes the sword as an object of splendour. A sense of balance has been restored to the conversation. Rabbi Eliezer, it now seems, was defeated because he was in a minority, not because his reasoning or knowledge of Scripture was at fault. However, at this point Rav Kahana makes what, on the face of it, is a remarkable objection. Is it conceivable, he asks, that the verse from Psalms is to be understood *literally*? Can we imagine a holy Jew, the author of the Psalms, glorying in a sword? Obviously not. Clearly, when the Psalmist says 'sword' he is using the word metaphorically. What he means is *scholarship*, wisdom, 'the words of Torah', knowledge of the sacred texts. To this, Mar son of Rav Huna gently replies (with a response that could equally be aimed at recent deconstructionist literary criticism) that whatever else a text may mean, it also means what it says.

'Now and then,' writes Lionel Trilling, 'it is possible to observe the moral life in the process of revising itself.'[4] The conversation we have just listened to is a striking example. Something has happened to Jewish life between first-century Israel and fourth-century Babylon. In the first century, rabbis could debate whether or not a weapon was an ornament and could be carried on the Sabbath. But they knew that a sword was a sword. By the fourth century, an outstanding scholar, Rav Kahana, no longer understands what the word means in a Jewish context. Doubtless he would recognise a sword when he saw one, but he can no longer recognise it *within the pages of Scripture*. It has become a metaphor for something else, for study, textual scholarship, the life of the mind. What has happened to the Jewish people in the intervening centuries, that makes one of its great sages immediately and instinctively translate 'sword' into 'words'?

The answer is: catastrophe. At the beginning of the first century Jews still constituted an autonomous nation, albeit under Roman patronage. Judaism was associated with a land – Israel – and a central place of worship, the Temple in Jerusalem. Within a short space of time that world was to be tragically eclipsed. In the year 66, under

[4] Lionel Trilling, *Sincerity and Authenticity*, 1.

increasingly harsh Roman rule, a 'Great Rebellion' took place, whose suppression led ultimately to the destruction of the Second Temple in the year 70, and to final defeat with the collective suicide of the last outpost of resistance in Masada in 72. Some sixty years later a further period of religious persecution under the emperor Hadrian led to a second uprising, the Bar Kochba rebellion. This too was brutally suppressed with massive loss of life. According to the Roman historian Dio, 'Nearly the entire land of Judaea was laid waste.' Jerusalem was completely destroyed and rebuilt as a Roman city, Aelia Capitolina, which Jews were forbidden to enter.

From a Jewish perspective it is almost impossible to overestimate the impact of these two events. The history of the Jewish people as a sovereign nation in its own land came to a close. It was not to be re-opened until the birth of the state of Israel in 1948. The biblical world of kings, priests and prophets had disappeared, with no imminent prospect of return. Over the next century the centre of Jewish life moved from Israel to Babylon. Jewish consciousness slowly became demilitarised, dehistoricised and depoliticised.

As these events unfolded, some Jews came close to despair. When disaster had struck six centuries earlier, with the loss of the First Temple, there had been prophets to offer consolation. Now there were none. In the event, the first Babylonian exile had lasted little more than half a century, but the second seemed to be stretching on indefinitely. Meanwhile, in Israel, Jews were being murdered for their faith. The Talmud contains a statement, probably dating from the period of the Hadrianic persecutions, that: 'From the day that a Government has come into power which issues cruel decrees against us and forbids to us the observance of the Torah and the commandments . . . we ought by rights to issue a decree not to marry and have children, so that the seed of Abraham our father would come to an end of itself.'[5] To the author of that statement, it seemed like the end of the Jewish world.

What was the condition of Judaism during this period? The picture which emerges during the late Second Temple era is of considerable fragmentation. According to Josephus, there prevailed

[5] Babylonian Talmud, *Baba Bathra*, 60b.

not one interpretation of Judaism but three: Sadducees, Pharisees and Essenes. Josephus is concerned with their doctrinal differences, but of greater interest are their respective spheres of activity.

The Essenes, a series of apocalyptic groups of whom the Qumran sect known to us through the Dead Sea Scrolls was probably one, had their strongholds in separatist communities[6] where they could live by rules of intense religious discipline, removed from the mainstream of society, waiting for the imminent 'end of days'.

The Sadducees formed an aristocracy of wealth and position. They were worldly and conservative, landowners and priests, Jewry's upper class. They were 'pre-eminently the party of Jewish statehood, in the sense that their Jewishness was principally expressed through the political institutions of a state and those religious institutions, such as the priesthood and the Temple, intimately bound up with statehood'.[7]

The Pharisees have suffered greatly from the portrait painted of them in early Christian texts. There is a large literature on how and why this happened, but let us bypass it, and instead call them 'the rabbis', for that is who they became. It was their way of life that held greatest appeal for the mass of ordinary Jews, emphasising as it did the personal sanctification of everyday life. Their leading institutions were the home, the synagogue and the 'house of study', and their overwhelming concern was with the study and practice of the Torah. One of the most famous early rabbinic traditions is of a conversation between Rabban Jochanan ben Zakkai and the Roman leader Vespasian in the year 69, as Jerusalem lay besieged. Against the prevailing militancy of the Zealots, Jochanan favoured a peaceful settlement with the Romans rather than a war which he foresaw would end in destruction. 'Leave me one thing,' he is reported as saying, '[the academy of] Yavneh and its sages.' Judaism could survive without a Temple so long as it had its scholars.

---

[6] According to Philo, however, the Essenes lived in the towns and villages of Judaea, where they engaged in agriculture or the crafts. They rejected the concept of private property and were for the most part celibate. Their intense communalism found re-expression in the twentieth century in the form of the Israeli kibbutz.

[7] Daniel Elazar, *People and Polity*, 160.

The rabbis organised perhaps the first genuinely universal system of education in history. Its evolution in the late Second Temple period is described in the Talmud: 'At first, if a child had a father, his father taught him; if he had no father, he did not learn at all . . . Then they introduced an ordinance that teachers of children be appointed in Jerusalem . . . Even so, if a child had a father, the father would take him to Jerusalem and have him taught there; but if he had no father, he would not go up there to learn. They therefore ordained that teachers be appointed in each district and that boys enter school at the age of sixteen or seventeen. But because a boy who was punished by his teacher would rebel and leave school, Joshua ben Gamla introduced a regulation that teachers of young children be appointed in each district and town, and that children begin their schooling at the age of six or seven.'[8] This structure was in place by the time of the destruction of the Temple. By the beginning of the fourth century, the sages were already regulating class size (a maximum of twenty-five per teacher), and debating whether incompetent teachers could be dismissed. A rabbinic dictum of the third century states that a town which lacks a school is to be excommunicated, on the grounds that 'the world only exists in virtue of the breath of children at school'.[9]

Concern with education did not begin with the rabbis. It has its roots in the ancient history of Israel. In the book of Genesis, for example, the sole explanation for the covenant with Abraham is: 'For I have singled him out, that he may instruct his children and his posterity to keep the way of the Lord by doing what is right and just' (Genesis 18:19). Abraham is chosen not because he is, like Noah, 'righteous' or 'blameless' but because he will hand his values on to future generations. In a passage which has a central place in the Jewish liturgy, Moses commands the Israelites: 'Teach these things diligently to your children; recite them when you stay at home and when you are away, when you lie down and when you rise up' (Deuteronomy 6:7).

The rabbis were therefore drawing on a long tradition when

[8] Babylonian Talmud, *Baba Bathra*, 21a.
[9] Babylonian Talmud, *Shabbat*, 119b.

they began to build their society around schools.[10] The same was true of their emphasis on the home and the synagogue. The book of Genesis is, among other things, a set of variations on the theme of family: Adam and Eve, Noah and his children, Abraham and Sarah, Isaac and Rebecca, Jacob and his domestic crises. The Hebrew Bible opens on a cosmic plane with the unfolding of the universe, but it quickly narrows its focus to the most intimate of human relationships, husbands and wives, parents and children. In sanctifying the home and making it the setting of many of Judaism's most sacred rituals, the rabbis were again continuing a central biblical motif. We do not know the historical origins of the synagogue, but it too was already an institution of long standing, probably dating back to the first Babylonian exile and the days of the prophet Ezekiel. The point about the synagogue as opposed to the Temple was that it was a gathering place for a community, as opposed to the nation.[11] It could be built anywhere, so long as there were ten adult males to constitute a congregation. The synagogue rapidly became the centre of communal life, as it was to remain throughout the Middle Ages, a place where people met not only for prayer, but also for study, the adjudication of disputes, the distribution of charity, and other collective welfare activities.

So the rabbis, in all respects, were continuing the tradition. But so too were the Essenes and the Sadducees, and this is the point. A tradition is not a system but a way of life. It contains many divergent, even conflicting, strands. It can be taken forward in different ways. A tradition never, in and of itself, resolves disagreements. Instead, it is the arena within which they take place. As Alasdair MacIntyre puts it: 'Traditions, when vital, embody continuities of conflict.'[12] At stake in the disagreement between rabbis, Essenes and Sadducees was a fundamental question about the nature of Judaism. For the rabbis it was the religion of a people in their everyday lives. For the Essenes it was the code of

[10] On these subjects, see my *Crisis and Covenant*, Manchester, Manchester University Press, 1992, and *Will We Have Jewish Grandchildren?*, London, Vallentine Mitchell, 1994.

[11] I have developed this theme in my book, *Community of Faith*.

[12] Alasdair MacIntyre, *After Virtue*, 206.

a pietist sect. For the Sadducees it was the religion of a state. In the years preceding the destruction of the Second Temple, these two latter alternatives held considerable sway.

With this background, we can now go back and sense the underlying drama of the rabbinic debate about the carrying of weapons on the Sabbath. In first-century Israel the relationship between religious fervour and armed resistance was still an open and much-debated issue. The great Jewish uprisings against Greek and Roman rule, from the Maccabees to Bar Kochba, were protests against the suppression of Jewish religious life. Jews were fighting for religious freedom as much as for national sovereignty. It was still possible for sages like Rabbi Eliezer to see the sword as a symbol of honour.

By the time we reach fourth-century Babylon, however, so greatly has Jewish consciousness changed that a sage as eminent as Rav Kahana can no longer understand that when the book of Psalms speaks about a sword it means a sword. The terms of Jewish life have been transformed. A war is still being fought for the survival of Judaism, but it is no longer physical but cultural. What must be protected are the boundaries, not of a country but an identity. The Ministry of Defence has become the Ministry of Education. Its fortresses are schools, its heroes teachers, and when religious texts speak about weapons, they refer not to a sword but to a book, the 'words of Torah'. In the course of a single extended conversation we are witnesses to the transformation of Jewish life from an autonomous nation-state built around a Temple to communities built around schools.

No less important is the fact that certain voices are missing from this conversation. There are no Sadducees or Essenes. Within a remarkably short space of time, these groups disappeared, leaving Pharisaic – now rabbinic – Judaism as the sole normative expression of Jewish life, a position it held with few serious challenges until the nineteenth century. Why? The Essenes had built communities but made no provision for their continuity over time. The Sadducees had predicated their religious life on the state, and there was now no Jewish state. Jews no longer had the instrumentalities of political society. They were a diaspora. They had a modicum of self-government, whether in Babylon or elsewhere in their long dispersion, but for eighteen centuries their normal situation was that of a religious and cultural minority with limited access to power. They were, to all intents and purposes, a voluntary association with branches worldwide. It was not until the nineteenth century that Jews were enfranchised as full participants in the political process in the West, and not until the mid-twentieth century, in Israel, that they had the opportunity to create their own society and state.

The survival of Jewish life depended, therefore, on two things: the institutions of civil society – families, congregations, communities and voluntary organisations – together with the transmission of an identity based on a distinctive way of life and its associated values. That way of life was not endorsed by the surrounding culture. For the most part Jews lived among Christians or Muslims who made frequent attempts to convert them, sometimes by intimidation or force. Education, and its reinforcement by the family and the community, was therefore critical to the maintenance through time of a civilisation and its way of life. By now I hope it has become clear why I chose to tell this story.

In the previous chapters I spoke about the gradual erosion of civil society in liberal democracies dominated by the concepts of the individual and the state. The analysis pointed to an unspoken but vital question: can such societies survive? The obvious answer is, of course they can. Given the present configuration of international politics, they are unlikely to be overrun by invading forces. They stand in no imminent danger of conquest and defeat. But as Lord Devlin warned almost forty years ago, 'Societies disintegrate from within more frequently than they are broken up by external pressures. There is disintegration when no common morality is observed, and history shows that the loosening of moral bonds is often the first stage of disintegration'.[13] From that perspective, many observers are today sounding the alarm. Violence, crime, family breakdown, drug abuse, and the rise of depressive illness, are symptoms of a civilisation in decline.

[13] Lord Devlin, *The Enforcement of Morals*, 13.

At such moments it is important to keep a sense of proportion. Things are almost never as bad as social commentators say they are. As Peter Berger and Hansfried Kellner amusingly remind us:

> If we take our minds back many millennia, back into the dawn of history, we may imagine the appearance of the very first intellectual. After centuries during which people did nothing but rhythmically bang away with stone implements and keep the fires from going out, there was someone who interrupted these wholesome activities just long enough to have an idea, which he or she then proceeded to announce to the other members of the tribe. We can make a pretty good guess as to what the idea was: 'The tribe is in a state of crisis.'[14]

However acute our contemporary pathologies, they pale into insignificance in the light of the crisis faced by Jews in the first and second centuries of the Common Era. They had lost their land, their independence and their Temple. Most of their cities, above all Jerusalem, had been laid waste. There was loss of life, given the smaller populations of those days, on the scale of the destruction of European Jewry during the Holocaust. Dio estimated that 580,000 Jewish fighters were killed, along with 'countless numbers' of women and children who died through 'starvation, fire and the sword', during the suppression of the Bar Kochba rebellion alone. Yet the Jewish story remains one of hope. Judaism survived this, as it would survive the many other tragedies of subsequent generations, none worse than in the twentieth century. But (leaving aside, in this non-theological work, the Divine promise) there was nothing inevitable about this survival. That is the significance of the fate of the Sadducees and the Essenes.

Post-biblical Judaism offers us a peculiarly focused way of testing a hypothesis about the maintenance of a social order. Religion is not a factor, since all three groups in the days of the Second Temple were religious, yet they did not fare equally. What turned out to be decisive was the specific way the groups were organised, the conception they had of the nature of identity, and above all the

---

[14] Peter Berger and Hansfried Kellner, *Sociology Reinterpreted*, Harmondsworth, Penguin, 1982, 143.

institutions to which they attached significance. Their options were not unlike ours. The Sadducees, like many today, vested their hopes in the state. The Essenes had no such hopes. They expected the apocalypse, and prepared themselves to meet it in small and separatist groups. Their counterparts today are not only the more extreme millennial sects like the Branch Davidians of Waco, but also pessimistic philosophers like Alasdair MacIntyre, who ends his lament for contemporary culture, *After Virtue*, with the remark that: 'What matters at this stage is the construction of local forms of community within which civility and the intellectual and moral life can be sustained through the new dark ages which are already upon us.'[15] This is a typical Essenian sentiment.

Neither Essenes nor Sadducees survived, but something else did: a way of life based on the family, the community, an educational system, and the dedicated transmission of practices and ideals from one generation to the next. Rabbinic Judaism was perhaps the first, and surely the most remarkable, example of a civilisation which sustained itself, without political power, as a civil society. It is no coincidence that as contemporary analysts search for a way out of our current impasse, they are beginning to rediscover the same themes that once inspired a group of teachers almost two thousand years ago.

[15] Alasdair MacIntyre, *After Virtue*, 245.

14

Communitarians, Old and New

[C]ollective activity is always too complex to be able to be expressed through ... the State. Moreover, the State is too remote from individuals; its relations with them are too external and intermittent to penetrate deeply into individual consciences and socialize them within. Where the State is the only environment in which men can live communal lives, they inevitably lose contact, become detached, and thus society disintegrates. A nation can be maintained only if, between the State and the individual, there is intercalated a whole series of secondary groups near enough to the individuals to attract them strongly in their sphere of action and drag them, in this way, into the general torrent of social life.

Emile Durkheim[1]

IN 1982 A YOUNG Harvard professor, Michael Sandel, published a book that, in the intervening years, has transformed the terms of philosophical and political debate. Entitled *Liberalism and the Limits of Justice*, it was a nuanced but devastating challenge to the prevailing liberal orthodoxy. Liberalism, he argued, at least in the terms with which it had been presented in the second half of the twentieth century, was simply too abstract to do justice to the kind of people we are. It had misconceived the individual and society.

This was a bold act of iconoclasm on Sandel's part, for his targets – the two other great Harvard philosophers, John Rawls and Robert Nozick – had seemed between them to have defined the only significant options within a liberal democratic order. Rawls had argued for an interventionist state, actively redistributing incomes and benefits for the sake of a more equal society. Nozick

[1] Emile Durkheim, *The Division of Labour in Society*, New York, Free Press, 1964, 28.

161

had argued for a minimalist, 'night watchman', state, leaving as many resources as possible in private ownership. Rawls had given philosophical expression to the welfare liberalism of the 1940s to the 1970s. Nozick had done likewise for the economic liberalism that would later prevail during the decade of Margaret Thatcher and Ronald Reagan. Sandel's contention was that they were both wrong, because they had left out a vital dimension of human nature and our social lives.

The work Sandel was primarily confronting was John Rawls' *A Theory of Justice*, published in 1971. Rawls had revitalised political philosophy by returning to the idea of the social contract. Rawls' question, somewhat different from that of Hobbes, Locke and Rousseau, was not so much 'What makes society possible?' but 'What would constitute a just society, one that, given a free choice, we would wish to construct?' To answer this question, Rawls proposed a brilliant theoretical device, the 'veil of ignorance'. Imagine that you are about to design a society. You can shape it any way you wish, but with this one proviso: you cannot know in advance what sort of person you are going to be, what talents, abilities and other advantages you will have. Rawls was making sophisticated use of a device parents have long used to teach their children the concept of justice: 'John, you can divide the apple any way you like, but Jane gets to choose which piece she takes.' Quite soon the child learns the meaning of justice-as-fairness.

The conclusions Rawls drew were these. The ideal outcome would be one in which 'Each person is to have an equal right to the most extensive total system of equal basic liberties compatible with a similar system of liberty for all'. In addition, 'Social and economic inequalities are to be arranged so that they are both (a) to the greatest benefit of the least advantaged, and (b) attached to offices and positions open to all under conditions of fair equality of opportunity.'[2] Rawls thus believed that justice-as-fairness involved the state in redistributive activity to establish the rights of its citizens.

Robert Nozick, who published his *Anarchy, State and Utopia* three years later, radically disagreed. For him the primary idea was

[2] John Rawls, *A Theory of Justice*, 302.

justice-as-entitlement, a philosophical version of another childhood maxim, 'I found it. It's mine.' For Nozick, we have a right to keep what we legitimately own, and for the state to take away what is mine, even for the purpose of distributive justice, is a violation of that right. The state is justified in performing only the minimal functions of protection against force, theft and fraud, and the enforcement of contracts. Beyond this it has a moral duty to do as little as possible. 'The minimal state treats us as inviolate individuals, who may not be used in certain ways by others as means or tools or instruments or resources . . . Treating us with respect by respecting our rights, it allows us, individually or with whom we choose, to choose our life and to realize our ends and our conception of ourselves, insofar as we can, aided by the voluntary co-operation of other individuals possessing the same dignity.'[3] How *dare* any state do more, or less, he asked.

Sandel challenged both views, not at their point of disagreement – justice as fairness or entitlement – but at their points of consensus, their shared ideas of rights, freedom, the nature of the individual and the role of the state. Rawls had argued that a just society does not try to cultivate virtue or encourage among its citizens any particular conception of the good. Instead its task is to provide a neutral framework of rights within which individuals can pursue their own private ideals and aspirations. So the state is merely procedural. It abandons the 'perfectionist project' of society as the pursuit of shared aims. 'The right is prior to the good', meaning that procedure takes precedence over substantive common goals. In addition, freedom is conceived as the right of individuals to choose their own values. This means that persons are imagined as unencumbered consumers freely shopping between alternatives, or to put it technically, 'the self is prior to its ends'. For Sandel, this was simply not an adequate description of the kinds of people we are. We are not lonely bearers of rights. We are 'situated selves' with loves, affiliations and attachments, not all of which we choose. Any political theory which ignores this fact does scant justice to human nature.

[3] Robert Nozick, *Anarchy, State and Utopia*, 333–4.

163

In an eloquent passage, he explains why we cannot think of ourselves wholly in terms of unfettered choices:

> [W]e cannot regard ourselves as independent in this way without great cost to those loyalties and convictions whose moral force consists partly in the fact that living by them is inseparable from understanding ourselves as the particular persons we are – as members of this family or community or nation or people, as bearers of this history, as sons and daughters of that revolution, as citizens of this republic. Allegiances such as these are more than values I happen to have or aims I 'espouse at any given time' . . .
>
> To imagine a person incapable of constitutive attachments such as these is not to conceive an ideally free and rational agent, but to imagine a person wholly without character, without moral depth. For to have character is to know that I move in a history I neither summon nor command, which carries consequences none the less, for my choices and conduct.[4]

Individuals have networks of belonging, and a good society will be one in which these are recognised and conserved. If so, our view of politics will be somewhat changed. In his recent work, *Democracy's Discontent*, Sandel says what he believes it to be. Governments will not be neutral between ends. Instead they will seek to cultivate in citizens the virtues necessary to the common good of self-government. Nor will they pursue freedom as the right of the individual to non-interference in his or her choices. Instead they will envisage it as being 'a member of a political community that controls its own fate, and a participant in the decisions that govern its affairs'.[5] Sandel, in other words, sought to bring back to politics talk about character, virtue, community and participation. The state as credit-card and the individual as consumer were too narrow a view of politics to sustain a civil society. We don't, and can't, live that way.

Sandel's views were echoed at around the same time by two other influential voices, Michael Walzer at Princeton, and Charles Taylor, then at Oxford. Taylor, too, argued against the primacy of

[4] Michael Sandel, *Liberalism and the Limits of Justice*, 179.
[5] Michael Sandel, *Democracy's Discontent*, 25–6.

rights and the 'atomic' conception of the individual. We are who we are, he suggested, because of the institutions which surround us, the family that brought us up, the culture we absorb, and the associations (universities, businesses, television stations) among which we live. These institutions 'require stability and continuity and frequently also support from society as a whole – almost always the moral support of being commonly recognized as important, but frequently also considerable material support'. They sustain us, therefore we have a duty to sustain them. Rights presuppose the responsibility to participate in and keep in good order the basic framework of society. This creates 'a significant obligation to belong', indeed actively to care about 'what the moral tone of the whole society is'.[6] If we want to pick the flowers we must help to tend the garden.

Walzer, in his marvellously rich survey of the ways different societies have distributed their benefits, *Spheres of Justice*, argued that it is impossible in principle to give the kind of abstract, universal account of justice that Rawls and Nozick had attempted to do. Particular goods – education, health care, even public recognition – have their own internal distributive logic. Besides which, distributions have histories, and different societies arrange things differently. Consider a sentence like 'To each according to his need.' What is a need so fundamental that it must be made available by public funds? For the ancient Greeks it was political participation, for rabbinic Judaism it was religious education, for post-war Britain it has been health care. Needs are not facts but values, and they are written into the history of a particular culture. This suggests that, instead of aiming at neutrality, one of the duties of a society is to protect its own character, not as set in stone, but certainly as the evolving joint creation of its citizens:

> By virtue of what characteristics are we one another's equals? One characteristic above all is central to my argument. We are (all of us)

---

[6] Charles Taylor, 'Atomism', in Shlomo Avineri and Avner de-Shalit (eds), *Communitarianism and Individualism*, 29–50. Taylor's views are developed at length in his books *Sources of the Self* and *The Ethics of Authenticity*.

culture-producing creatures; we make and inhabit meaningful worlds. Since there is no way to rank and order these worlds with regard to their understanding of social goods, we do justice to actual men and women by respecting their particular creations. And they claim justice, and resist tyranny, by insisting on the meaning of social goods among themselves. Justice is rooted in the distinct understandings of places, honours, jobs, things of all sorts, that constitute a shared way of life. To override those understandings is (always) to act unjustly.[7]

These works, intricately argued and forcibly expressed, were in one sense hardly revolutionary. Their authors were philosophers. They had no political programme. But they were injecting into academic discourse a series of substantive moral claims that philosophy had not heard for a long time. There was, though, something familiar about their concerns, because, spanning a distance of a century and a half, they brought to mind both the anxiety and the hope of one of the first and most insightful observers of liberal democracy, Alexis de Tocqueville.

Tocqueville, as we saw in earlier chapters, chronicled the birth of two tendencies which have dominated free societies ever since: the rise of individualism and the growth of the state. His antidote was simple: 'Among the laws that rule human societies,' wrote Tocqueville, 'there is one which seems to me more precise and clear than all others. If men are to remain civilized or to become so, the art of associating together must grow and improve in the same ratio in which equality of conditions is increased.'[8]

Tocqueville's fundamental question was simple. Could freedom survive in a democracy? The United States offered a quite different model to that of France. It was a new society. There had been no need for a violent overthrow of established interests. There was no established church to be contained. The vast extent of America allowed individuals the space for privacy. Its geographical isolation meant that it did not have to be on constant alert for war. Its seemingly open-ended capacity for growth meant that people could aspire to wealth without envying others, reliant instead on

[7] Michael Walzer, *Spheres of Justice*, 314.
[8] Alexis de Tocqueville, *Democracy in America*, 408.

166

their own efforts. Even a fortune lost could, in the space of a single lifetime, be rebuilt. There seemed to be no reason why the United States should not become and remain a peaceable kingdom, each of its members pursuing 'self-interest rightly understood'.

Tocqueville, though, was haunted by one fear. A liberal, democratic, capitalist society would, he believed, eventually lose its own liberty. This would come about not by revolution but through a slow erosion of the ties that bind people to one another. It would evolve because of the very phenomena that so captured his interest: individualism – the retreat of individuals into the private sphere – and the growth of the state, that 'immense and tutelary power'. It would take place gradually and without resistance, partly because the state was benign and supplied people's needs, but more importantly because it was democratic. Under such circumstances, he wrote, people 'console themselves for being in tutelage by the reflection that they have chosen their own guardians'. The loss of liberty is not always sudden or painful or even opposed, but it is a loss none the less. Tocqueville searched for a phrase to describe this, to him, quite novel danger. At times he called it 'administrative despotism'. At others he used the term later taken up and made famous by John Stuart Mill, 'the tyranny of the majority'.[9]

What might protect a nation against such a fate? Tocqueville had no doubt. It was the strength of 'associations', the institutions of civil society. His argument was this. In a traditional society individuals are bound to one another by deep ties of history, habit and custom. Those ties are broken by the constant turmoil of the modern world. The only way a sense of fellowship can be regained is by voluntary association, and it was this that formed the defence of liberty in a democratic society. Tocqueville was amazed and at times amused by the vigour of such groups in the United States. 'Americans of all ages, all conditions and all dispositions constantly form associations . . . If it is proposed to inculcate some truth or foster some feeling by the encouragement of a great example, they form a society.'[10] But this activity had a significant effect. It

[9] Ibid., 103.
[10] Ibid., 403.

accustomed people to work together. It reminded 'every citizen, and in a thousand ways, that he lives in society'. It broke down the barriers of self-interest and self-preoccupation. It was a constant education in virtue and fellow-feeling. 'Liberty of association', he concluded, 'has become the necessary guarantee against the tyranny of the majority.'

Tocqueville was particularly struck by the role of four institutions: the family, religion, local government, and voluntary organisations. The American family was more egalitarian than its European counterparts. Women were educated to be independent. Parents and children were bound less by authority than affection. But the home was no less strong for being more democratic. 'There is certainly no country in the world', he wrote, 'where the tie of marriage is more respected.' The family gave stability to society as a whole. It guarded against the 'taste for excesses, a restlessness of the heart, and fluctuating desires' that could be observed in some European countries. The American, he said, 'derives from his own home that love of order which he afterwards carries with him into public affairs'.[11]

The place of religion in the United States at first bewildered him and ran counter to all his expectations. It had no power but immense influence. It 'took no part in the government of society' but it was 'the first of their political institutions'. Unlike France, where 'I had almost always seen the spirit of religion and the spirit of freedom marching in opposite directions', religion in America was regarded as one of the main guardians of freedom, 'indispensable to the maintenance of republican institutions'. Far from being weakened by the separation of church and state, religion was strengthened by it. It meant that the church had to stand apart from politics, and was thus spared the divisions and resentments that the political arena inevitably involves. Tocqueville had made a fundamental discovery, that in a democracy religion flourishes when it takes up residence in civil rather than political society. 'In the United States religion exercises but little influence upon the laws and upon the details of public opinion; but it directs

[11] Ibid., 183–4.

the customs of the community, and by regulating domestic life, it regulates the state.'[12]

Local government and voluntary associations helped to bridge the distance between the individual and a remote governing power. They formed an ongoing tutorial in the arts of citizenship. 'Town meetings are to liberty what primary schools are to science; they bring it within the people's reach, they teach men how to use and how to enjoy it.'[13] The large measure of devolution helped to counter-balance the power of central government. 'The townships, municipal bodies, and counties form so many concealed break-waters, which check or part the tide of popular determination.'[14] Most importantly, it created a sense of public-spiritedness. 'If an American were condemned to confine his activity to his own affairs, he would be robbed of one half of his existence.' This, Tocqueville believed, was the single most important guarantor of liberty. 'I am persuaded that if ever a despotism should be established in America, it will be more difficult to overcome the habits that freedom has formed than to conquer the love of freedom itself.'[15]

Tocqueville's view is a classic account of what is sometimes called 'republican' political theory, and shares some of the features of the biblical tradition, as well as the concerns of contemporary thinkers like Sandel, Taylor and Walzer. It rejects the libertarian reduction of politics to the choosing individual and the supplying state, for it is convinced that a free society cannot be created by political or economic structures alone. It requires virtues, or what Tocqueville himself termed 'habits of the heart'. Nor do these exist in a vacuum. They are born and sustained in particular institutions, the family, the congregation, the neighbourhood, the voluntary organisation, which give shape to our individuality and moral substance to our sociability. When these are in good order, the qualities of character needed for liberty are in constant exercise. Tocqueville called this

12 Ibid., 182–7.
13 Ibid., 49.
14 Ibid., 160.
15 Ibid., 142.

'the slow and quiet action of society upon itself'.[16] Without these local arenas of duty to others, we would never acquire the sense of responsibility necessary for citizenship. 'How', asked Tocqueville, 'can a populace unaccustomed to freedom in small concerns learn to use it temperately in great affairs?'[17]

Clearly there are differences between Tocqueville and his modern heirs. He was an observer, they are philosophers. He was concerned with liberty, they with the sense of identity. But what they hold in common is absolutely fundamental. It goes against the grain of post-Enlightenment thought, yet it captures something we know to be true. We are not what Hobbes and so many of his successors thought we were, isolated individuals pursuing self-interest, nor can a society be constructed on these lines. We have attachments and affiliations, loyalties and loves. These cannot be reduced to contractual alliances for the temporary pursuit of gain. They are covenantal, which is to say that they are both moral and fundamental: they enter into our identity, our understanding of the specific person we are. This kind of thought recaptures what the Enlightenment sought to abandon, namely the significance of the particular, that which is neither unique nor universal but communal. That is why it has come to be known as *communitarianism*.

Slowly this perspective has moved from cloistered reflection to practical politics. Perhaps the first person to introduce it into modern public debate was the late Robert Kennedy in the 1960s. Before almost anyone else he sensed that something was going wrong with the relationship between state and people. Governments had grown too large, too impersonal. Individuals had lost their rootedness in associations where they knew their contribution made a difference. 'Bigness, loss of community, organizations and society grown far past the human scale – these are the besetting sins of the twentieth century, which threaten to paralyze our capacity to act.' He lamented 'the destruction of the sense, and often of the fact, of community, of human dialogue,

16 Ibid., 276.
17 Ibid., 70.

the thousand invisible strands of common experience and purpose, affection and respect, which tie men to their fellows'. Community, he said, 'demands a place where people can see and know each other, where children can play and adults work together and join in the pleasures and responsibilities of the place where they live'.[18] These were the themes that more than a decade later were to be elaborated into philosophical systems.

Robert Kennedy was ahead of his time. But by the 1990s a new mood was taking shape. Amitai Etzioni, a Washington professor, had created a movement, the 'Responsive Community', which sought to encourage a more active participation in families, schools and neighbourhoods. In his book, *The Spirit of Community* (1993), he argued that 'strong rights presume strong responsibilities' and that if the 1980s were the 'I' decade, the 1990s must become the decade of 'We'. It was not always clear whether the 'communitarian agenda' was a political campaign or a programme of moral renewal, but in a sense it was both. Essentially Etzioni was asking governments to help communities and families to help themselves.

A year earlier, also in the United States, David Osborne and Ted Gaebler had published their best-selling work, *Reinventing Government*. Among other things, they cited evidence to show that communities, churches, charities and self-help associations were often better at delivering services than governments. They were closer to people, they understood their needs better, they were more participative, and as a result they were simply more effective in solving problems by involving, and thus changing, the people who were affected. Governments create clients, communities create citizens. Governments give rise to dependency, communities to competence. Governments encourage people to think in terms of what they lack, communities foster people who think in terms of what, collectively, they can do. Osborne and Gaebler told some marvellous stories of what happened when deprived groups in drug-ridden neighbourhoods got together to act, and between them worked transformations that had defeated the best efforts of outside agencies. Theirs was a balanced case.

---

[18] I owe these quotations to Michael Sandel, *Democracy's Discontent*, 301.

Community and voluntary action could not solve all problems, but it could solve some, in particular those that require commitment to other people, personal attention, and a comprehensive, holistic approach. It was the best way of 'enforcing moral codes and individual responsibility for behaviour'. They called for a new partnership between governments and the 'third sector', neither private nor public but communal.[19]

So community had passed from rhetoric to philosophy to plan of action. Slowly, too, it passed from the United States to Britain where, in 1996, two leading political philosophers, Roger Scruton on the right, John Gray on the left, published their own versions of the communitarian case.[20] It was an idea whose time had come. Faced with the failure of the second liberal revolution – libertarianism – thinkers and activists alike turned to earlier political traditions and rediscovered there a truth that had become obscured: that we are and have our being in networks of belonging, which form the matrices of identity and moral purpose. If those older traditions preserved an insight that had been lost in the clamour of modernity, might this not lead on to a re-evaluation of the role of tradition itself?

[19] David Osborne and Ted Gaebler, *Reinventing Government*, especially 49–75, 311–48.
[20] Roger Scruton, *The Conservative Idea of Community*; John Gray, *After Social Democracy*.

15

Education and the Limits of Autonomy

> Civilization hangs suspended, from generation to generation, by
> the gossamer strand of memory. If only one cohort of mothers and
> fathers fails to convey to its children what it has learned from its
> parents, then the great chain of learning and wisdom snaps. If the
> guardians of human knowledge stumble only one time, in their
> fall collapses the whole edifice of knowledge and understanding.
>
> Jacob Neusner[1]

A RECOLLECTION. ALMOST my first memories as a child are
of evenings spent in my grandparents' house celebrating Passover,
the Jewish festival of freedom. For days before, the place had been
a flurry of activity. Rooms were cleaned, dishes changed, crumbs
tracked down like unwanted intruders. We were doing the things
that Jews have always done at this time, clearing the house of bread
and leaven, and getting ready to re-enact the formative experience
of the Jewish people, the exodus from Egypt and the long journey
across the wilderness. When *seder* night eventually arrived – the
evening when we recited the *Haggadah* and told the story – we
would gather together as a vast extended family, aunts and uncles,
cousins and distant relatives, along as always with sundry visitors
who had no family of their own.

As the youngest, I quickly realised that I had the starring part.
The entire ritual is set in motion and constructed around the
questions asked by a child. So I practised and learned the *Mah
Nishtanah*, the 'Why is this night different from all other nights?',
that for me, as for most other Jewish children, formed my first
introduction to Jewish history. We ate the *matzah*, the unleavened

---

[1] Jacob Neusner, *Conservative, American and Jewish*, Lafayette La., Huntington
House, 1993, 35.

'bread of affliction', and drank the four cups of wine, each one symbolising a stage on the road to redemption. For me the best part was the traditional game of hide-and-seek. I was given the *afikoman*, part of the middle *matzah*, to hide, and when the time came for it to be eaten I knew I would be offered a gift in return for disclosing its whereabouts. The evening ended, after midnight, with the rousing songs added to the ritual in the Middle Ages, most of them designed to keep sleepy children awake. It was heady, magical and fun, and like most Jewish children I have never forgotten it.

What was happening in this ritual? I didn't know it then, but I was being inducted into an identity and a series of moral commitments. I was becoming part of a people, its shared experiences and hopes. The historical details of the exodus are lost in the oubliette of the past. But this was not history but memory. It was in the process of becoming 'my story'. As the narrative began, and my grandfather lifted the *matzah* and declared: 'This is the bread of affliction which our ancestors ate in the land of Egypt', all of us there were making the leap across more than three millennia and turning ancient events into our own. With a single sentence my grandfather, *zeida* as we called him, was bringing past and present together and extending both to the future by offering it as his legacy to his children and grandchildren. We would take the story forward, knowing as Jews that we too were part of the same journey, towards freedom, away from tyranny, and that on the way we would have to recognise affliction when we saw it and learn to overcome it, in faith and together. This was moral education, not education as the act of making choices, but as the process of learning who we are, where we came from, and the language of ideals of which we are a part. Passover is about the handing on of Jewish memory across the generations.

Nor did I understand then that such celebrations of memory can themselves change history. My maternal grandfather came from Israel, then Palestine, where his family had been among the early nineteenth-century pioneers. He had been forced to leave because of a dispute with the local Arab population, a foreshadowing of greater tensions yet to come and still unsolved. He would have known Theodor Herzl, the Viennese journalist traumatised by the anti-Semitism he saw in France at the time of the Dreyfus trial. After deep reflection between the years 1894 and 1896, Herzl came to the conclusion that if the Jews of Europe were to be safe they would need a home in Israel, and so Zionism as a worldwide movement began. I later discovered that Herzl too had been profoundly influenced by his memories of Passover and the story of the Israelites' flight from persecution across the desert to a land of their own. He provides us with an account of his feelings in his semi-autobiographical novel, *Altneuland*. Herzl, thinly disguised in the character of Dr Friedrich Loewenburg, the assimilated Jew who attends a *seder* service and rediscovers his identity, describes his emotions as he too undergoes the transformation from history into memory:

> And so the ritual went on, half religious ceremony and half family meal, moving for anyone who had a heart to be moved by ancient custom. For this most Jewish of Jewish festivals reached back farther into ancient times than any living customs of the civilized world.
>
> It was celebrated now exactly as it had been observed for hundreds and hundreds of years. The world had changed, nations had vanished from the face of the earth, others had made their way into the annals of history . . . and only this one nation was still here, cherishing its ancient customs, true to itself, remembering the sufferings of its ancestors. It still prays in the ancient language and the ancient formula to the Eternal God, this nation of slaves and now of free men – Israel.[2]

Loewenburg discovers, as Michael Sandel, Charles Taylor and Michael Walzer have argued, that to have moral commitments, even an identity, we must first belong.

But this is a radically different account of moral education than that which has prevailed since the days of Locke and Rousseau. According to this view the child is a *tabula rasa*, a clean slate, on which it can write any script it chooses. It learns words, language, ideals by itself. It learns the way a scientist learns, by observation and experience, putting aside all preconceptions, 'prejudices', it has inherited from those around it. Not only is this the way we

[2] Theodor Herzl, *Altneuland*, translated Paula Arnold, Israel, Haifa Publishing Co., 141–2.

learn, but according to Kant it is the way we must learn if we are truly to be moral agents. To do something because others do it, or because of habit or custom or even Divine command, is to accept an external authority over the one sovereign territory that is truly our own: our own choices. The moral being for Kant is by definition an autonomous being, a person who accepts no other authority than the self. By the 1960s this was beginning to gain hold as an educational orthodoxy. The task of education is not to hand on a tradition but to enhance the consciousness of choice. As in politics, 'the self is prior to its ends'. Curricula were devised in 'values clarification', teaching children simply to articulate their personal preferences. Critical to this process were non-judgementalism and relativism on the part of the teacher. No one way of life was to be singled out as preferable to, or less fulfilling than, any other. The procedural state found its equivalent in the value-free classroom.

But this is not how we learn. It is not the way we learn anything, let alone the most important question of all, namely how to live. To learn any skill, as Aristotle noted, we need to see how master-practitioners practise their craft. We need to watch and imitate, at first clumsily, then with growing fluency and confidence. We need to set foot within a practice, finding our way around it from the inside. This presupposes distinctive attitudes: authority, obedience, discipline, persistence and self-control. To learn music, painting, football, woodwork, we have to enter a tradition, a 'form of life', and one that has acknowledged and socially recognised exponents. Only much later on in the process do we begin to learn that what we have been doing informally has rules, an inner logic, a grammar of its own.

There is a stage at which we put those rules to the test. We assert our independence, we challenge, ask for explanations, occasionally rebel and try quite other ways of doing things. Eventually we reach an equilibrium. The rules have been internalised. We understand them. We know why they are this way rather than that. We may choose to reject them, but in doing so we are conscious that we have thereby exiled ourselves from a particular way of life, perhaps something small like a game, but also and more rarely something of greater moment, like the way of life handed on to us by our parents – a decision rarely taken without a sense of personal crisis, even bereavement. For the most part, though, we stay within the world as we have inherited it, just as for the most part we stay with our mother-tongue, capable now of self-critical reflection on its strengths and weaknesses, perhaps working to change it from within, but recognising that its rules are not a constraint but the very possibility of shared experiences and relationship and communication. Autonomy – the capacity to act and choose in the consciousness of alternatives – is a late stage in moral development, the achievement of mastery and maturity. It is not where it begins. More importantly, autonomy takes place *within* a tradition, just as artistic creativity, as Ernst Gombrich has shown,[3] always takes place within the history of a genre. It is not a state of traditionlessness, but the high-point of tradition itself.

The modern thinker who has done most to rehabilitate these ideas is Alasdair MacIntyre. His *After Virtue*, appearing in 1981, was the counterpart in moral philosophy to the work of Michael Sandel in political thought. Like Sandel, he argued that the idea of an 'unsituated self', free to make choices unencumbered by attachments, was radically incoherent. Such an individual, even supposing one could exist, would have no reason to choose this rather than that. He or she would lack an identity. Life would consist in a set of disconnected episodes and events, not unlike a series of MTV pop videos, without a connecting narrative to explain why this, not that. Even to have a reason for acting, we need to have some sense of ourself as a character within a drama, of whose script we are (with others) the co-authors, but which at least has a plot and point, a sense of continuity from one scene to the next. As he put it:

I can only answer the question 'What am I to do?' if I can answer the prior question, 'Of what story or stories do I find myself a part?' We enter human society, that is, with one or more imputed characters – roles into which we have been drafted – and we have to learn what they are in order to be able to understand how others respond to us and how

3 In his books *Art and Illusion*, Oxford, Phaidon, 1988, and *Meditations on a Hobby Horse*, London, Phaidon, 1978.

our responses are to be construed. It is through hearing stories ... that children learn or mislearn both what a child and what a parent is, what the cast of characters may be in the drama into which they have been born and what the ways of the world are. Deprive children of stories and you leave them unscripted, anxious stutterers in their actions as in their words.[4]

This, in Jewish terms, is what the Passover is about. As MacIntyre makes clear, the need for stories and traditions is neither Jewish nor religious, but simply human. Nor was this insight left at the theoretical level alone. In the United States it was taken up by William J. Bennett who, as chairman of the National Endowment for the Humanities and Secretary of Education under the Reagan and Bush administration, fought for the reinstatement of this classic view of learning. In his words, 'To be a citizen is to share in something common – in common principles, common memories, and a common language in which to discuss our common affairs.'[5] Recognising the value of stories as the shared heritage of memory and moral imagination, in 1993 he published *The Book of Virtues*, a seemingly unfashionable collection of the stories, poems, parables, legends and inspirational literature which earlier generations of parents had taught their children. He grouped them under the headings of the various virtues: self-discipline, compassion, responsibility, friendship, work, courage, perseverance, honesty, loyalty and faith. Nothing like it had been seen in decades, but to everyone's surprise it became an immense public success, staying near the top of the best-seller lists for over a year.

Like MacIntyre, Bennett took his inspiration from Aristotle and the idea of virtue as habituation, and like him he believed that over and above precept, habit and example, children require stories, 'moral literacy', before they can confront the great dilemmas of adult life. He argued that: 'We must not permit our disputes over thorny political questions to obscure the obligation we have to offer instruction to all our young people in the area in which we have, as a society, reached a consensus: namely on the importance

[4] Alasdair MacIntyre, *After Virtue*, 201.
[5] William J. Bennett, *The De-valuing of America*, 54.

of good character, and on some of its pervasive particulars.'[6] In Britain, as I write, the National Forum for Values in Education and the Community is preparing its recommendations to the School Curriculum and Assessment Authority, as yet unpublished.[7] They too discovered that consensus was relatively easy to reach, and the group, including teachers, employers, religious leaders and academics, converged on the virtues of compassion, equality, fairness, freedom, justice, respect, responsibility and truth – strikingly similar to the chapter-headings of Bennett's book. Like Bennett and MacIntyre they believed that these virtues were under threat in a society which valued 'success, self-interest, wealth, winning and not getting caught'.

There is a deeper point behind the reinstatement of virtue and moral literacy within the curriculum, obvious but rarely alluded to in the literature. Like Sandel, MacIntyre was primarily concerned with the nature of personal identity and its relationship to a political and moral culture. But there is an altogether more fundamental reason why human beings throughout history have sought to pass on their traditions to their children. Moral experience takes time, often more than a single generation. It took millennia for people to learn that slavery is morally unacceptable, or that men and women share equal dignity and responsibility, or that the possession of a minority faith is not sufficient reason to be deprived of citizenship rights. These are not new ideas. They are implicit in the opening chapter of Genesis, where the human person as such is declared to be 'the image of God'. But it took many centuries of painful experience before these principles worked their way through to consciousness and implementation. When civilisations forget their past, they too, like individuals, become 'anxious stutterers in their actions as in their words'. Tradition is to morality what memory is to personality, and when we lose it we become prey to a kind of collective Alzheimer's Disease.

It was the error, perhaps even the hubris, of the Enlightenment to suppose that human nature could be studied in the same way

---

[6] William J. Bennett (ed.), *The Book of Virtues*, 13.

[7] *Daily Telegraph*, 13 August 1996.

as physical nature, through a kind of scientific methodology that discarded the past and proceeded as if the entire extant heritage of human wisdom could be ignored – a frame of mind we can trace all the way from Descartes' attempt to start philosophy on new foundations to A. J. Ayer's dismissal, in a mere twenty pages of *Language, Truth and Logic*, of the whole of ethics, aesthetics and religious belief as 'meaningless'. We now know, thanks to the work of Michael Polanyi and T. S. Kuhn,[8] that even science does not work this way. It too is a tradition–guided activity.[9] But if it were the case that human beings were atoms and a part of nature, then it seemed plausible to suppose that there could be a science of human behaviour, and that older understandings were no more than superstitions.

At some time around the eighteenth century, as Raymond Williams has shown,[10] a whole series of words began to acquire new saliency. Prior to that time, for example, the word 'modern' had an unfavourable connotation. It meant 'altered', not necessarily for the better. Subsequently it came to mean 'improved'. Words like 'progress', 'evolution', even 'civilisation', began to carry with them the implication that the new is inevitably a higher, more developed, stage than the old. Moral justification, which had previously referred to something in the past (a promise undertaken, a command given, a covenant accepted), now began to point towards the future, most famously in the case of utilitarianism, where actions are judged by their consequences. In time, even individual deliberation about behaviour came to seem less relevant to the condition of society. For Marx, human behaviour was the

[8] Michael Polanyi, *Personal Knowledge: Towards a Post-Critical Philosophy*, Chicago, University of Chicago Press, 1974; T. S. Kuhn, *The Structure of Scientific Revolutions*, 2nd ed., Chicago, University of Chicago Press, 1970.

[9] Traditions can, of course, face crises: this is the theme of Kuhn's book, as it is of Alasdair MacIntyre's *Whose Justice? Which Rationality?*, and Edward Shils' *Tradition*. The point, however, is that we cannot pursue knowledge by standing outside traditions any more than we can create art outside genres or formulate speech outside language.

[10] Raymond Williams, *Keywords: A Vocabulary of Culture and Society*, Flamingo, 1976.

product of economic structures. For Darwinians it was carried in genetic codes. For behaviourists it was the result of 'operant conditioning'. If social change was sought, it could be brought about by social engineering, or political revolution, or economic incentives, or new patterns of stimulus-response. If human beings were indeed part of nature, then they could be pacified and manipulated through some form of socio-technology. One way or another, what mattered in decision-making were purposes not antecedents, futures not pasts, ends not beginnings. Tradition could be discarded as so much unnecessary baggage.

The mistake, and it was profound, lay in a failure to understand the significance of the fact that, though *Homo sapiens* is a part of nature, persons are a part of culture. We pass on our moral instincts not only genetically but also and primarily through what we say and do and what we teach our children to say and do. What makes man unique, and uniquely adaptable, among the animals, is that we possess the capacity for language. Cultural transmission is altogether more subtle and sensitive than genetic transmission. It takes the work of more than a lifetime to know and draw workable conclusions from the whole of human history thus far. That is why all cultures develop codes, rituals, stories, and heroes, which summarise and exemplify in simple form what an entire people and its sages have learned over the centuries. Traditions are the collective shorthand of experience.

The point was made by the sociologist Edward Shils in his massive work, *Tradition*, published in the same year as MacIntyre's *After Virtue*. Human beings, he wrote, 'do not fare well in a disordered world. They need to live within the framework of a world in which they possess a chart . . . The loss of contact with the accomplishments of ancestors is injurious because it deprives subsequent generations of the guiding chart which all human beings, even geniuses and prophets, need. They cannot create these for themselves in a stable and satisfying way.' He added: 'The destruction of these cognitive, moral, metaphysical and technical charts is a step into chaos.'[11]

[11] Edward Shils, *Tradition*, 326.

In the last work he wrote before he died, the influential economist and liberal Friedrich Hayek turned his attention to the nature of traditions. His posthumously published *The Fatal Conceit* (1988) sets out the argument that the consequences of our ethical choices are so far-reaching, lasting and unpredictable that we can never know them in advance. Only with long hindsight are we able to judge the effectiveness of a social order, and the best test of a moral system is that it has survived. The idea that we can make sound decisions rationally, autonomously, and by disregarding the past, is misconceived and potentially tragic. Humanity has survived only through its capacity to acquire habits whose significance we rarely if ever fully understand. 'It is not our intellect that created our morals,' he wrote, 'rather, human interactions governed by our morals make possible the growth of reason and those capabilities associated with it. Man became intelligent because there was tradition – that which lies between instinct and reason – for him to learn. This tradition, in turn, originated not from a capacity rationally to interpret observed facts but from habits of responding.'[12] With this argument, Hayek turned the Enlightenment on its head. Rationality could not replace tradition. Instead, it depended on it.

These thoughts, too, echo ideas articulated long ago but subsequently forgotten. Most famously it was Edmund Burke who had argued that society was a partnership extending over time. 'As the ends of such a partnership cannot be obtained in many generations, it becomes a partnership not only between those who are living, but between those who are living, those who are dead, and those who are to be born.'[13] One aspect of that relationship was the handing on of understanding. 'We are afraid to put men to live and trade each on his own private stock of reason; because we suspect that this stock in each man is small, and that the individuals would do better to avail themselves of the general bank and capital of nations, and of ages.' Inherited wisdom (Burke called it 'prejudice') has the effect of rendering

---

[12] F. A. Hayek, *The Fatal Conceit*, Routledge, 1990, 21–2.
[13] Edmund Burke, *Reflections on the Revolution in France*, 96.

'a man's virtue his habit; and not a series of unconnected acts'. His duty 'becomes a part of his nature'.[14]

Understandably but wrongly the concept of tradition has come to be associated with a reactionary disposition, the defence of an existing order and hostility to change. In fact, over the past two centuries, its most famous protagonists – Burke himself, G. K. Chesterton, T. S. Eliot and Michael Oakeshott – have been cultural conservatives. But a tradition can also be revolutionary. The Passover tradition is a notable example. Its themes – liberation, redemption, the building of a new social order – have inspired revolutionary movements in Britain and America since the seventeenth century.[15] Just as we can hand on to our children the desire to conserve a status quo, so we can hand on to them the desire to change it in ways we have not yet succeeded in doing. We can convey to them our ideals, not only our necessarily imperfect achievements. Tradition has nothing to do with a conservative disposition. It has to do with the fact that experience takes time to acquire, and ideals many generations to enact.

The failures of value-free education have become well-known since the publication, in the late 1980s, of Allan Bloom's *The Closing of the American Mind*. That work, and many others which followed in its wake, focused on the state of the humanities at university level. But it rapidly became clear that the same problems could be traced back to elementary and secondary schooling, which in Britain and America had suffered, since the introduction of new methodologies, from falling levels of literacy and numeracy, strikingly so in comparison with other countries where more traditional methods were still practised. The American story is told at length in Charles Sykes' pungently titled *Dumbing Down Our Kids*, subtitled *Why American kids feel good about themselves but can't read, write or add* (1995). Melanie Phillips gives a parallel account of the British scene in her equally powerful indictment, *All Must Have Prizes* (1996). These books are savage in their critiques. I do not share their sense of indignation. Teachers are among a civilisation's

14 Ibid., 87.
15 See Michael Walzer, *Exodus and Revolution*.

most precious assets, and it is wrong retroactively to blame those who faithfully implemented the prevailing wisdom of their time. But a re-evaluation is called for, one that restores to education its true dignity as the citadel of cultural continuity, and to teachers the honour due to those who are the trustees of society's bequest to its children.

Education is the transmission of a tradition. A civilisation is like an ancient but still magnificent building. Different ages have added new wings here, an altered façade there, rooms have been redecorated, old furniture restored. Over the generations paintings have been acquired, some hanging, others – currently out of fashion – stored away. We inherited the house from our parents, and we want to leave it in good order to our children. We know that they will adapt it to their needs, indeed we want them to. Nor can we say in advance how they will do so or what the house will look like in the future. But as its temporary guardians, we know that we must teach our children its history, why it was built and how it was changed. We must do our best to ensure that, in time, they will come to love it as we do, so that when they come to change it, as they will, they will do so harmoniously, not destructively, according to their best understanding of what it represents to them and those who came before them. That is the goal of education as articulate autonomy. Education is not, and cannot be, a matter of handing a child an architectural encyclopaedia on the one hand, a heap of bricks on the other, and telling it to build its own house. 'Values clarification' is a sophisticated form of values obfuscation.

Traditions are never lost. They can be renewed or re-invented. All it takes is for them to be cherished. Cultures survive the way post-biblical Judaism survived: when they attach the highest priority to schools and teachers, and when they see at least part of the role of education as developing individuals articulate in the language of their heritage. Individuality is not a gift of birth. It is a cultural achievement of a high order. The more widely this form of education is available, the more at-home-in-the-universe our children will feel. But as my Passover example suggests, education needs more than schools. Above all else, it needs families.

16

Family Matters

Like a marriage, a family is a commitment, one that places heavy
burdens on its members, burdens that the experience of history has
shown must nevertheless be shouldered if people are to be happy
and society is to prosper. These burdens may be light and bearing
them can be a joy, or they may be heavy and bearing them can
be an affliction. Whichever is the case, one can no more choose
to take the joy and ignore the afflictions than one can choose to
live a life that is both solitary and happy ... We learn to cope
with the people of this world because we learn to cope with the
members of our family. Those who flee the family flee the world;
bereft of the former's affection, tutelage, and challenges, they are
unprepared for the latter's tests, judgements and demands.

James Q. Wilson[1]

OVER A CENTURY ago, Charles Dickens revolutionised the
way we thought about children. In novel after novel – *Oliver
Twist, Great Expectations, Bleak House* – he took his readers behind
the façade of Victorian England and brought them face to face
with scenes of poverty, abandonment, exploitation and cruelty that
shocked and awoke the conscience of a generation. There were
many other campaigners at the time, but Dickens' voice was the
most effective because he taught people to view the world through
the eyes of a child. He made people see what was around them but
which they had not fully noticed before: that though Britain ruled
a vast and distant empire, it was neglecting its own children.

If Dickens were to come to life today and witness what had
changed, there would be much that would give him immense
satisfaction. He would see standards of medical care, schooling,
welfare and social support that would amaze him. He would

---

[1] James Q. Wilson, *The Moral Sense*, 163.

see centres of relative deprivation, but he would be astonished by the advance in absolute living standards. Above all he would see a revolution in the freedom and independence of children. He would see much for which to give thanks.

But he would also be perplexed. He would discover that in the United States, every three hours, gun violence takes a child's life; that every nine minutes a child is arrested for a drug or alcohol offence; that every minute of the day an American teenager has a baby; and that every twenty-six seconds a child runs away from home. He would find that among young people, suicide is the third highest cause of death, that a 1990 survey revealed that 15 per cent of teenagers had contemplated it and 6 per cent attempted it. He would find that between 16 and 19 per cent of young people suffered from a depressive condition, and some two and a half million of them were without a permanent home.[2] He would note that among those aged between twelve and twenty-five, 2 per cent are using cocaine, 4 per cent crack, 13 per cent cannabis, 13.2 per cent hallucinogens, and that 20 per cent regularly abuse alcohol.[3] He would learn that between 1985 and 1990, the murder of babies under one year old doubled, and of children between one and four quadrupled.[4]

Turning to Britain he would find that in the last decade the crime rate among youth has risen by 54 per cent, that drug addiction among the under-18s has increased fourfold during the same period, that illegitimate births have increased six times, as have abortions among teenage girls.[5] He would learn that reported cases of child abuse are running at three times the level they were in the 1970s, and that the number of children in psychiatric hospitals has risen by 65 per cent in the last five years.[6] He would then be in a position to understand how, in an age of rising living standards, a 1995 MORI opinion poll

[2] David Walsh, *Selling Out America's Children*, 3–5.

[3] Rosalind Miles, *The Children We Deserve*, 4.

[4] Patrick Dixon, *The Rising Price of Love*, 142.

[5] Miles, op. cit., 3–4.

[6] Ibid., 6.

showed that of those interviewed, 53 per cent believed that the world their children would inherit would be worse than the one they knew as children. Only 13 per cent thought things had improved.

He would want to know what had happened. On investigation, he would find that since the 1960s the divorce rate has multiplied six times; the number of children born outside marriage has risen five times; the number of dependent children living with a lone parent has risen three times. He would further discover that in this respect Britain and America, though they led some of the trends, were not alone. He would be struck by the observation of the French demographer Louis Roussel, that beginning around the mid-1960s there has been 'a general upheaval across the whole set of demographic indicators, a phenomenon rare in the history of populations'.[7] Throughout the industrialised world, birth and marriage rates fell, while those of divorce and illegitimate births rose, in most countries by massive margins. Dickens would find himself bewildered by the extreme fluidity of new family arrangements: cohabitation, single parenthood, divorce, serial monogamy, and virtually every imaginable combination of alternative lifestyles. Nothing in his Victorian upbringing would have prepared him for this possibility. But then, nothing in anyone's upbringing would have done so. Different societies at different times have had different marital and family structures. But none before has tried them all together and all at once.

He would want to know the connection between these two phenomena, the breakdown of marriage and the rise in child pathologies. He would discover the following: Research undertaken by the Joseph Rowntree Foundation and published in 1994 showed that children from families that had experienced separation or divorce were twice as likely as those from intact families to have problems with emotional and physical health, behaviour and achievement at school. They were more likely to have low self-esteem and find it difficult to make friends. They were four

[7] Quoted in Mary Ann Glendon, *Rights Talk*, 132.

times more likely to suffer stress-related problems and four times more likely to need psychiatric treatment.[8]

Further surveys have shown that the effects of divorce on children are long-lasting. According to one, almost half the children of broken marriages 'entered adulthood as worried, underachieving, self-deprecating, and sometimes angry young men and women'.[9] According to another, among a cohort of British children born in 1946, those who had experienced their parents' divorce were three times more likely to be unemployed in their late teens and early twenties, and by the age of thirty-six twice as likely to be in the lowest income bracket. They are also more likely to repeat in their own lives the pattern of disrupted relationship they witnessed in their parents'. Girls are more likely to have teenage births, premarital births and failed marriages; boys less likely to establish a successful marriage or retain a job.[10]

For children of single-parent families the results are less bad but still chilling. In America they are twice as likely to drop out of high school, or if they remain, to have poorer academic and attendance records.[11] Girls living with a single parent are two-and-a-half times more likely to become single mothers. The majority of young people in prison either come from single-parent homes or have lived with someone other than their natural parents.[12] Single parents are more likely to use 'abusive forms of violence' with their children than two-parent households.[13] In 1993, social commentator Barbara Whitehead concluded that: 'The social science evidence is in: though it may benefit the adults involved, the dissolution of

[8] John Tripp and Monica Cockett, 'Children living in re-ordered families', *Social Policy Findings No. 45*, Joseph Rowntree Foundation, 1994.

[9] Judith Wallerstein and Sandra Blakeslee, *Second Chances*, New York, Ticknor & Fields, 1989, 299.

[10] The evidence is summarised in Patricia Morgan, 'Conflict and Divorce', in Robert Whelan (ed.), *Just a Piece of Paper?*, 19–35.

[11] Deborah Dawson, *Family Structure and Children's Health*, Washington DC, National Center for Health Statistics, 1991.

[12] William J. Bennett, 'What to do about the children', *Commentary*, March 1995, 23–8.

[13] Patrick Dixon, *The Rising Price of Love*, 141.

intact two-parent families is harmful to large numbers of children. Moreover . . . family diversity in the form of increasing numbers of single-parent and step-parent families does not strengthen the social fabric but, rather, dramatically weakens and undermines society.'[14] In Britain, in a much-quoted verdict, Professor A. H. Halsey concurred. The evidence showed, he said, that children of single parents tend 'to have more illness, to do less well at school, to exist at a lower level of nutrition, comfort and conviviality, to suffer more unemployment, to be more prone to deviance and crime, and finally to repeat the cycle of unstable parenting from which they themselves have suffered'.[15]

Dickens, finally, might be driven by curiosity to ask how this situation had come about, what logic lay behind it, what reasoning led people to make these sorts of choices. We would, I imagine, try to explain to him the changes in attitudes that have taken place since his day. We would say that nowadays we believe that individuals should have the freedom to choose their own lifestyle, that none is intrinsically better or worse than any other, that marriage is only a contract and therefore has no special priority or bindingness, and that relationships have only one test of acceptability, namely that they take place between consenting adults. At that point I imagine Dickens, who has followed the argument thus far, asking one question. 'I understand the principle of consenting adults. *But what about the children?*'

It is a good question, the essential question. But I want to ask another. I have imagined a hypothetical Dickens, returned to life more than a century after his death, surveying our social landscape and passing a quizzical eye over some of our habits. But where is *our* Dickens? Where is the contemporary novelist, artist or film-maker willing to raise the mirror and let us see our world from the perspective of a child, abandoned, disregarded, left alone, vulnerable and verging on despair, and show us in the way that Dickens did that though we can now see distant galaxies and

---

[14] *Atlantic Monthly*, April 1993; quoted in Norman Dennis and George Erdos, *Families Without Fatherhood*, xvi.

[15] Foreword to Dennis and Erdos, op. cit., xii.

understand the birth of the universe, we sometimes fail to see those closest to us and fail to understand the moral implications of the birth of a child?

With this we come to one of the most troubling features of our cultural predicament. There has been lively academic debate about political institutions, in the wake of the work of Sandel, Taylor and Walzer. There has been equally vigorous argument, following the writings of Alasdair MacIntyre, about morality and the place of virtue. But about the family, despite the vast cumulative weight of empirical research, the conversation has been strained and tense. It has not been an arena of rational debate. Despite the fact that in Britain the strongest defenders of the family have come from the left – A. H. Halsey, Melanie Phillips and Norman Dennis – the persistent charge is that those who express concern about it are seeking an excuse for reduced welfare expenditures or a more authoritarian approach to crime. It is almost impossible to speak about the family without being accused of launching a moral crusade, blaming the victim, or hitting at the most vulnerable – as if what was at stake were the self-esteem of the parents, instead of the concrete suffering of those who matter in this situation, namely the children.

In 1994, an eminent child psychiatrist, Dr Clifford Yorke, delivered a disturbing series of radio talks on 'Childhood and Social Truth'. He suggested that responses to the plight of children in contemporary society amounted to 'a *denial* of massive proportions: a denial of the needs and rights of children. The needs and wishes of adults come first, and unconsciously they take advantage of an amnesia for the early childhood they themselves once experienced. At the same time, they make unwitting use of child-like wishful fantasy and, in doing so, seek and strive to promote public support.'[16] That denial is, I believe, a central issue at stake in the possibility of a renewed politics of community.

Consider this. In 1996 two British philosophers, John Gray on the left, Roger Scruton on the right, published pamphlets in defence of communitarianism. Both argued that we should

---

[16] Dr Clifford Yorke, *Childhood and Social Truth*, five broadcast talks, BBC Radio 4. The quotation is taken from the third lecture, deliverd on 9 November 1994.

abandon any attempt to reinstate the family. For Gray, any wish to restore 'vanished or dying forms of family' should be rejected as a 'form of nostalgia'.[17] For Scruton 'it is self-defeating to make the family and family values into an object of policy' and 'the more it is held forth as an ideal and an example, the more it will wither and disintegrate under the strain'.[18]

I respect these thinkers greatly and admire their work. But I question their conclusions. From all we know from the assembled findings of a century of research in anthropology, sociology and child psychology, the stable family is not a dispensable institution. Communities like the Israeli kibbutz have tried, and after long experience have reverted to more traditional patterns. We know, from the work of Le Play and Emmanuel Todd,[19] how many and varied are the types of kinship structure, but we know equally that no society has been able to exist without some framework of rules establishing marriage as a legal institution, and defining responsibilities for child nurture.

We know more than this, namely that the family is the crucible of much that matters in later life, the growth of sympathy and trust and sociability. It is where we acquire our identity, self-confidence, responsibility, attachment, fellow-feeling, the moral sentiment itself. It is where we learn who we are, where we came from, and where we belong. It is where we become, in Michael Sandel's phrase, 'situated selves'. Above all, it is the matrix of the belief that lies at the heart of hope itself, namely that love given is not given in vain, that in the sharing of vulnerabilities we discover strength. Burke and Tocqueville were not wrong to see the family as the citadel of liberty and the origin of our larger 'public affections'. Dickens was not wrong to see that a society which harms its children, whatever else it is, is not a place in which one can live at ease. Hayek was not wrong to suggest that a society which cannot sustain families cannot survive. Nor, as Lord Macaulay said,

[17] John Gray, *After Social Democracy*, 19.

[18] Roger Scruton, *The Conservative Idea of Community*, 25, 21.

[19] Emmanuel Todd, *The Explanation of Ideology: Family Structures and Social Systems*, Oxford, Blackwell, 1985.

are we entitled to have 'periodical fits of morality'. Heaven help us if, as a society, we are judged by history to have campaigned for the protection of animals, birds, rare plant species and rain-forests while failing to heed the cry of our own children.

In one sense Gray and Scruton are right. It is not that there are no government policies that would, over the course of time, bring healing to the fractured family. There are. We could end tax discrimination against married couples. We could institute curricula in parenting and personal relations. We could resource widespread premarital counselling. We could make divorce more difficult. We could use the instrumentalities of law, education and fiscal policy to send a clear message that marriage, though not the only, is none the less the socially preferred context of childrearing. Far from this being impossible, it was the norm throughout the Western world for most of its history until the 1960s. Indeed in strict economic terms there are overwhelming reasons for doing so. The cost of divorce, welfare, social and psychiatric services, drug and alcohol rehabilitation, law enforcement and crime prevention arising out of the undersocialisation of a large section of a generation are high and rising and will, of themselves, create budgetary crises of a formidable order. Quite apart from this, Francis Fukuyama has recently advanced the argument that families form the core of what he calls 'social capital', which is itself a factor in economic growth.[20] For that reason alone the West may be overtaken in the twenty-first century by the high-technology but still strongly familial cultures of China and South East Asia.

So the strengthening of the family can be done and, even on strictly non-moral grounds, should be done. But Gray and Scruton have correctly intuited this, that it will not be done. The political will is lacking. For a government to identify one way of life as inherently preferable to another is the ultimate crime against the concept of the abstract individual and the procedural state, the self which is prior to its ends and the right which is prior to the good. If the stable family is one of society's ideals, then not all choices are equal, and we shrink from this conclusion. But I believe they

[20] Francis Fukuyama, *Trust: The Social Virtues and the Creation of Prosperity.*

have not fully understood that if the communitarian argument fails here, it fails everywhere. If we cannot summon the political will to strengthen families, we cannot do so to strengthen communities of any other kind. The case stands or falls on this: are we prepared to accept some limit on the pursuit of private interest? If we are not prepared to do so for the sake of children, then we are not prepared to do so *tout court*.

A politics of institutions is not a politics of interests, it is a politics of the common good. To exist at all it must be prepared to make moral judgements, not indeed to legislate on them, but at the very least to bring them within the domain of public debate, so that in time we may be able to create a political will that is not currently there. With grave trepidation, therefore, I want to say what others, surely no less wise, believe cannot be said.

If we have any moral responsibilities at all, then we have moral responsibilities to those we brought into being. Our duty to our children is constitutive and inalienable. This is not my view alone. It was shared by the most radical libertarian the British tradition has produced, John Stuart Mill, who wrote: 'The fact itself, of causing the existence of a human being, is one of the most responsible actions in the range of human life.' He continued, with rare moral fervour: 'To undertake this responsibility – to bestow a life which may be either a curse or blessing – unless the being on whom it is to be bestowed will have at least the ordinary chances of a desirable existence, is a crime against that being.'[21] To have a child and then walk away is an abandonment of the most ultimate kind, whatever the cause or circumstance.

If we have a duty to fulfil any undertaking, we have a duty to honour the pledge of marriage. For in marriage we ask for and offer a commitment to share not this or that aspect of life but life itself. Marriage is the supreme example of a moral bond. Like all things seriously worthwhile it involves the realisation of a possibility at the price of self-imposed exclusion of others. Every relationship has its rows, its tensions, its disappointments, its languid passages, but

[21] John Stuart Mill, *Utilitarianism, On Liberty and Considerations on Representative Government*, 177.

marriage is where we live through these things in the knowledge – given by commitment, renewed by love's rituals – that they will not drive us apart. Marriage is surrounded by a wall (the rabbis called it a 'hedge of roses') that we may not cross. On the other side is adultery.

If marriage is holy, adultery is a sin. If it is moral, then adultery is a wrong. There are some moral judgements we cannot avoid making if we are to protect the things worth having, and this is one. Adultery is wrong because it is a betrayal – of a partner, a commitment, a promise, a trust. If adultery is undiscovered, then one of the partners to a marriage is living a lie and the other an illusion. If it is discovered, there is no way of avoiding the pain. If the adulterous partner drops the affair and goes back to his or her marriage partner, then one person is abandoned – used, spent, discarded – and between the couple there is now the slow poison of suspicion and mistrust. If the affair continues and the marriage breaks up, a relationship built on a pledge of love has been destroyed. Nor can the new partnership ever recover the sense of stability with which the old began. Both partners know that one of them in the past has broken a vow and may do so again, and that both have purchased their happiness at the cost of someone else's pain. If both the marriage and the affair continue, then neither can continue to be what they once were. The marriage is no longer a promise of mutual loyalty. The affair has lost the allure of illicit pleasure. And this is to say nothing of the children who may be involved. Adultery has no saving graces.

Understanding why adultery is wrong allows us to understand more generally why morality matters, and why so few acts are truly private. Like most immoral acts, adultery involves putting short-term pleasure ahead of lifelong happiness. It sets my desires above my feeling for, and obligation to, others. It devalues the currency of commitment: the word spoken, the pledge given, the promise undertaken. And like so many ostensibly unpublic acts, it affects the world around us. What we do today others may do in the future, affected, consciously or unconsciously, by our example. We tacitly teach our partners, friends, and above all our children, that despite our most serious undertakings, the word of another person cannot be trusted. When that happens, we are all diminished.

Attacked once by muggers in the street, we think twice about going out alone. Robbed once, we think twice about leaving our door open. A single breakdown of order introduces into our horizons a note of mistrust and we are never as free again. Betrayed once as partners or children, we are reluctant to give ourselves wholly and unconditionally to another person. We keep our distance, lower our expectations, stay cool, aloof, separate. When that happens, something of our world has been lost, nor is it something small. Love freely given and freely received, the sharing of a life, is the most profound redemption ever experienced from loneliness, the point at which the political and moral enterprise begin. A world of safe distances, of reservations and precautions, can never hope to recapture that state. We, individually and collectively, are the guardians of the world of trust, and the family is its birthplace.

Gray, Scruton and others who are reticent to speak about the family are right and wrong, right to believe that change cannot be brought about politically, wrong to ignore the fact that it can be brought about morally. Reconnecting morality and politics – what I have been doing throughout this work – is the genesis of hope, because morality restores to politics the idea that there are things I can change. I am bound to others, and together we are the co-authors of our world. Of this, the supreme example is the family. Far from being the institution we can least affect, it is the one we can most affect, because it is made or unmade by our choices. More than any other, it is the domain in which what you and I do makes a difference to other lives.

We can reinstate marriage in the simplest possible way, by revaluing it, cherishing it in our own lives, and teaching it to our children. It takes courage to make the great commitment – the leap of faith – of marriage itself. Within our culture the many things that were once combined – sex, affection, friendship, love, bringing new life into the world, caring for it and one another – have all been separated so that the one is no longer expected to entail the other. Nothing else has contributed more to the fragmentation of our lives, to the sense, in the words of John Donne, that "Tis all in pieces, all coherence gone'. So it takes moral courage to take the risk of marriage in a culture in which such commitment is neither valued nor supported. But of all commitments it justifies the risk, for there are few greater achievements of which we can be the artists than a love hazarded and reciprocated and expressed in a moral bond, and none more awe-inspiring than bringing new life into the world. More than any other institution the family turns the everyday into unselfconscious beauty: it is the celebration of ordinary virtues, life made a blessing by being shared.

These values will not speak to everyone. They never did. Nor will we live up to them all the time. We never do. But unless they live as ideals at the heart of our civilisation, it will not survive. The devaluing of the family and the legitimation of sexual licence, whether it takes place in ancient Greece or contemporary Britain, is the beginning of the end of a social system. If there are any objective limits to a moral order they lie here, for the human person needs to learn a 'Thou' before it can coherently pronounce the 'I'. We need to be cared for before we can learn to care for others. We need the formative experience of personal stability if as adults we are to make the sacrifices necessary to sustain a stable social order.

The family will only die if we lose faith in it. We have not lost faith in it, therefore it will not die. People learn. When I was making a television documentary about the family, I spent time with a single mother in East London, chosen by the director of a single-parent action group as a representative voice. She was indeed a delightful person, with two charming and self-confident children. I discovered this, that she was living with her happily married parents, and she had decided that she would never let her son do what the fathers of her children had done: walk away. For her, and for a generation, the nuclear family had been replaced by the extended family, but she knew this could not last for ever, and she was already teaching her children not to repeat her mistakes.

The family has not died. Most people marry, and even in Britain stay married for the rest of their lives. The idea that most people prefer unfettered freedom is a fantasy created and sustained by an elite that has temporarily lost its sense of responsibility, but that will change. Humanity has survived because of its capacity to impose the sacrifices necessary to protect its young. Our moral sense will not allow children to continue to be neglected, for if there is a moral wrong that cries to heaven, it is the blighted lives of too many children today. The family will prove to be the axis on which our moral world will turn, for in reaffirming it, as we will, we will discover the fatal fallacy of libertarianism. Though it seems to promise paradise – a world where we are free to choose anything we like – that world lacks the very possibility of happiness itself. For it is a world systematically deprived of the good we enjoy – the good which exists – only because it is shared.

17

The Common Good

Society consists wholly of persons. It has no distinct personality separate from and superior to those of its members. It has, indeed, a certain collective life and character. The British nation is a unity with a life of its own. But the unity is constituted by certain ties that bind together all British subjects, which ties are in the last resort feelings and ideas, sentiments of patriotism, of kinship, a common pride, and a thousand more subtle sentiments that bind together men who speak a common language, have behind them a common history, and understand one another as they can understand no one else. The British nation is not a mysterious entity over and above the forty odd millions of living souls who dwell together under a common law. Its life is their life, its well-being or ill-fortune their well-being or ill-fortune. Thus, the common good to which each man's rights are subordinate is a good in which each man has a share. This share consists in realizing his capacities of feeling, of loving, of mental and physical energy, and in realizing these he plays his part in the social life, or, in Green's phrase, he finds his own good in the common good.

L. T. Hobhouse[1]

IN AN EARLIER chapter I spoke about Regent's Park, the great garden close to where I live. It had, I suggested, a beauty that went beyond its physical attributes, its excellence as an example of nineteenth-century English landscape gardening. It has a moral beauty: it is a public space. We can all go there, and when we do we go on equal terms. No one person owns it more than any other. It is an environment where, rich or poor, newcomer or long-standing resident, we stand as equal citizens. To be a Londoner is at least partly to share in the pride that such places bring. They are part

[1] L. T. Hobhouse, *Liberalism and other writings*, 61.

of our environment, our civic space, and the number and beauty of such parks – and the fact that we can go there safely, knowing our person and privacy will be respected – in part contributes to the landscape of our social existence, our being-as-part-of-society.

Now imagine the following scenario. It is announced that the park will be divided up into lots and sold to the highest bidders. The money raised will be accredited to the national budget, with the result that for a year we will all pay a fraction less in taxes. Those who are able to purchase lots find themselves in possession of a prime residential site in the heart of London. New homes go up, some of them palatial. Who gains in such a situation, and who loses? In a sense each of us gains. We all pay less tax for a year. We each have a chance to buy a section of the park, though not all of us have the resources to make a realistic bid and only a few actually succeed. But something is lost none the less: the park itself, and the fact that while it was there it was ours – we could go there and enjoy it without money or any other condition of entry. It was something that none of us individually could have afforded to own or maintain, but each of us individually could enjoy in our own way. It was a public space, *not* an aggregate of private spaces, and while it was there, whether or not we took advantage of it, it contributed to our possibilities of enjoyment. We might well feel that the gain achieved by privatising it – selling it to individual buyers – was outweighed by the loss of keeping it as a shared, public possession. Indeed it is almost impossible to imagine such a proposal going ahead without vigorous public protest.

None the less, something very much like this did happen in England not long ago with little public consternation, namely the deregulation of Sunday as a day of public rest. Until 1995, with a few exceptions, shops did not open. Increasingly, with the secularisation of British society, the law came to seem like an anachronism, a Christian institution in the heart of a society that was no longer predominantly churchgoing, or even Christian in any active sense. Britain contains many secularists, humanists and atheists, as well as many Christians who do not observe the Sabbath in the traditional way. It contains other religious groups – Jews, Muslims, Sikhs, Hindus, Zoroastrians and Buddhists – for whom Sunday is not a holy day. It seemed altogether absurd to maintain an institution to which the majority of the population did not owe doctrinal allegiance. On the face of it, the argument for liberalisation was overwhelming. Those who observed the Sabbath could continue to do so. Those who did not, now had their freedom of choice significantly extended. They could shop, as for some time they had been able to go to theatres, football matches, and pubs. Everyone would gain. No one would lose. It was a perfect win-win situation.

This argument is at the very heart of the libertarian case: a free society is one where everyone has the opportunity to pursue his or her own vision of the good. 'Whatever view we take,' writes Ronald Dworkin in a different context (he is speaking about abortion and euthanasia), 'we want the right to decide for ourselves, and we should therefore be ready to insist that any honorable constitution, any genuine constitution of principle, will guarantee that right for everyone'.[2] It is a seductive case, for how can one argue against it? How can we sensibly maintain that *not* everyone should have the opportunity to do what he or she likes on the seventh day? The traditional Sunday is a Christian institution. Why then impose it on a diverse society, thus penalising non-Christians? Surely the mere idea had already begun to be obsolete in the nineteenth century when it was recognised that Catholics, Jews and dissenters had a right to enter civil society on equal terms?

None the less, both my predecessor Lord Jakobovits and I opposed the change in the law. Clearly, Sunday deregulation was of enormous benefit to the Jewish community, especially to religious Jews. The Jewish Sabbath – Saturday – is a day on which we may neither work nor buy or sell, and this carries with it significant disadvantages in a society in which Saturday is the principal shopping day. Deregulation meant that, for the first time, religiously observant Jewish families could go shopping together during the weekend. It meant that some individuals would find it easier to gain employment, since they were willing to work on

[2] Ronald Dworkin, *Life's Dominion*, 239.

Sunday but not Saturday. In terms of *interests*, therefore, the change in the law clearly benefited Jews, as it did other non-Christian or non-religious groups.

But Sunday was not only a Christian institution. Just as the park is public space, so Sunday was public time. It was a day in which the commercial pulse of Britain was at rest. There was quiet in the streets. Families did things together which did not involve buying or selling. They cleaned the car, dug the garden, had lunch together, went for walks. Like the park, Sunday was a world of equal citizens. Its enjoyment could be shared alike by those who had money and those who did not, by those who had a job and those who did not. It was a time when relationships of power or exchange were suspended, when we were valued for what we were, not for what we owned or could buy. That is precisely why it existed within the framework of biblical legislation, and why, having been instituted by Judaism, it was taken up by other civilisations. Having experienced slavery in Egypt the Israelites were commanded to rest on the seventh day so that no one could force anyone else to work, and so that they could contemplate creation as belonging to God, not to its many and private owners. A society needs something very much like the Sabbath if it is to celebrate and sustain the values of freedom and equality. There must be places and times where we exist, and relate to one another, and are valued, not for what we have or the power we wield but simply because we are beings of unconditional value, 'ends in ourselves' as Kant put it, or 'the image of God' as the Bible more metaphysically and forcibly expressed the same idea.

A day of shopping and private recreation is not the same as a public day of rest. It introduces inequalities. Not all of us can shop; not all of us have the money to do so. Some of us must work, others have no work to go to. The replacement of the church by the supermarket as a central symbol of our culture may represent a gain in individual freedom, but it is the loss of a public good, precisely as if Regent's Park had been divided up and sold. It was not Christians alone who benefited from Sunday, but everyone, believer or non-believer. For in the most concrete and tangible way it communicated certain messages within a normative framework of shared meanings: that consumption is not everything, that there are things valuable which cannot be bought, that work is only part of our lives, that the world is not ours to manipulate as we wish, and that there is a universe of worth outside individual recreation and exchange. The Sabbath was and is an ongoing tutorial in freedom, equality, human dignity and the independent integrity of the environment as a creation whose guardians and trustees we are, and its privatisation meant that these values lost one of their most powerful embodiments in public, as opposed to private, life. That is why a Jew – or a Hindu or an atheist – might well have felt that private gain was outweighed by public loss. Sunday was an example of the common good.

The argument for Sunday was lost, and I do not wish to re-open it. None the less it is a useful point of entry into a reconsideration of the great political ideals, liberty, equality and fraternity, as the French Revolution conceived them, or as the American constitution put it, 'life, liberty and the pursuit of happiness'. Are these things private possessions, or is there an important sense in which they, too, belong to the common good?

In 1992 the American political commentator Mickey Kaus published a fascinating work entitled *The End of Equality*. The title was misleading, because Kaus remained committed to an egalitarian society, and one in which equality meant more than the equal opportunity to succeed (or fail). However, he had come to the conclusion that a certain kind of politics had reached an end. He called this 'money liberalism', the attempt to secure greater equality through redistribution of income. After half a century or more of egalitarian politics, American society had not become more equal; it had become less so. It was not merely that the income gap between the poor and rich had widened, which it had, but that the United States had now become a segregated society. The well-off and the urban poor no longer lived in the same neighbourhoods, sent their children to the same schools, used the same health services or public transportation. Americans might still be committed in principle to social egalitarianism, but 'give the affluent two more decades to grow comfortable in their gated suburbs, two more decades to revile the underclass and avoid the cities as if they were a dangerous foreign country, two more decades to isolate their "gifted" children from their supposed inferiors, two decades of "symbolic analysis" and assortative mating, and we might wake up to discover that Americans aren't such egalitarians at all any more'.[3]

Kaus argued for a different kind of politics, 'civic liberalism', which instead of trying to equalise monetary outcomes concentrates instead on increasing the range and significance of areas in which 'money does not count'. His arsenal of proposals includes 'class-mixing' institutions like national community service, along with 'rebuilding, preserving and strengthening community institutions in which income is irrelevant', such as libraries, parks, schools and public transportation. One of Kaus's canonical texts is the remark of R. H. Tawney:

> What is repulsive is not that one man should earn more than others, for where community of environment, and a common education and habit of life, have bred a common tradition of respect and consideration, these details of the counting house are forgotten or ignored. It is that some classes should be excluded from the heritage of civilization which others enjoy, and that the fact of human fellowship, which is ultimate and profound, should be obscured by economic contrasts, which are trivial and superficial.[4]

Kaus's argument was simple: 'In the money sphere . . . not *everyone* can succeed. But everyone, even the economy's losers, should be able to pass the test necessary for equal dignity in the public sphere.'[5] But this requires the strong existence of public facilities and activities through which a sense of worth is freely accessible. Though Kaus argues for government action to enhance and multiply the range of 'class-mixing' contexts, it is clear that what he seeks to achieve is something more intangible, a social environment rather than a political outcome, namely a public culture of equal respect, where what we participate in matters no less than what we own.

Liberty too depends on a social climate no less than on a political

[3] Mickey Kaus, *The End of Equality*, 180.

[4] R. H. Tawney, *Equality*, 113.

[5] Kaus, op. cit., 78.

structure of laws and their enforcement. Virtually all writers on society in the eighteenth and early nineteenth centuries shared the view that without strong and widely diffused virtues of lawfulness and self-control, the result would be not freedom but oppression. Burke's famous remark, that people are 'qualified for civil liberty in exact proportion to their disposition to put moral chains upon their appetites', was echoed, in 1840, by John Stuart Mill, who argued that one of the preconditions of a stable political order was a system of education whose 'one main and incessant ingredient was restraining discipline' by which the individual was trained 'in the habit, and thence the power, of subordinating his personal impulses and aims, to what were considered the ends of society'.[6]

Their point, and it is surely indisputable, is that freedom 'to' presupposes freedom 'from'. Our sense of liberty to pursue our own purposes depends to a considerable degree on the security with which we feel we can do so without fear of unpredictable assault on our person or integrity. It rests on a degree of confidence in the underlying orderliness of things, which in turn rests on public habits of respect. A society in which we are afraid to walk in streets and parks, or to open the door to a stranger, or to engage in debate with an audience which does not share our views, has become a less free environment, because there are fewer things we can do 'freely', without precautions. When confidence in order breaks down, the appeal of authoritarian politics rapidly rises and the call is heard – as it has been recently in both Britain and the United States – for heavier policing, more intrusive surveillance, harsher judicial sentences, and the curtailing of freedoms for those under suspicion. Liberty, as Friedrich Hayek argued, depends on shared moral habits:

> We understand one another and get along with one another, are able to act successfully on our plans, because, most of the time, members of our civilization conform to unconscious patterns of conduct, show a regularity in their actions that is not the result of commands or coercion, often not even of any conscious adherence to known rules, but of firmly established habits and traditions. The general observance of these conventions is a

[6] John Stuart Mill, *Essays on Ethics, Religion and Society*, 133.

necessary condition of the orderliness of the world in which we live, of our being able to find our way in it, though we do not know their significance and may not even be consciously aware of their existence.[7]

Equality and liberty, then, are social goods which cannot be reduced to state action on the one hand, or the private pursuit of interests on the other. Still more obviously is this the case with fraternity, for it is precisely when this is conceived as a political value that it begins to lose all human resonance. This was Aristotle's charge against Plato's Republic, that in a society where there were no families, there would be no affection. The ties that bind parents and children would become, he said, 'as a little sweet wine mingled with a great deal of water'.[8] The 'brotherhood of man', as an abstraction, is predicated on the belief that if we love no one in particular, we will love everyone in general. The opposite is at least as likely to be the case. As Benjamin Nelson aptly observed, 'all men have been becoming brothers by becoming equally others'.[9]

The value of fraternity is that of belonging, of holding a secure place of affection or regard within a wider group. Because we are social animals, our relationship with other people and their attitude to us, matters to us intensely, and for that reason membership within groups has often been regarded as a primary good, even a human need. That is why exclusion (or excommunication) can be acutely painful, and why group membership enters so strongly into our sense of identity. Fraternal groups are moral associations. Within them I acknowledge duties to the other members which go beyond mere contractual obligation. As Ronald Dworkin points out, a fraternal association is different from even a long-standing contractual relationship in that 'it has a life of its own: each partner is concerned not just to keep explicit agreements hammered out at arm's length but to approach each issue . . . in a manner reflecting special concern for his partner as partner'.[10] This is what I have

---

[7] F. A. Hayek, *The Constitution of Liberty*, 62.

[8] Aristotle, *Politics*, II, 4.

[9] B. N. Nelson, *The Idea of Usury*, Princeton, 1949, 136; quoted in Ferdinand Mount, *The Subversive Family*, 184.

[10] Ronald Dworkin, *Law's Empire*, 200.

elsewhere called a covenantal relationship, one that goes beyond the joint pursuit of interest to embrace a sense of shared destiny. Not surprisingly, fraternal associations have the feel and some of the moral character of an extended family.

Fraternity matters to us because it expresses the I–Thou rather than the I–It dimension of social life. It is personal rather than procedural. It is also the most powerful context of altruism – action for the sake of others – and the two facts are related. As Adam Smith noted long ago, whenever we feel that the fate of others is our personal responsibility, we are far less likely to stand idly by. That sense of connection makes it likely that your suffering will prompt not only my sympathy but also my active response. From Charles Darwin onward, evolutionary biologists have been intrigued by the presence of altruism in virtually every human society, because it seemed to run counter to the instinct for survival. People do sacrifice their interests, sometimes even their lives, for the sake of others. None the less, as Darwin himself intuitively understood, altruism goes to the core of our being as social animals. 'Any animal whatever, endowed with well-marked social instincts, would inevitably acquire a moral sense of conscience, as soon as its intellectual powers had become as well developed . . . as in man,' he wrote. Recently, in a fascinating series of experiments with computer-simulated populations, Robert Trivers and Robert Axelrod have shown that under conditions of uncertainty, groups with a code of reciprocal altruism will flourish and grow relative to others.[11]

Not all societies, however, develop fraternity, altruism and mutual trust to the same degree. As we saw in an earlier chapter, Alexis de Tocqueville attributed the public-spiritedness of Americans to the great variety of voluntary associations they created, seemingly at the slightest pretext. Elsewhere, he wrote, things were different, 'For in a community in which the ties of family, of caste, of class, and craft fraternities no longer exist, people are far too much disposed to think exclusively of their own interests, to become self-seekers practicing a narrow individualism and caring

[11] The story is told in Robert Wright, *The Moral Animal*, 180–209.

nothing for the public good.'[12] The strength of fellow-feeling in society depends, in no small measure, on the health of the institutions in which it is expressed.

It might seem strange to add the pursuit of happiness to the list of social goods. Whatever else happiness is, it is surely a personal possession. But my argument in this chapter is that not everything we enjoy personally can be divorced from a social context. From the days of the Psalms and Aristotle's *Ethics* people have debated the meaning of happiness, and this is not the place to enter the debate, but a rough-and-ready definition would be *lasting and justified satisfaction with one's life as a whole*,[13] and it has at least some connection with the idea of socially (or in the case of religions, divinely) recognised achievement. But this places, if not the attainment, then at least the pursuit of happiness within a social context, because the values within a society can affect the range and accessibility of human striving.

Charles Murray asks a fascinating question: how are we to construct a society so that anyone, no matter what his gifts, can reach the age of seventy, look back on his life, and be able to say it has been a happy life, filled with deep and justified satisfactions?[14] His answer is this. In a properly run society someone should be able to say such things as:

> I was a good parent to my children.
> I was a good neighbour.
> I always pulled my own weight.

These achievements are available. They are not narrowly distributed like fame, wealth or success. They are things for which I can claim personal responsibility, and thus see them as a source of justified pride. They presuppose relationships (families, neighbourhoods, teams) and thus networks of mutual recognition.

[12] Alexis de Tocqueville, *The Old Regime and the French Revolution*, xiii, quoted in Mary Ann Glendon, *Rights Talk*, 118.
[13] Charles Murray, *In Pursuit*, 44.
[14] Ibid., 282.

A society in which such ordinary virtues are highly prized will be one that optimises the pursuit of happiness.

To sum up: I have suggested that there are certain goods which cannot be privatised without loss. They range from parks to days of rest to a public culture which sustains liberty, equality, fraternity and the pursuit of happiness. These goods are essentially social. They are enjoyed by each of us as individuals but none of us could create and maintain them as individuals. Nor could they be brought into being by political means alone. Liberty cannot be created by law. Equality cannot be brought about by simple income redistribution. Fraternity is not established by contract. The pursuit of happiness depends on the possibilities within a social system.

This, ultimately, is what makes libertarianism so unsatisfactory an account of who we are and what our culture should be like. The most convincing case for libertarianism is that in a world in which we were each free to do what we like so long as we do not harm others, everyone would gain and no one lose. The truth is, though, that we would all lose, for we would lose the social domain, the realm of the public good within which we discover our identity and allegiances, our loyalties and common strivings, our sense of liberty and equal regard. A world without public meanings – like one without parks and public holidays – would be one in which important dimensions of human security, worth and happiness, would be missing. It might be that in the fullness of time we would grow so accustomed to the loss that we would no longer miss it. But that seems unlikely, for man is a social animal, not a private one.

The libertarian society was created with the highest of intentions, to maximise the scope of individual freedom. But though freedom is in some respects like a private garden it is also like a public park, and it needs powerful habits of self-restraint if it is not to be quickly ruined by litter, graffiti and wanton damage. A society whose values are monetary – advertising, consumption, and the pursuit of wealth – will be inegalitarian, not just because there are differences of income but because in it money matters too much. A society which neglects the socialising effects of the family will be increasingly unfree, not because there are too many laws but because order depends on them too much. A society in which relationships are based on contract rather than loyalty will create places where we happen to be, but not places where we belong. The result is inevitably that, while standards of living may rise, quality of life declines.

When L. T. Hobhouse wrote the quotation which heads this chapter (the book from which it is taken was published in 1911), the great expression of the common good was the nation-state. Today we would surely see it as more complex. It would include international movements like environmental groups, non-institutionalised phenomena like the media, and most powerfully of all, local arenas like the neighbourhood, the congregation, businesses and schools. The quality of life they sustain, the place they give to integrity, respect, courage and admiration, affects us all, as does its opposite, a culture of cynicism, self-interest and exploitation. What this suggests is that virtue cannot be privatised, nor can happiness itself. We have our being in relationship with others and we breathe a common air. There can be no articulate 'I' without a coherent 'We'. The goods we share are no less significant than those we privately own.

18

Beyond the Moral Maze

> Getting right outside morality would be rather like getting outside
> the atmosphere. It would mean losing the basic social network
> within which we live and communicate with others, including
> all those others in the past who have formed our culture.
> If we can imagine this deprived state at all, it would be a
> solitary condition close to that of autism or extreme depression
> – a state where, although intelligence can still function, there is
> no sense of community with others, no shared wishes, principles,
> aspirations or ideals, no mutual trust or fellowship with those
> outside, no preferred set of concepts, nothing agreed on as
> important.
>
> Mary Midgley[1]

THE SOCIAL DOMAIN, I have been arguing, is in essence a
moral domain, and to reclaim it means that we must recover a
shared moral language. But is that possible? Do we not know
by now that there are too many differences between us in our
multi-faith, multicultural society to be able to resolve them with
any hope of agreement? This, our new consensus-that-there-is-no-
consensus, is reinforced by virtually every media presentation we
see of moral issues. Typically these take the form of a panel of
experts in conversation with a series of witnesses, or an audience, or
both. Their subject is usually a moral dilemma – abortion, perhaps,
or euthanasia – and by the end of the discussion we know, if we
did not beforehand, that conflicting, irreconcilable views can be
held with conviction and argued with cogency. The conclusion
seems inevitable. There is no single, absolute, uncontroversial
moral truth. There are alternatives between which we must
choose. Morality is what the relativists or subjectivists claim it

---

[1] Mary Midgley, *Can't We Make Moral Judgements?*, 8.

to be: nothing more or less than what we choose it to be. We are trapped in a moral maze.

The simplest reply was given by the Archbishop of Canterbury during the course of the debate on morality in the House of Lords. Speaking shortly after a widely televised football competition, he noted that we take it for granted that you cannot play a game of football without rules. 'Rules do not get in the way of the game, they make the game possible. It is strange that what we take as so obvious for games we deem unnecessary for life.' Participative activity requires rules, which need to be understood and internalised by those who take part, and if necessary, enforced. To refute the idea that we can do without shared rules we need do no more than imagine a country in which drivers were free to choose the side of the road on which they preferred to drive. The short answer is: soon they would prefer to walk.

The analogy is good but it does not go far enough. A critic might agree that football needs rules, but he would go on to argue that not everyone need play football. There are other games. Just as there is cricket, tennis and rugby, so there are different moral systems, and that is precisely our contemporary situation. Is cohabitation without marriage 'living in sin' or merely an alternative and no less valid form of relationship? Is abortion the murder of an innocent person, the unborn, or is it the fundamental right of a woman to do what she wishes with her own body? Our dilemma is simply this, that there are many moral 'games' and hence no one set of rules that constitutes the good life. The best we can do is to create a society in which we are free to choose the game we wish to play.

The critic would probably go further. What sense, he might ask, does it make to say that football is a 'better' game than tennis? Each has its own distinctive feel, its particular challenges and excitements. No game is comparable to any other, and there is no meta-game, no Platonic form or ideal type, against which we can judge the respective merits of the particular games we have so far developed. This, he would continue, is precisely the thesis of the relativist. There are many ways of understanding morality, many ways of living a good life, many ways of resolving ethical dilemmas, and there is no metamorality which has the power to rule one way better than another.

Of course, he would admit, people would loudly disagree with what he says. Christians, Jews, Muslims, Sikhs, Hindus, new age mystics, utilitarians and secular humanists of various shades would all claim that they did possess the truth, unique and indivisible. 'But,' he would add, 'isn't that just my point? These claims cancel one another out. Their disagreement, which is interminable, proves that on morality we cannot agree. At best we can agree to disagree. A Christian is convinced of the truth of Christianity because that is how he was brought up, or that is what she chose. So morality is after all relative, to our upbringing, our education or our choice. Needless to say, so long as you practise Christianity, you are convinced that it is the sole and sufficient truth. But then, so long as you are playing football, your mind is on the game and you are not conscious of the rival attractions of other ways of spending your time. But in your more reflective moments you know that there are other games. All I ask is that we are reflective enough to realise that outside our moral world are many others, each of which is entitled to equal dignity and respect, and none of which may make claims on society that are exclusive of any other. Whether you lament the fact or celebrate it, moral diversity defines the world in which we live.'

How true is this analysis? One is tempted to reply with the famous parable of the elephant. Four blind men approach an elephant. One feels its trunk and concludes that it is a snake. Another feels its tusk and decides that it is a spear. A third touches its side and says that it is a wall. A fourth touches its leg and declares that it is a tree. Morality is not one thing but many, and generalising on the basis of one or other of its different aspects can yield conclusions which seem reasonable but in fact screen from us the larger reality. What, then, can we say about the phenomenon we call morality?

Firstly, there are moral institutions – marriage, the family, and friendship are obvious examples. These are the closest to the Archbishop's analogy of a 'game' or what Wittgenstein called a 'form of life'. They are constituted by rules, which can vary from culture to culture but which have to be shared for the institution to exist. Anthropologists have charted for us the many types of family structure, but there are virtually no societies without rules of kinship and child-care responsibilities, and in almost all, the family is defined by marriage, a public contract that gives sanction to the sexual union of a man and a woman and attaches to that fact socially enforced duties and restrictions.

Beyond that there are virtues, dispositions of character, what Tocqueville called 'habits of the heart'. One way of understanding virtue is to think again about games. Though the various forms of sport are different from one another they tend to require a similar set of skills – physical fitness, brain–eye coordination, and the capacity to be part of a team. So there are different skills that we need to acquire if we are to achieve any long-term goal. They include such attributes as resolution, persistence, fortitude, self-control and courage. There are others we need if we are to coexist with others over an extended period of time, such as honesty, trustworthiness, courtesy, punctuality, generosity, sympathy and reliability.

Beyond this again are the great rules which have been arrived at independently in one culture after another, and which seem to sum up what we know about the universal requirements of society as such. C. S. Lewis, in his protest against moral relativism, *The Abolition of Man*, called these by their Chinese name, the *Tao*, the 'way'. In the Judaeo-Christian tradition we think in this context of the Ten Commandments or the great summations to be found elsewhere in the Bible. For Lewis they included the law of general beneficence (the prohibition of murder, the command to love our neighbour), the law of special beneficence (the love of kin), duties to parents, ancestors and elders, duties towards children, and the laws of justice, honesty, mercy and magnanimity.[2] These principles are configured somewhat differently from one civilisation to another, but they share sufficient of a family resemblance to suggest that they form the objective boundaries of social life as such,

[2] C. S. Lewis, *The Abolition of Man*, 49–59.

and that without them and their maintenance no assemblage of human beings will find it possible to live stably together for long.

Over and above these universals are the specific virtues and rules we need to develop if we are to coexist peaceably in a society in which there is considerable diversity. These do not always come to the fore, precisely because not all societies have been marked by internal variety of codes and creeds. Villages, traditional societies, and religious orders are often marked by strong internal cohesion. Their members are linked by common adherence to a highly articulated set of rules and a vision of the good. But there are other environments in which individuals of quite different convictions live and strive to get along with one another. Traditionally the home of such encounters has been the city, which is why the virtues associated with them often carried linguistic reference to it. We speak of a certain type of person as 'civilised', 'cosmopolitan' or 'urbane'. The characteristic features of this ethic are an emphasis on tolerance, fairness, dignity as opposed to honour, rights attaching to the individual as such, and the ability to respect differences and evolve practical compromise. These are the so-called 'liberal virtues', and constitute the historically remarkable achievement of Western societies since the eighteenth century. It was the great insight of liberalism to see that the new and more complex order being brought about by industrial and post-industrial society would require a new cluster of virtues not often associated with more close-knit communities. It was the error of some of its more extreme proponents to see these as the totality – or at least the dominant feature – of the moral life instead of a mere part of it.[3]

None of these phenomena suggests that morality is relative, subjective, chosen, invented, the product of will, whim or desire. Why then has relativism come to seem so compelling an account of morality? One reason is that much of our moral conversation, from philosophical treatises to media presentations, has focused on one area of the moral life at the expense of others: dilemmas. Jean-Paul

[3] For a defence of the 'cosmopolitan self' as against other, more communal identities, see Jeremy Waldron, 'The Cosmopolitan Alternative', in Will Kymlicka (ed.), *The Rights of Minority Cultures*, 93–119.

Sartre described one of the most famous of these in his account of the young Frenchman during the war, torn between his duty to his invalid mother, and the claims of the French Resistance which needed him to leave home. Sartre quite rightly suggests that in such conflicts we are faced with an inescapable but fateful, 'existential', choice, that cannot be resolved by any general rules, or indeed by anyone else other than the individual concerned.[4]

But this is hardly the revelation Sartre thought it was. Such dilemmas occur in virtually every moral system. We know of them from the Hebrew Bible. Should Abraham accept or challenge the decree of Heaven condemning the cities of the plain? Should Moses concur in God's verdict that the Israelites should be destroyed after the making of the golden calf? Should Job accept his fate as the will of Heaven or should he argue his innocence before Heaven itself? These conflicts, between the claims of justice and obedience, are a continuing theme within the moral drama of the Hebrew Bible, as are the clashes between kings and the prophets, among the earliest 'existential' heroes. This is enough to tell us that even the most sublime religious faith does not guarantee a life free of moral conflict – indeed that the desire for such a life is misconceived.

Dilemmas arise not because there are no moral absolutes, but precisely because there are, and because they can sometimes conflict. In Sartre's example the problem arises only because the young man recognises the call of duty, on the one hand as a son, on the other as a citizen and defender of freedom. The conclusion we should draw is not that there are no objective duties, but that one of the great failings of the philosophical quest for a rational basis of morality has been its search for a single coherent set of principles which would unequivocally answer all moral questions. These principles, whether they take the utilitarian form of 'the greatest happiness for the greatest number' or the deontological mode of a fixed hierarchy of duties, fail to do justice to one of the most striking features of the moral life, namely that there *are* dilemmas in which doing the right thing

---

[4] Jean-Paul Sartre, *Existentialism and Humanism*, London, Methuen, 1989.

involves doing something which in other circumstances would be wrong.[5]

To be moral, in such circumstances, is to feel anguish and something close to remorse, but also to have wisdom, courage, trust and the self-knowledge that one has done the best one could in difficult circumstances. Fortunately such occasions are rare (though perhaps more frequent in public than in private life, which is why some people, for moral reasons, prefer not to enter the political arena).[6] They suggest that morality does not consist in a single set of principles, but rather in a constellation of rules, virtues and practices which for much of the time happily coexist, but which sometimes, and tragically, come into collision.

Another error arises when we confuse what P. F. Strawson has called 'social morality' with 'individual ideal'.[7] Undeniably, we have different visions of the ideal life, which can range from a life of public service to one of domestic duty, from the pursuit of fame to the quiet satisfaction of a job well done. Strawson calls this the ethical as opposed to the moral domain, and suggests that it is a realm in which there are 'truths' rather than 'truth'. But at the same time there are rules, practices, conventions, without which we could not achieve the minimum of social co-operation needed to achieve even the most basic of our aspirations. It may well be that our ethical ideal comes closer to our sense of self (the thing that only I can do or am called on to do) than does our sense of moral obligation (the duties I share with others). Morality, then, gains its importance as the 'condition of everything that matters', and moral uniformity becomes the ground of ethical diversity, but this is not to deny its binding character. It is simply to remind us that individuality depends on society which in turn depends on morality.

One of the greatest errors of relativism is to be over-impressed by the sheer variety of the sources of our moral inspiration. We

[5] For different approaches to this subject, see Christopher Gowans (ed.), *Moral Dilemmas*, New York, Oxford University Press, 1987.

[6] See the essays in Stuart Hampshire (ed.), *Public and Private Morality*.

[7] P. F. Strawson, *Freedom and Resentment*, London, Methuen, 1974, 26–44.

come to the broad places of our moral life through many streets and starting-points – religious conviction, habit, the example of our parents, the influence of our friends, the messages conveyed by the media, and sometimes long and hard personal reflection. The fact that we have different points of departure – even different systems of justification – does not imply that we cannot arrive at something like consensus, and it is on this that modern societies depend. Jacques Maritain put this well:

> Thus it is that men possessing quite different, even opposite, metaphysical or religious outlooks, can converge, not by virtue of any identity of doctrine, but by virtue of an analogical similitude in practical principles, toward the same practical conclusions, and can share in the same practical secular faith, provided that they can similarly revere, perhaps for quite diverse reasons, truth and intelligence, human dignity, freedom, brotherly love, and the absolute value of moral good.
>
> We must therefore maintain a sharp and clear distinction between the human and temporal creed which lies at the root of common life and which is but a set of practical conclusions or of practical points of convergence, on the one hand; and on the other, the theoretical justifications, the conceptions of the world and of life, the philosophical or religious creeds which found, or claim to found, these practical conclusions in reason.[8]

We can agree on much that is fundamental to our moral life without necessarily agreeing on why.

What then is morality? I want to suggest that moral systems are our *languages of relationship*, and that an insight into language helps us understand morality. John Locke, one of the key figures in the development of political liberalism, was also a pioneer in the study of language. He believed that the mind of a child is a blank sheet of paper, on which over the course of time it paints pictures by reflecting on experience. The child learns words by generalising from what it perceives. It is not difficult to see, in this charming portrait of the child as a kind of miniature scientist working alone in the laboratory of the sensations, some of the key themes of the

[8] Jacques Maritain, *Man and the State*, Chicago, University of Chicago Press, 1951, 111.

Enlightenment: the solitary individual, the rejection of anything beyond sense-experience and reason, and the use of inductive science as the model of knowledge.

We now know, thanks to the work of Wittgenstein, Chomsky and others, that this account is false. Language is a social phenomenon, based not on private experiences but on shared understandings and rules. Though there are many languages, underlying them all is a universal grammar which we seem genetically conditioned to acquire. It is, so to speak, part of our computer hardware, or what Steven Pinker calls our 'language instinct'. Without this we cannot account for the speed and consistency with which children learn languages. They simply could not do it the way Locke thought they did, by unaided inference from the available data.[9]

This suggests an old-new insight into the nature of morality. We do not learn how to behave by private reflection on the basis of experience. We do so by acquiring socially constituted rules, from our first faltering conversations with our parents, to our ever-widening dialogue with others. Just as there are many languages, so there are many moral systems, and we can no more move between them than we can learn a new language without painstaking effort. None the less there is a deep structural similarity between the great moral traditions, akin to Chomsky's universal grammar. The difference between moralities led some people to regard them as relative. The similarities between them led others to think of them as universal. We can now see that both are half-truths.

Particular forms of moral life – specific codes and virtues, traditions and institutions – are as varied as the forms of human speech. Nevertheless, we do not think of our language as 'relative'. Instead we regard it as our essential vehicle of self-expression. It is true that we can adopt another language, but only at the cost of becoming part of another culture, a different form of life. Moralities also share certain universals – those already mentioned, such as the prohibition against murder, theft and dishonesty – but this is only at a high level of generality. In the real world of moral

9 See Steven Pinker, *The Language Instinct*, London, Penguin, 1995.

experience, universals are translated into codes and customs, our moral language as Britons or Americans in the late twentieth century. It was the mistake of the Enlightenment to concentrate on universals while failing to understand the critical importance of particulars – the actual ways of life of families, communities and traditions. But a grammar without a language is not yet speech. The result, as Charles Taylor rightly calls it, has been an 'ethics of inarticulacy'.[10]

Morality is like a language: subtle, complex, but with its own distinct coherence, its rules of syntax and semantics, its grammar and vocabulary. Within a language there is an open-ended variety of things we can say, and each of us makes sentences that have never been said before. But as individuals *we do not make the language*. We learn it. We inherit it. We enter its unique yet universal configuration of virtues. We become part of its history, extending it into the future, developing it perhaps, but also participating in its continuity. In the West we are heirs to a moral heritage, Judaeo-Christian in origin, but amplified and enlarged by a host of other influences, the way English has grown from its Anglo-Saxon roots, borrowing in the process words, phrases and constructions from other tongues. It is part of our culture; consciously or unconsciously it shapes who we are. Like language we learn morality through a series of conversations and encounters, most markedly in early childhood, but in a sense throughout our lives. The idea that we invent it – making it through our choices or by reasoned reflection on private experience – is as incoherent as Locke's theory of the way we learn words. No language could be acquired that way.

The analogy between morality and language explains why I take issue with the pessimism of Alasdair MacIntyre, who argues that, since the Enlightenment, the possibility of a shared moral life has disappeared. MacIntyre's argument is this. The 'Enlightenment project' was the search for a morality independent of revelation, based, in other words, on reason and human nature alone. The only such effort which had hitherto succeeded was that of Aristotle, who

[10] Charles Taylor, *Sources of the Self*, 53–90.

was able to define virtue in terms of a *telos* or ultimate purpose of human life. We now no longer believe that humanity has a unique or given purpose. Therefore we cannot arrive at a shared morality. We live in an 'after virtue' age.[11]

This is an all-or-nothing view which does injustice to the way we actually live. There are indeed groups of human beings who share a view of the purpose of human life: religious communities are a good example. But we do not need a single view to prevail before we can have a common life. We have families, communities, professional associations and voluntary groups, each of which involves a rich repertoire of rules and virtues. Beyond these we have society, and the attributes and dispositions – the 'liberal' virtues – which allow us to get along together despite our differences, and these too involve distinct moral claims. Vesting the moral vision in the utopian project of society-as-a-single-community, a religious order, say, or Aristotle's Greek city-state, is to invite disillusionment and MacIntyre's lament about 'the new dark ages'. A Jewish view would be more realistic, namely that the messianic age has not yet arrived, but that does not stop us making a blessing over the present and trying to make it better.

In his book *The Language Instinct*, Steven Pinker relates a remarkable fact, and one that should give us hope. During the bleak days of slavery, plantation owners deliberately mixed slaves from different countries and language backgrounds in order to make it difficult for them to communicate and organise. For the minimum understanding necessary to give and obey orders, they used a basic set of words and phrases known as a 'pidgin' (Pinker gives the example of the South Pacific islanders who greeted Prince Philip in Pidgin English as *fella belong Mrs Queen*). Pidgin is not a language. It has a vocabulary but not a grammar. However, the linguist Derek Bickerton discovered that pidgin can be transformed into a full and complex language within a few years. All it takes is for children to be exposed to it at the age when they acquire their mother tongue. Bickerton found that children 'injected grammatical complexity where none existed before, resulting in a

[11] Alasdair MacIntyre, *After Virtue*, 49–59.

brand-new, richly expressive language'.[12] A pidgin that becomes a language is called a creole.

In *After Virtue*, Alasdair MacIntyre argued that our moral language has become fragmented beyond hope of recovery. The evidence is that language is *never* fragmented beyond recovery. Given the right conditions a pidgin becomes a creole, and we learn again how to link words together, availing ourselves of the universal grammar that seems to be written into not only our language instinct but also our moral instinct. We develop languages because we seek communication. We develop moralities because we seek community. The task of restoring community and morality is one and the same, and derives from the same need: to rescue the self from solitude, so that in finding the 'We' we can learn to say 'I'.

---

[12] Steven Pinker, *The Language Instinct*, 33.

19

Politics and the Art of Balance

We may now define virtue as a disposition of the soul in which, when it has to choose between actions and feelings, it observes the mean relative to us, this being determined by such a rule or principle as would take shape in the mind of a man of sense or practical wisdom.

Aristotle[1]

We are bidden to walk in the middle paths, which are the ways of right and good, as it is said, 'And you shall walk in His ways' (Deut. 28:9).

Moses Maimonides[2]

ARISTOTLE AND MAIMONIDES agreed on the need for balance, the right measure, the due proportion, and saw this as the key to moral and political wisdom. To be sure, there are profound differences between Greek and Jewish ethics. For Aristotle, the state is prior to the individual, for Judaism the individual prior to the state. For that reason the Greece of Plato and Aristotle placed a primacy on political involvement whereas their Jewish counterparts emphasised education, the family, and the moral and spiritual dimensions of community.[3] That, perhaps, is why Jews survived and Greek civilisation did not, other than in the realm of ideas. Political structures are simply more short-lived than moral institutions.

Despite the difference, however, Aristotle and Maimonides

---

[1] Aristotle, *Nicomachean Ethics*, 2:6.

[2] Moses Maimonides, *Mishneh Torah, Deot*, 1:5.

[3] See the instructive chapter on this contrast in Michael Walzer, *Spheres of Justice*, 64–94.

agreed on the central significance of the idea of due proportion, the golden mean, the middle way. For that reason, their visions lacked the utopian grandeur of other schemes within their respective traditions, Plato's Republic, for example, or the dream of Jewish national rebirth to be found in Maimonides' more mystical-romantic predecessor, Judah Halevi. By contrast, theories of balance seem middle-aged, middle-class and prosaic. Nevertheless they stand the test of time for one reason: they map their theories against the contours of reality. They aspire, not to utopian perfection, but to making the best out of imperfection. Politics, I believe, has to recover its sense of balance.

Balance comes in different shapes and sizes, and corresponds, in the field of politics, to different kinds and conceptions of society. There are organic or hierarchical views of the *polis*, to be found among thinkers as different as Burke and Hegel. On these views, society is a complex knitting together of individuals into a seamless whole, each in his or her due place, and each fulfilling, in F. H. Bradley's phrase 'my station and its duties'. There is no more magnificent description of this kind of order, and its breakdown, than that given by Shakespeare's Ulysses:

> The heavens themselves, and the planets, and this centre,
> Observe degree, priority, and place,
> Insisture, course, proportion, season, form,
> Office, and custom, in all line of order . . .
> Take but degree away, untune that string,
> And, hark, what discord follows! each thing meets
> In mere oppugnancy . . .
> Force should be right; or rather, right and wrong –
> Between whose endless jar justice resides –
> Should lose their names, and so should justice too.
> Then everything includes itself in power,
> Power into will, will into appetite,
> And appetite, an universal wolf,
> So doubly seconded with will and power,
> Must make perforce an universal prey,
> And last eat up himself.[4]

---

[4] Shakespeare, *Troilus and Cressida*, I, iii.

Altogether less majestic and metaphysical, there is a second kind of balance: the kind to be found in Montesquieu's account of the three branches of government (legislature, executive and judiciary), or the *Federalist Papers'* view of counter-balancing factions, or the different religious groups within the Ottoman empire. On this view, society is not a harmonious whole, but a mix of different powers, functions, interests and even cultures whose natural relationship is one of conflict. The task of government is not to embody a pre-existing order, but to constitutionalise the relationship between different groups so that each is guaranteed a measure of integrity, while each checks the powers of the others. At times, this may be no more than a *modus vivendi*, at others it may result in the interactive play of forces within a single constitutional arena. But here too, no less than in organic societies, there is a formal structure in which all things have their place.

But there is a third and far more modest kind of balance which aims at no structure, but simply at the health of the various elements within the system, recognising that failure in one may adversely affect the others, because of the interdependence of all things. Such a balance is not metaphysical or political but, rather, *ecological*. There is no precise formula we can give for the point at which the destruction of rain-forests, or the pollution of the atmosphere, or the demise of a species of wildlife, begins to threaten the viability of life on earth. Nor, perhaps, do we seek one. Ecological concern is not only instrumental – this as a means to that – but also essential – this as valuable in its own right. The death of the last animal of a species impoverishes us, not only because we know that somewhere, sometime, it will have a chain-effect on the bio-system, but also because our world has grown smaller. The pursuit of balance, ecologically conceived, is less a science than an art.

I have been arguing, in these chapters, for an ecological approach to politics, not one that denigrates the significance of the individual and the state, but one that maintains that these are not all there is, or all we need, for political health or even individual happiness. The third domain of the *polis* – the families, communities and voluntary networks that make up so much of our lives – has been unduly neglected, philosophically for several centuries, practically for the last fifty years. Now the balance needs to be restored.

Those who have argued the case for 'mediating structures' have done so for a variety of reasons, each of which merits our concern. For Alexis de Tocqueville, they were important as a defence of liberty. Active participation in local politics and voluntary organisations were the best protection against the separation of individuals from one another, a condition in which they would slowly but willingly invite the government to play an ever greater part in the management of their lives. Strong families were a particularly important part of the ecology of freedom. 'As long as family feeling is kept alive,' he wrote, 'the opponent of oppression is never alone.' D. H. Lawrence, perhaps mindful of his Nottingham childhood, agreed. 'It is marriage,' he said, 'which has given man the best of his freedom, given him a little kingdom of his own within the big kingdom of the State . . . Do we then want to break marriage? If we do break it, it means we all fall to a far greater extent under the direct sway of the State.'[5]

Conservatives like Edmund Burke were less interested in liberty than order. He saw the 'little platoons' as defenders of tradition and cohesion, of the multiple loyalties that gave a society its continuity and strength. 'We begin our public affections in our families,' he wrote in a famous passage. 'No cold relation is a zealous citizen. We pass on to our neighbourhoods, and our provincial connections. These are our inns and resting places. Such divisions of the country as have been formed by habits, and not by the sudden jerk of authority, were so many little images of the great country in which the heart found something which it could fill.'[6] Far from being a defence against the state the family was the birthplace of loyalty and patriotism. Not only this, but it was as children and parents that people most clearly understood that they belonged to a past and a future of which they were the trustees. For Burke this was a crucial dimension of citizenship, for if people saw themselves as no more than 'temporary possessors

[5] I owe these quotations to Ferdinand Mount, *The Subversive Family*, 2.

[6] Edmund Burke, *Reflections on the Revolution in France*, 198.

and life-renters' of society they would have no sense of, and thus respect for, the link between the generations. The 'whole chain and continuity of the commonwealth would be broken. No one generation could link with the other.' People would become, in his arresting metaphor, 'little better than the flies of a summer'.[7]

Ethical socialists like A. H. Halsey and Norman Dennis are motivated more by the ideal of the 'fellowship of sharing', the strengthening of bonds of mutual attachment to the point at which 'All members of such a society flourish in freedom because they are held together by mutual regard.'[8] Like R. H. Tawney, they would argue that 'Civilization is a matter, not of quantity of possessions, but of quality of life,'[9] and go on to suggest that quality of life is diminished when the more vulnerable members of society become casualties of a money-based culture and a remote and impersonal state.

For an economist like Francis Fukuyama, the institutions of civil society are important simply because they contribute to prosperity. A society without trust and the institutions that sustain it will be one in which a significant part of the national energy – and hence its wealth-producing capacity – will be devoted to litigation and the prevention of crime. The strength of civic institutions is, he argues, a form of 'social capital', the result of collective investment in the maintenance of long-term relationships. When this deteriorates, a nation becomes as preoccupied in protecting itself against internal conflict as it would be in securing itself against an external enemy.[10] The administration of law becomes a kind of national self-defence.

I, for one, am moved by all these concerns, because they are interdependent. A nation without freedom, order and a sense of continuity quickly becomes a society of strangers, in which the bonds of fellow-feeling grow weak and the motive of mutual exploitation grows more compelling. Nor do I believe that

[7] Ibid., 95.
[8] Norman Dennis and A. H. Halsey, *English Ethical Socialism*, 1–2.
[9] R. H. Tawney, *The Radical Tradition*, Harmondsworth, Penguin, 1964, 174.
[10] Francis Fukuyama, *Trust: The Social Virtues and the Creation of Prosperity*.

prosperity can be left out of the equation. There have indeed been poor societies that were free, stable and cohesive. But they were also places where deprivation, disease and ignorance were rampant, and they are not an option for the post-industrial democratic West. The creation of wealth allows us to achieve many things, collectively and individually, which are of value in themselves, not least, helping others and welcoming strangers. Declining societies are not often generous societies.

My own view is that social goods are not merely means to an end. They are ends in themselves. They are the institutional framework of moral relationships, and these are intrinsically valuable. As I put it elsewhere:[11] Morality matters because we cherish relationships and believe that love, friendship, work and even the casual encounter of strangers are less fragile and abrasive when conducted against a shared code of civility and mutuality. It matters because we care for liberty and have come to understand that human dignity is better served by the restraints we impose on ourselves than those forced on us by external laws and punishment and police. It matters because we fear the impoverishment of significant groups within society when the only sources of value are material: success and wealth and physical attractiveness. In most societies – certainly ours – these are too unevenly distributed to be an adequate basis of self-worth.

Morality matters because we believe that there are other and more human ways of living than instinctual gratification tempered by regret. It matters because we believe that some projects – love, marriage, parenthood – are so central to our being that we seek to endow them with as much permanence as is given to us in this unpredictable and transitory life. It matters because we may not abdicate our responsibility for those we brought into being, by failing to provide them with a stable, caring environment within which to grow to maturity. It matters because we believe that there are other routes out of the Hobbesian state of nature – the war of all against all – than by creating a Leviathan of a state. It matters

[11] This, and the next two paragraphs, are taken from my *Faith in the Future*, 20–1.

because as long as humanity has thought about such things, we have recognised that there are achievements we cannot reach without the collaborative bonds of civil society and the virtues which alone make such a society possible.

Morality matters, finally, because despite all fashionable opinions to the contrary, we remain moved by altruism. We are touched by other people's pain. We feel enlarged by doing good, more so perhaps than by doing *well*, by material success. Decency, charity, compassion, integrity, faithfulness, courage, just being there for other people, matter to us. They matter to us despite the fact that we may now find it hard to say *why* they matter to us. They matter because we are human and because, in the words of Sir Moses Montefiore, we are worth what we are willing to share with others.

The cumulative weight of these several concerns is bringing about a paradigm shift in our thinking about politics. T. S. Kuhn coined the phrase 'paradigm shift' in his book, *The Structure of Scientific Revolutions*.[12] In it he argued that science did not simply proceed by the slow accumulation of knowledge, the gradual accretion of experimental data. At any given time, scientific disciplines are dominated by an accepted theory, a 'paradigm', which governs the experiments people undertake and the results they expect. For long periods of time they are confirmed. Contrary results are explained away. But gradually the counter-evidence accumulates. The theory is placed under increasing strain. Eventually a new theory emerges – Einstein's relativity in place of Newtonian physics, for example – and people begin to see the world in a new way.

That is what has been happening for more than a decade within the sphere of politics, although it has yet to be translated into action in any systematic way. The individual-state model of libertarianism simply fails to account for the many phenomena we see daily, from rising crime to the dismembered family. The new paradigm, whether it comes from the left or right, places community and civil society at the heart of the social equation. In place of the

[12] T. S. Kuhn, *The Structure of Scientific Revolutions*, 2nd ed., Chicago, University of Chicago Press, 1970.

politics of interests it proposes a politics of institutions. Instead of autonomy, rights, and contracts, it argues for a vocabulary of duties, character and virtue. Needless to say, as with the emergence of any new theory, it has its critics – defenders of the old paradigm – and these too deserve to be heard.

Its libertarian opponents, drawn equally from the right and the left, argue that 'communitarian' or 'civic' politics is essentially nostalgic, looking back on a world that is no more and perhaps never was. It is also systematically vague. What is community and where is it to be found?[13] Moreover it is unfeasible, for if the combined impact of governments, markets and social forces has eroded the sense of community, how can it be restored? If these were not sufficient objections, there is a stronger and more fundamental claim which needs to be listened to with the utmost seriousness.

Not for nothing, say the libertarians, did the Enlightenment seek to break the hold of tradition, custom and local association. Communities have in the past been a source of prejudice, authoritarianism, narrowness, bigotry and persecution. As Roger Scruton puts it with disturbing frankness, the real price of community is 'sanctity, intolerance, exclusion, and a sense that life's meaning depends upon obedience, and also on vigilance against the enemy'.[14] The 'quest for community', which can seem so desirable in the atomised world of British and American cities, can look quite different from the perspective of Northern Ireland or Bosnia or Lebanon or India or a dozen other places where communitarian values look more like ancient tribalism of a particularly bloodthirsty kind. It would be as wrong to take the achievements of the Enlightenment for granted, and thus risk losing them, as it was for the Enlightenment itself to devalue the vital contributions of religion, family and moral habit.

Undeniably, belonging involves exclusion. The concept of an

[13] For a powerful presentation of the opposing case, see Jeremy Waldron, 'The Cosmopolitan Alternative', in Will Kymlicka, *The Rights of Minority Cultures*, 93–119.
[14] Roger Scruton, *The Philosopher on Dover Beach*, 310.

'us' presupposes a 'them'. It unites but it also divides. The more strongly we identify with a society of friends, the more powerfully we become conscious of the presence of strangers, which threatens to disturb the order we have so painstakingly constructed. Michael Walzer reminds us that: 'Admission and exclusion are at the core of communal independence. They suggest the deepest meaning of self-determination. Without them, there could not be communities of character, historically stable, ongoing associations of men and women with some special commitment to one another and some special sense of their common life.'[15] The sense of kinship can create estrangement from those who are not like us. In *The Fall of Public Man*, Richard Sennett describes how a strong feeling of community can polarise a neighbourhood, making different groups resentful of one another's presence.[16] In its most extreme forms the attempt to create an organic national community can lead to ethnic cleansing, holocaust and genocide. No one, least of all a writer who is a Jew, can ignore these dangers.

However, my argument has not been for a politics of community alone. Instead it has been for a restoration of balance in the body politic. Without a state there is anarchy. Without a respect for individuals as individuals there is tyranny. But without morality and the civil institutions within which it lives, breathes and has its being, there is too little to prevent the pendulum swinging between tyranny and anarchy. A *polis* comprised only of the procedural state and the abstract individual – the situation to which liberal democracies have been tending with ever-increasing speed in the twentieth century – is both unsustainable and impoverished in its view of the human situation. It externalises too much of what, in a viable human order, should be internalised. Virtue is externalised in the form of government action, through the universal replacement of generosity by taxation. Law-abidingness is externalised in the form of police, surveillance, bolted doors and barricaded windows. Worth is externalised in the worship of wealth, consumption, fame and physical attraction.

[15] Michael Walzer, *Spheres of Justice*, 62.
[16] Richard Sennett, *The Fall of Public Man*, 294–312.

In such a society there is too little *socialisation*, too little internalising of the history of which we are a part and the civilities in whose maintenance we have a share. Perhaps the most striking symbol of this is the role of *memory* in contemporary society, our ability to pass on to our children knowledge of the great events, heroes and battles which brought us to where we are. Traditional societies lived with the past as an eternal present. It was the narrative which connected them to their ancestors, and thus to their children, and thus to a coherent sense of human history as a journey towards a destination. Today, computers have massive memories, while we have lost ours.

Community is not everything, but it is not nothing. It represents our most deep-seated protest against the atomisation or politicisation of our sociability. It is the attempt to bring together in a stable, structured, even gracious form our sense of relatedness to others in a manner in which we are neither manipulated nor manipulative. It is the attempt to give expression to the idea that our worth as individuals is related to what we do to recognise the worth of other individuals, and as we would wish our own worth to be recognised, not for what we own, or the power we wield, or our physical attractiveness, but for what we are, and what we cherish, and what we strive to be.

Communities are neither mysterious, nor consigned to the past, nor brought about by government action or inaction. They arise in an open-ended variety of forms at all times when we, as moral agents rather than as political beings, come together to achieve together what we cannot achieve alone, when we substitute collective action for individual effort on the one hand, or on the other, pressure for some other body to act. They are more than associations of people with common interests, what Robert Bellah calls 'lifestyle enclaves', distinguishing the two by pointing out that 'enclaves' tend to bring people together only during recreational time, and are limited to people with the same lifestyles, whereas communities are both more diverse and more involving.[17] They are, above all, moral institutions whose existence depends on more

[17] Robert Bellah et al., *Habits of the Heart*, 71–4.

than the joint pursuit of interests, but on mutual commitment and the shared pursuit of the good-held-in-common.

I have argued for a communitarian politics of institutions and responsibility which, while not neglecting the unique and the universal (the individual and the state), restores to public discourse a respect for the neglected third sector of our human ecology, *society* as the 'community of communities', the domain populated by families, congregations and associations, on whose health so much else in our culture depends. The view I have advocated belongs to the tradition of classical liberalism as opposed to libertarianism, which I see as liberalism wrongly transferred from the political to the moral domain. Classical liberalism saw the cultivation of virtue and the protection of the institutions in which it was sustained as one of the great responsibilities of the *polis,* one that formed the basis of a tacit partnership between governments and individuals alike. Libertarianism, by reducing transactions to distribution and consumption, contracts and rights, tends to destroy our social ecology in the name of personal autonomy. This is seen as a gain in personal freedom. Instead, I have argued, it involves us all in loss.

A liberal environment respects the integrity of communities and their traditions, but it does not forget the lessons of the Enlightenment: that we must respect one another across boundaries, that we must engage (as Jews, Christians and others have been doing for the past half-century) in constant dialogue, and that there are certain liberal virtues, such as tolerance and the capacity to moderate our claims in the light of public interest and national tradition. It values communities not only in themselves but for the virtues they cultivate and the contribution they make to the collective good. But it makes this proviso, that in a liberal society communities are voluntary associations. We are free to leave without ceasing to be part of society. That freedom, to join or to secede, together with the other constraints of a liberal order, means that communities can be strong without threatening hard-won liberties elsewhere. They are not the whole, but simply part, of the ecology of freedom. How then do we move towards that goal?

20

Why Civilisations Fail

I met a traveller from an antique land
Who said, 'Two vast and trunkless legs of stone
Stand in the desert. Near them on the sand,
Half sunk, a shattered visage lies, whose frown
And wrinkled lip, and sneer of cold command,
Tell that its sculptor well those passions read
Which yet survive, stamped on these lifeless things,
The hand that mocked them and the heart that fed.
And on the pedestal these words appear:
"My name is Ozymandias, king of kings:
Look on my works, ye mighty, and despair!"
Nothing beside remains. Round the decay
Of that colossal wreck, boundless and bare,
The lone and level sands stretch far away.'

Shelley[1]

THERE IS NOTHING inevitable about the survival of civilisations. The pages of history are littered with the debris of cultures
that seemed impregnable in their day, but which, soon thereafter,
faded and disappeared. Humanity has one distinct evolutionary
advantage over the dinosaurs: our capacity to sense when things
are going wrong, and then to change.

Unique among life forms, we do not merely adapt to our
environment; we consciously shape it as well. We are creatures of
foresight and deliberation. Isaac Bashevis Singer put it pithily: 'We
have to believe in free will. We've got no choice.' Because we have
freedom, nothing is inevitable in the human situation: not survival,
and not decline. The most important resource we have in mending

[1] P. B. Shelley, *Ozymandias*.

our damaged social environment is simply the clear awareness that it *is* damaged and that we, severally and collectively, must put it right. Changing dysfunctional behaviour is hard but not impossible. The real danger to any culture lies elsewhere, in the inability to recognise when it is in danger. Few have put this more sharply than Jean-Jacques Rousseau:

> Nations, like men, are teachable only in their youth; with age they become incorrigible. Once customs are established and prejudices rooted, reform is a dangerous and fruitless exercise; a people cannot bear to see its evils touched, even if only to be eradicated; it is like a stupid, pusillanimous invalid who trembles at the sight of a physician.[2]

My thesis has been that we are perilously close to this situation. The collapse of moral language, the impoverishment of public discourse, the tyranny of two words – autonomy and rights – which have between them power to flatten any tradition or institution, are systematically insulating us from the tragedy of the breakdown of the family and the collapse of community, two institutions essential to our humanity. But what if I am wrong? What if I am a mere traditionalist sighing *eheu fugaces* and lamenting the passing of the years? What if the libertarians are right, that our social ecology is not disintegrating, merely changing, and that the models of the past are themselves outmoded and dysfunctional? Is there any objective line of proof, any scientific demonstration, that the classic institutions of civil society are not dispensable, that they form a necessary element of human flourishing? That is what I want to argue here as I drive my case to its close. I want to approach our social situation by a different route to show the non-relativity of the position I have been articulating, and hence the danger we face if we do not begin to change. Is there any guarantee that, on our present trajectory, liberal democracy will survive?

One of the turning-points of modern economic history was the famous observation of Adam Smith, in *The Wealth of Nations*: 'It is not from the benevolence of the butcher, brewer or baker

[2] Jean-Jacques Rousseau, *The Social Contract*, 88–9.

that we expect our dinner, but from their regard to their own interest. We address ourselves not to their humanity but to their self-love.'[3] In a single dazzling insight, Smith resolved one of the great tensions of Western culture, between self-interest and altruism, the pursuit of individual and collective gain. There is, he suggested, no conflict. On the contrary, the one led to the other. The power of the division of labour and the free economy was that it harnessed private energies and turned them to the common good. You feel, in Smith, an almost religious awe in the face of this felicitous feature of the market. He gave it a quasi-religious name: the 'invisible hand'. Like the theological concept from which it was derived, divine providence, it pointed to a larger pattern in events, one beyond the intentions of individual agents. Out of the seemingly disconnected decisions of millions of people, each pursuing their own advantage, emerged something vast, benign and unexpected: economic growth. To promote the gain of all, all we had to do was to concentrate on ourselves. The 'invisible hand' would do the rest.

This, the central dogma of market economics, was later disputed by the great political alternatives of the modern world, socialism and communism, but by the end of the twentieth century they were in retreat, even defeat. While democratic capitalism was winning its battle against rival economic systems, though, a quite different challenge was taking shape. The story is one of the most fascinating chapters in the history of modern thought, involving as it does the convergence of three disciplines – mathematics, evolutionary psychology and the power of computing – and resulting in a paradigm-shift in our understanding of survival itself.[4]

It began in 1944 with the invention of a new branch of mathematics, games theory, devised by one of the twentieth century's most formidable intelligences, John von Neumann (1903–1957). Born in Hungary, the son of a successful banker, he went to the United States in 1930, where he played a leading part in

---

[3] Adam Smith, *The Wealth of Nations*, 119.
[4] The story is best told in Robert Wright, *The Moral Animal*; Matt Ridley, *The Origins of Virtue*, and Francis Fukuyama, *The Great Disruption*.

the development of thermonuclear weapons, ballistic missiles and the theory of nuclear deterrence. One particular memory, though, stayed with him from childhood: the conversations his father held around the dinner table about the problems of running a bank. In time this led von Neumann to conclude that economic analysis failed to do justice to a central feature of human decision-making. It is one thing to choose the best of several alternatives when the consequences can be calculated, but life is rarely that simple. Usually the outcome of my choice depends on the reactions of others, and these cannot be predicted. Games theory was an attempt to produce a mathematical representation of action under conditions of uncertainty. Six years later, it yielded its most famous application, the Prisoner's Dilemma.

The dilemma imagines the following scenario: Police arrest two men on suspicion of a serious crime. They lack, however, the evidence to convict. At most, they have enough information to prove them guilty of a lesser offence. The aim of the police, therefore, is to get at least one to inform on the other. They put them in separate rooms with no possibility of communication. They then offer each of the suspects a deal. If one informs and the other stays silent, the informant will go free and the other will receive a jail sentence of ten years. If they both inform on one another, each will receive five years. If they both stay silent, they will be found guilty only of the lesser offence, and each will face a year in prison.

It does not take long to work out that for each, the optimal decision is to inform. The result, though, is that each receives a five-year jail sentence, whereas if they had both stayed silent they would only have been imprisoned for a year. The reason that neither opts for this strategy is that they cannot be sure that the other will do likewise. The Prisoner's Dilemma looks like a mathematical curiosity, but it is far more significant than that. What it did was to challenge the central premise of Smithian economics, namely that several people, each pursuing their own self-interest, generate an outcome which is beneficial to all. It showed, to the contrary, that two people, both acting rationally, produce a result that is bad for both of them.

For many years this remained a paradox, until insight came from another direction. There had long been a tension in Darwinian biology, of which Charles Darwin was himself aware. In the struggle for survival, the fittest wins. Despite this, almost all human societies value altruistic behaviour and hold it out for emulation. What evolutionary advantage could possibly flow from the sacrifice of one's own interest to that of the group? The group might benefit, but the individual would not. How then would his genes flourish into future generations? As Darwin noted, the bravest individuals 'would on an average perish in larger number than other men'. The hero 'would often leave no offspring to inherit his noble nature'.[5] Altruism should not survive, yet it does.

The answer eventually came through reflection on the Prisoner's Dilemma, which showed that self-interested action did not always yield optimal outcomes. What if the paradox was due to the fact that the parties met only once? What if they met repeatedly? Might they not eventually work out that there was a better strategy, namely co-operation: 'I will stay silent if you do'? I would then be acting in your interest because it was in my interest to do so. This pattern, though, would only emerge once I had a chance to learn; if, in other words, I found myself repeatedly in the same situation, the so-called Iterated Prisoner's Dilemma. This might then solve a problem not only in economics but also in biology. It would explain the origins of altruism.

By the late 1970s, the power of computers was great enough to simulate such encounters. A political scientist, Robert Axelrod, announced an international competition to find the programme that did best at playing the Iterated Prisoner's Dilemma against itself and other opponents. The winner was devised by a Canadian, Anatole Rapoport, and called Tit-for-Tat. Its procedure was dazzlingly simple: it began by co-operating, and then repeated the last move of its opponent. It worked on the principle 'What you did to me, I will do to you', or what the Bible and Shakespeare call 'Measure for measure'. The more aggressive programmes did well in the short run but lost out in the end by

[5] Charles Darwin, *The Descent of Man*, vol. I, 163.

provoking retaliation. What Tit-for-Tat showed was the survival value of reciprocal altruism.

Even more fascinating was the discovery, in the late 1980s, of a programme capable of beating Tit-for-Tat. Devised by Martin Nowak and called 'Generous', it overcame the one weakness of Tit-for-Tat, namely that when it met a particularly nasty opponent it was drawn into a destructive cycle of reprisal, of a kind all too familiar from the politics of Bosnia, Northern Ireland and the Middle East. Generous avoided this by randomly but periodically forgetting the last move of its opponent, thus allowing the relationship to begin again. What Nowak had produced, in fact, was a computer simulation of the human virtues of forgiveness and reconciliation.

The search for the perfect programme did not end there, but already we can state its remarkable implications. Against the whole tendency of modern thought, it suggests that we *can* establish a rational basis for ethics, indeed a specific form of ethics. What Tit-for-Tat and Generous show is that individuals and populations thrive when they practise the two fundamental principles of the Judeo-Christian tradition, reciprocity and forgiveness, otherwise known as justice and mercy. It is no accident, therefore, that these two faiths have survived while so many other civilisations have disappeared. They turn out to be deeply rooted in biological reality. To say this is not to commit the fallacy of identifying 'is' with 'ought' – deriving moral imperatives from a set of facts – but it does offer fresh insight into the biblical connection between morality and social stability. A just and forgiving society will endure; a corrupt or cruel one will not.

We are also in a better position to understand the evolutionary advantage of *Homo sapiens* against other species. Survival turns out to depend not so much on individual strength as on habits of co-operation. One man loses against a lion, but ten men stand a good chance of winning if they can co-ordinate their efforts. It now seems likely that the distinctive features of human beings – the 300 per cent increase in brain size since our species split from the other primates, and the development of the use of language – derive from the advantages of extended sociality. There is even a close correlation amongst mammals between brain size and social group: the bigger the brain, the larger the group. Interestingly, this measure suggests that the optimum size of a human group is about 150. That, on average, is the maximum number of people we can know well and count as friends. Here is a tantalising hint that community, that social construct, has a biological base.

Returning, now, to Adam Smith's principle of self-interest, we recall that it seemed to be contradicted by the Prisoner's Dilemma, which showed that self-regarding action often failed to produce optimal outcomes. The conflict was resolved when the game was played many times by the same participants. Eventually they learn to co-operate; and co-operation is predicated on trust, the belief that you will reciprocate, now or later, the actions I take that benefit you. So fundamental is this principle that economists have given it a name. They call it *social capital*, meaning the level of trust in a society.

Where and how is social capital created? It comes about precisely through the Iterated Prisoner's Dilemma, namely through repeated interactions between the same human beings. That is why, for example, acts of robbery or incivility are more frequent in cities than in villages. I am more likely to take advantage of you if I think I will never see you again than if I have to meet you tomorrow and the day after in the local shop or pub. Habits of co-operation depend on the existence of long-term relationships.

Now we can say why families, communities and neighbour-hoods, Burke's 'little platoons', play so vital a role in social ecology. There is nothing mystical or mysterious about it. They are simply the homes of the Iterated Prisoner's Dilemma, the places where we form long-term relationships with other people and interact with them repeatedly over time. That is why they have the power to inculcate the habits of co-operation on which social life depends. They are the environments in which we learn the choreography of reciprocity and forgiveness. They are where we are there for other people, knowing that they are there for us. They are, in short, the matrix of trust.

It follows that Adam Smith's principle is neither inevitable nor universal. Not all cultures generate a market economy. That, in fact, calls for quite a delicate balance between conflicting forces: the competitive mentality of the market and the co-operative habits learned among family and friends. Too much competition destroys trust; too little stifles creativity. It takes a particular cultural configuration to generate a new economic order. David Landes, the Harvard historian, points out for example that China was technically far in advance of Europe in the Middle Ages. It was the first country to invent printing, paper, explosives and porcelain. Yet it was Europe, not China, that gave birth to the Industrial Revolution.[6] Max Weber famously argued that what led to capitalism was Puritanism, not because it had any interest in economics but because its ethic promoted honest behaviour among people unrelated to one another. Its highly internalised religious code combined individualism with trustworthiness. It created the necessary mix of markets and morals.

The market, in other words, depends on virtues not produced by the market, just as the state depends on virtues not produced by the state. The question then becomes: once a market economy comes into existence, is it self-sustaining, or does it, like so many other social systems in the past, contain the seeds of its own disintegration? One of the most significant figures to take the second view was the Austrian economist Joseph Schumpeter. In his *Capitalism, Socialism and Democracy* (1942) he argued that while capitalism creates economic success, it also leads to social breakdown. The climate it engenders, a 'perennial gale of creative destruction', eventually sweeps away its own foundations:

> Capitalism creates a critical frame of mind which, after having destroyed the moral authority of so many other institutions, in the end turns against its own; the bourgeois finds to his amazement that the rationalist attitude does not stop at the credentials of kings and popes but goes on to attack private property and the whole scheme of bourgeois values.[7]

It didn't happen quite like that, but something else did and for the very reason Schumpeter predicted. The consumer ethic, with its

[6] David Landes, *The Wealth and Poverty of Nations*, 45–59.
[7] Joseph Schumpeter, *Capitalism, Socialism and Democracy*, 143.

emphasis on choice and its devaluation of loyalty, proved to be one of the great solvents of marriage and the family, neighbourhood and community. The way in which it did so is complex and many-sided. We have traced some of the factors already. The process was slow and has only reached a critical point after several centuries, in the stage known as 'late capitalism'. Michael Walzer paints a graphic portrait of where we are now:

> We are perhaps the most individualist society that ever existed in human history. Compared certainly to earlier and Old World societies, we are radically liberated, all of us. Free to plot our own course. To plan our own lives. To choose a career. To choose a partner or a succession of partners. To choose a religion or no religion. To choose a politics or an anti-politics. To choose a lifestyle – any style. Free to do our own thing, and this freedom, energizing and exciting as it is, is also profoundly disintegrative, making it very difficult for individuals to find any stable communal support, very difficult for any community to count on the responsible participation of its individual members. It opens solitary men and women to the impact of a lowest common denominator, commercial culture. It works against commitment to the larger democratic union and also against the solidarity of all cultural groups that constitute our multi-culturalism.[8]

It was the Harvard political scientist Robert Putnam who in 1995 gave the phenomenon a metaphor and name. Noting that more Americans were going ten-pin bowling than before, but fewer were joining leagues, he called it 'Bowling alone'.[9] His argument was that social capital was in decline throughout the liberal democracies of the West. This could be seen not only in the breakdown of families and communities, but across the whole range of civic and social engagements. Fewer people were joining voluntary groups. Church attendance was down. People spent less time with their neighbours. The young were markedly less interested than their parents in politics. The 'habits of association' that had so impressed the young Alexis de Tocqueville a century and a half

[8] Michael Walzer, *Citizenship and Civil Society*, part 1, 11–12.

[9] Robert Putnam, 'Bowling Alone: America's Declining Social Capital', *Journal of Democracy*, January 1995, 65–78.

before were being lost, and the consequence was inevitable. The Iterated Prisoner's Dilemma implies that repeated interaction with a stable group of others is essential to the birth and maintenance of trust. When a society loses these contexts, individuals become more guarded and suspicious. They feel themselves surrounded by strangers, not friends. Putnam and others measured this loss. They found that people were more suspicious about the motives of others and more cynical about politicians. The proportion of Americans saying that most people can be trusted fell from 58 per cent in 1960 to 37 per cent in 1993. There was a generalised loss of confidence in authorities and institutions. To that extent Schumpeter was right. Democratic capitalism is a self-consuming artefact. It depends on, but eventually destroys, trust.

The irony is that Adam Smith seems to have known this all along, for he wrote not one masterpiece but two: not only *The Wealth of Nations* (1776) but also, and first, *The Theory of Moral Sentiments* (1759). In that earlier work, far from championing self-interest, he wrote that 'to feel much for others, and little for us . . . constitutes the perfection of human nature'. German scholars, puzzled by the apparent contradiction between the two books, called it *das Adam Smith Problem*. The resolution, though, should by now be clear. There is an economic system and a moral one. The first belongs to the market, the second to the concentric circles of family, friends, community and society. When the moral system encompasses the economic one, it produces the virtues of industry, honesty, reliability and trust on which the market depends. It is when the economic system subverts the moral one that bad things happen: in Smith's words, 'luxury, wanton and even disorderly mirth, the pursuit of pleasure to some degree of intemperance, [and] the breach of chastity'. In Smith's day that applied only to a wealthy elite. Today, an affluent society has democratised decadence. Therein lies the fragility of its future.

One recent restatement of this case is worth noting, coming as it does from one of the contemporary heirs of Adam Smith, George Soros. In *The Crisis of Global Capitalism*, subtitled 'Open Society Endangered', he writes that in the 1950s business depended on the slow building of relationships. Now it has become 'transactional', a series of one-off encounters. The result is the destabilisation of the social order. 'In a perfectly changeable, transactional society the individual is paramount. From the point of view of the individual it is not necessary to be morally upright to be successful; indeed it can be a hindrance ... In a society where stable relationships prevail, this is much less of a problem because it is difficult to be successful if you violate the prevailing social norms. But when you can move around freely, social norms become less binding, and when expediency becomes established as the social norm, society becomes unstable.'[10]

I have argued, then, that there is nothing nostalgic or subjective about concern for the institutions of civil society. They are rooted in the biological bases of the human condition. Without stable association with others over extended periods of time, we fail to acquire the habits of co-operation which form the basis of trust on which the economics and politics of a free society depend. Self-interest alone does not generate it; indeed self-interest without trust yields outcomes that are individually and collectively destructive. There is nothing wrong with our economics or our politics. The failure lies with our unwillingness to make sacrifices in the short-term to ensure the health of our families and communities in the long-term. No politician or economist holds our collective future in their hands. No government can make us solicitous, law-abiding, honest, public-spirited or reliable. No law or economic incentive can make families stay together, or neighbours help one another, or parents spend more time with their children. That lies with us, each of us; and in that fact lies the glory and moral challenge of our freedom. The politics of hope is born the moment we locate responsibility within ourselves, knowing that we can change and that we are not alone.

Thoughtful observers have long known that liberal democracy – the free economy, the free society – was a rare and precarious achievement, full of risk. At the end of his great essay on liberty, Isaiah Berlin remarks that it may be that our form of society 'is only the late fruit of our declining capitalist civilization: an ideal

---

[10] George Soros, *The Crisis of Global Capitalism*, 80.

which remote ages and primitive societies have not recognized, and one which posterity will regard with curiosity, even sympathy, but little comprehension'.[11] More portentously, Michel Foucault writes that 'man is an invention of recent date, and one that may well be coming to an end'.[12] That is what is at stake. But can we reverse social trends? Can what I propose be done?

[11] Isaiah Berlin, *Four Essays on Liberty*, 172.
[12] Michel Foucalt, *The Order of Things*, 386–7.

21

Can It Be Done?

Philanthropy made a massive contribution to reducing human
misery in the nineteenth century, but in practice it meant much
more than a simple wish to relieve the suffering or to uplift the
benighted. Humanitarian impulses were certainly a characteristic
of charitable activists, but in a culture so profoundly voluntarist,
philanthropy was an essential sphere of politics and social relations,
an expression of local democracy and civic life, of individual hope
and aspiration.

Frank Prochaska[1]

'THERE IS NO community in England.' This has been the central
argument of a growing number of social commentators and analysts,
and it has been mine. We can reverse the increase in crime, the
failures of education and the breakdown of morality, if only we
can restore the structures – the families and neighbourhoods –
which were once so vital a part of our life. The critics do not
necessarily disagree. They merely argue that it is impossible. Times
have changed. You cannot bring back the past. We can no more
reverse social trends than Canute could turn back the tide. So a
central question is: can it be done? Can we bring back the habits
and institutions which once made our collective life so much more
hopeful than it is today?

The quotation provides an answer. It was not written in the
1990s. It is taken from a novel published in 1845 by a writer who
would eventually become Prime Minister: Benjamin Disraeli. In
Sybil, or the Two Nations, Disraeli painted a bleak picture of life in
Britain in his day, the social injustices, the growing gap between
rich and poor. But what struck him with particular force was the

[1] Frank Prochaska, *Royal Bounty: The Making of a Welfare Monarchy*, 67.

collapse of ordinary relationships, the loneliness and isolation that lay beneath the noise and bustle of city life. People had lost a sense of community. He continued:

> There is aggregation, but aggregation under circumstances which make it rather a dissociating than a uniting principle . . . It is a community of purpose that constitutes society . . . without that, men may be brought into contiguity, but they still continue virtually isolated . . . In great cities men are brought together by the desire of gain. They are not in a state of cooperation, but of isolation, as to the making of fortunes; and for all the rest they are careless of their neighbours. Christianity teaches us to love our neighbour as ourself; modern society acknowledges no neighbour.[2]

This passage, summing up the central concern of this book, provides us with both perspective and hope. Despite the scale of our problems, we have been there before. Victorian society in the 1840s was undergoing vast, destabilising changes on a scale similar to today. The industrial revolution was changing the way people worked. It was creating huge movements of population from countryside to towns, breaking up old communities and weakening traditional patterns of life. The size of cities, the devastation of the landscape by factories and mills, the new working conditions, the abuse of children, the centres of poverty in the midst of affluence, the squalor of inner cities, the sheer pace of change: all these raised fears of the death of the familiar and the reign of the unknown, a juggernaut careering out of control.

Crime was a major problem. A century earlier another writer, Daniel Defoe, had addressed a pamphlet to the Lord Mayor of London on the problems of street violence – 'mugging' – and the breakdown of order. 'The Whole City, My Lord, is alarm'd and uneasy,' he wrote. 'Wickedness has got such a Head, and the Robbers and Insolence of the Night are such that the citizens are no longer secure within their own Walls or safe even in passing their Streets, but are robbed, insulted and abused, even at their own Doors.' That was in 1730. By 1751, Henry Fielding, who

[2] Benjamin Disraeli, *Sybil, or the Two Nations*, Harmondsworth, Penguin, 1954, 71–2.

combined novel writing with a career as Chief Magistrate at the Bow Street court, wrote that London had become 'a vast wood or forest, in which a thief may harbour with as great security as wild beasts do in the deserts of Arabia or Africa'. A year later Horace Walpole wrote that 'one is forced to travel, even at noon as if one were going to battle'.[3] By the end of the eighteenth century, a Middlesex magistrate, Patrick Colquhoun, was arguing that crime rates were rising because 'the morals and habits of the lower ranks in society are growing progressively worse'. He blamed this on the decline of religion and the influence of pubs and the popular music of his day.[4]

There were other worries strikingly like our own. Disraeli was concerned about the materialisation of culture, its loss of non-commercial values, and its new underclass, the industrial proletariat. 'To acquire, to accumulate, to plunder each other by virtue of philosophic phrases, to propose a Utopia to consist only of Wealth and Toil, this has been the breathless business of enfranchised England for the last twelve years, until we are startled from our voracious strife by the wail of intolerable serfage.' A few years earlier Coleridge had posed the question of whether change had brought an increase in the quality of life. 'Has the national welfare, have the weal and happiness of the people, advanced with the increase of the circumstantial prosperity? Is the increasing number of wealthy individuals that which ought to be understood by the wealth of the nation?' Like us, Coleridge was disturbed that rising living standards had not brought about a general sense of well-being, a 'feel-good factor'. Instead they had created widespread suffering and unease. There were centres of high unemployment. There was an erosion of the social bond. Society seemed to be ruled, not by a sense of mutual responsibility but by the hard calculations of 'a contemptible democratical oligarchy of glib economists'.[5]

Like ours, the early Victorian period was a transitional society. It

[3] I owe these quotations to Robert Reiner, 'How to Break the Crime Wave', *Manna* 42 (Winter 1994), 2.
[4] L. Radzinowicz, *A History of the English Criminal Law*, London, Stevens, 1956, 275.
[5] Quoted in Raymond Williams, *Culture and Society 1780–1950*, 72–3.

was experiencing the upheavals of the industrial revolution, as we are encountering the dislocations of a post-industrial, information-technology age. They asked the same questions we do. How do you control crime? How do you heal institutions like the family that are in disrepair? How do you make the city a more bearable place in which to live? How do you cope with poverty and unemployment? Where we have drug addiction, the Victorians had drunkenness. Where we have broken families, they had neglected and often brutalised children. Their problems were palpably like ours, and they were obsessed by them. They debated them, wrote about them, and at times seemed haunted by them. But there was a difference. The Victorians had what we seem to have lost: hope. In the vast array of literature they produced, the absent note is despair. In the mid-nineteenth century, there was none of the anger, denial, relativism, scepticism, confusion, cynicism, none of the 'not worsening, only changing' rhetoric, that so mark and diminish our time. The Victorians believed that if there are social problems they should be honestly faced and practically addressed. More than any previous society, they engaged in collective debate out of which emerged not only new programmes but a new culture.

By the end of the nineteenth century crime rates were down. In a remarkable and well-documented transformation, the mid-nineteenth century witnessed a reversal in historical patterns of criminal behaviour. Law-breaking and violence, which had risen steadily until 1850, then began, and continued, to fall. Ted Robert Gurr found that in London 'the numbers of murders, assaults, and thefts of almost all kinds which came to police attention declined irregularly, but consistently, for half a century or more' as did the numbers of persons arrested and convicted for such offences.[6] So too did illegitimacy, one of the indicators of the strength or weakness of the family as an institution. By the end of the century, the rate of births outside wedlock was down to half of what it had been in 1845. Most strikingly, in East London, the poorest section of the city, it was below the national

[6] Ted Robert Gurr, 'Contemporary crime in historical perspective', *Annals* 434, 114–36.

average.[7] These changes defy conventional wisdom. They took place in a period of urbanisation, industrialisation, and widespread immigration, the very factors which are associated with a breakdown of social order. There were ample reasons for, and occasional manifestations of, unrest. We know them: they are a continuing theme of Victorian literature. Nevertheless, families were strengthened, law-abidingness increased, alcoholism declined and schools improved. Nor was this confined to England. The same trends, during the same period, can be documented for the United States as well, and they were brought about in the same way. How did it happen?

The English Victorians and their American counterparts brought to their problems a very marked set of assumptions. They sought to create social change, and they deliberated about how to do so. They had a considerable wealth of theoretical models on which to draw. From Hobbes they knew about the power of governments. From Mandeville and Adam Smith they knew about the strength of self-interest as channelled through markets. These have been our primary resources in the second half of the twentieth century: social engineering brought about by government policy on the one hand, economic individualism on the other. Thoughtful individuals a century and a half ago rejected both these alternatives. Instead they concentrated on a single word, which became the title of a famous book by Samuel Smiles. The word was *character*.

The Victorians on either side of the Atlantic were not what today would be called 'communitarians'. They valued independence, self-reliance, initiative and courage. Their focus was on the individual rather than on the community. But they were not individualists in the modern sense. They knew that the heart is 'deceitful above all things'. They did not take human character as they found it. To the contrary, they had seen how the narrow pursuit of self could lead to decadence among the affluent, addiction and child-neglect among the poor, and a growing gap between different sections of society, the 'two nations' of which Disraeli spoke.

Above all else they wanted to shape a free society in which the

[7] Gertrude Himmelfarb, *The De-Moralization of Society*, 222–3.

individual was an independent source of dignity and well-being. For that reason they were hesitant about using the state as an instrument of control. They were mindful of Dr Johnson's warning, 'How small, of all that human hearts endure,/That part which laws or kings can cause or cure!' In their debates about welfare and the poor laws, they spoke in terms which have only now begun to resurface in the mainstream of political debate. They expressed concern that actions taken to remedy social problems might in the long run aggravate them, by creating dependency and a breakdown of family and personal responsibility. In short, they came to the conclusion that if you want to change society you have to change the individuals who constitute it. But you cannot do it coercively. You have to do it in and through the individual: through education, will-power, self-control, support, encouragement and example. The mid-nineteenth century had access to an insight which is the source of all hope: we can change the world because we can change ourselves.

The sociologist David Riesman has spoken about the particular kind of character that emerges in transitional societies. He called it the 'inner-directed personality'. Unlike the 'tradition-directed' type of earlier eras and the 'outer-directed' character he saw coming to the fore in the second half of the twentieth century, the inner-directed individual has a strongly internalised moral system 'implanted early in life by the elders and directed toward generalised but nonetheless inescapably destined goals'. The social order in such ages is created less by established custom ('shame' societies) or by prevailing fashions in public opinion ('anxiety' societies), than by an internalised sense of right and wrong ('guilt'). The result is the emergence of a 'rigid though highly individualized character'.[8]

It was just such individuals, driven by a strong sense of self-help on the one hand, social responsibility on the other, that Thomas Jefferson saw as the bedrock of the new American republic, and which in England emerged as the ideal of Victorian virtue. In both countries, self-reliance was regarded as a precondition of personal growth. 'Dependence', wrote Jefferson, 'begets subservience and venality, suffocates the germ of virtue, and prepares fit tools for the

[8] David Riesman, Nathan Glazer and Reuel Denney, *The Lonely Crowd*, 19–48.

designs of ambition.'[9] In England, Samuel Smiles' famous book *Self-Help*, published in 1859, became the canonical text of this approach. 'Help from without', he declared, 'is often enfeebling in its effects, but help from within invariably invigorates.' Law was a vital part of a well-ordered society, but 'no laws, however stringent, can make the idle industrious, the thriftless provident, or the drunken sober. Such reforms can only be effected by means of individual action, economy and self-denial; by better habits rather than by greater rights.'[10]

Self-reliance did not lead to a culture of self-interest, because against it was set that other great nineteenth-century claim: duty. Again Samuel Smiles wrote a book under that title, arguing that 'it is every man's duty, whose lot has been favoured in comparison with others, who enjoys advantages of wealth, or knowledge, or social influence, of which others are deprived, to devote at least a certain portion of his time and money to the promotion of the general well-being'.[11] The feeling was widespread. As a result, an age which was deeply engaged in industrial development, economic growth and international trade became at the same time one of the great periods of voluntary and philanthropic endeavour.

Throughout the length and breadth of Britain one could find missions, temperance societies, voluntarily established hospitals, dispensaries, schools, benevolent societies, children's aid societies, and orphanages. The French commentator Hippolyte Taine, writing in the 1860s, was frankly astonished at this outburst of public-spiritedness:

> There are swarms of societies engaged in good works: societies for saving the life of drowning persons . . . for the advancement of science, for the protection of animals, for the suppression of vice, for the abolition of tithes, for helping working people to own their own houses, for building good houses for the working class, for setting up a basic fund to provide the workers with savings banks, for emigration, for the propagation of economic and

[9] Thomas Jefferson, *Notes on Virginia 1782*, quoted in George Will, *Statecraft as Soulcraft*, 104.
[10] Samuel Smiles, *Self-Help*, new edition, London, IEA Health and Welfare Unit, 1996, 1.
[11] Samuel Smiles, *Duty: With Illustrations of Courage, Patience, and Endurance*, London, 1880, 261.

social knowledge, for Sabbath day observance, against drunkenness, for founding schools to train girls as schoolteachers, etc. etc.[12]

The same phenomenon had amazed his fellow-countryman Alexis de Tocqueville in his visit to the United States a generation earlier.

Nineteenth-century benevolence was rooted in certain assumptions about character, assumptions shared by both Aristotelian philosophy and the Judaeo-Christian ethic. Individuals were not born good or evil. They were made by their own choices. It was of critical importance, therefore, that they should understand the long-term consequences of those choices. Education had a key role to play in teaching discipline, perseverance, courage, duty and honour. Society too had to promote such virtues, and therefore citizens were also role-models, expected to display civility, good manners and uprightness. But the matrix of personality was the home. Thomas Chalmers, in his *Christian and Civic Economy of Large Towns* (1821–6), set the terms of the argument, insisting that the way to address social problems was to work through the family. Not all problems could be solved within the home. Hence the need for orphanages, asylums and other protective institutions. But almost all charities of the Victorian age sought to strengthen the family and project it as the citadel of education, healing and mutuality.[13]

These values were internalised by each of the different social groups in what was still a heavily class-based society, with a result well described by Robert Roberts in his reminiscences of life in the slums of Salford: 'Despite poverty and appalling surroundings parents brought up their children to be decent, kindly and honourable and often lived long enough to see them occupy a higher place socially than they had ever known themselves: the greatest satisfaction of all.'[14] The key, then, to the development of character was the strength of the social institutions through which the individual came

[12] Hippolyte Taine, *Notes on England*, trans. Edward Hyams, London, 1957, 167–8.

[13] Frank Prochaska, *Royal Bounty*, 71–2.

[14] Robert Roberts, *The Classic Slum: Salford Life in the First Quarter of the Century*, Harmondsworth, Penguin, 1971, 24.

to learn the difference between ways of life which led to happiness and those, however attractive, that led to misery, ill-health, and dependence on others. It is all the more remarkable that these institutions came into being without social planning or government intervention, but simply through a sustained, voluntary and informal effort of national self-improvement, inspired by a group of writers, religious leaders and philanthropists who became, through teaching and example, the pioneers and heroes of a new ethos.

Looking back at this period, Richard Herrnstein and James Q. Wilson come to the conclusion that crime rates fell, quite simply, because of the success of a generation in inculcating habits of self-restraint. Religious revivals, a growth in church attendance, and especially the institution of the Sunday school, all played their part in teaching order, punctuality, manners, duty and a respect for law and for 'respectability' itself. 'In myriad ways but with extraordinary singleness of purpose,' they write, 'Americans (and Englishmen) invested heavily in programmes designed to inculcate self-control and thereby enhance character. These efforts were directed at what reformers took to be the causes of crime and disorder – impulsiveness and a lack of conscience.'[15]

The result, in England, was one of those developments often thought impossible: a profound transformation in national character. Visiting London in 1766, Benjamin Franklin observed: 'There is no country in the world in which the poor are more idle, dissolute, drunken and insolent.'[16] By 1944, George Orwell, who had spent much of his life exploring the darker side of human society, could write that: 'An imaginary foreign observer would certainly be struck by our gentleness; by the orderly behaviour of English crowds, the lack of pushing and quarrelling . . . And except for certain well-defined areas in half-a-dozen big towns, there is very little crime or violence.'[17]

More, though, was achieved than individual advancement and

[15] James Q. Wilson and Richard J. Herrnstein, *Crime and Human Nature*, 434.

[16] Quoted in Marvin Olasky, *The Tragedy of American Compassion*, 43.

[17] Quoted in Christie Davies, 'Moralization and Demoralization', in Digby Anderson (ed.), *The Loss of Virtue*, 6.

law-abidingness. Frank Field has recently argued that the mutual aid societies and co-operatives which sprung up in working-class groups in the Victorian age created an environment of collective solidarity through their combination of self-help and association. They allowed people to achieve together what they could not achieve alone. 'The mutual aid movement held out the prospect of an organizational form through which members were able to advance their independence and gain control over the vagaries of life,' the ever-present dangers of poverty, unemployment and alcoholism. It was, he says, 'the means by which *de facto* citizenship was attained'.[18]

Voluntary societies played a crucial role in easing class and other divisions. Some were places where different classes could mix; others helped more precarious groups to develop their own resources of strength. The vast network of *hevrot* (societies), synagogues, schools, houses of study, welfare organisations and *landsmanschaft* groups which characterised immigrant Jewish communities, and which so impressed the young Beatrice Webb, helped the new arrivals from Eastern Europe to integrate into Britain without losing their religious or ethnic identity.[19] Frank Prochaska is surely correct in his judgement that voluntary associations in the nineteenth century 'were a most promising way for diverse social groups, which were often culturally vulnerable or politically isolated, to forge a relationship with the wider society'.[20] Aimed at developing self-reliant individuals, they had the effect of promoting the values of community and of knitting together the multiple strands of society.

For a long time the Victorian age has had a reputation for intolerance, repressiveness, paternalism and hypocrisy. That negative judgement was part of the process through which later generations felt able to liberate themselves from its claims. As Harold Bloom has argued, those who find themselves late arrivals on a cultural

[18] Frank Field, 'State-Run War of Attrition on Self-Improvement', The Allen Lane Foundation Memorial Lecture, 26 March 1996.

[19] See Gertrude Himmelfarb, *The De-Moralization of Society*, chapter 6; and my *Community of Faith*.

[20] Frank Prochaska, *Royal Bounty*, 72.

scene create space for themselves by 'misreading' their predecessors: that is the oedipal way in which civilisations progress.[21] Already in 1859, the year in which *Self-Help* appeared, John Stuart Mill had published his essay *On Liberty*, his protest against what he felt to be the stifling impact of social rectitude and propriety. His contemporaries, though, found it hard to understand what he was complaining about. Lord Macaulay, perplexed that Mill should be arguing for individuality in an age in which it was receiving its highest expression, accused him of 'crying "Fire" in Noah's flood'. In the same vein another reviewer observed that the book sounded as if it had come from 'the prison-cell of some persecuted thinker bent on making one last protest against the growing tyranny of the public mind' instead of from a society which more than most valued strong voices and independent minds. Indeed, as Gertrude Himmelfarb has carefully documented, *On Liberty* is strangely at odds with the rest of Mill's work. In his *Autobiography* the judgement he passed on his age was quite different. There he wrote of 'the great advance in liberty of discussion' which he held to be 'one of the points of difference between the present time and that of my childhood'.[22]

Speaking personally, I cannot forget that Victorian Britain and the United States of that time were generous enough to permit a vast immigration of Jews and others fleeing from persecution, an openness not repeated after 1914. It allowed a born Jew, Benjamin Disraeli, to become Prime Minister. Though he had been baptised as a child, Disraeli never hid his religious and ethnic origins nor spoke about them publicly without pride. It held another Jew, Sir Moses Montefiore, in great esteem, *The Times* honouring him with long editorials on his ninety-ninth and hundredth birthdays. In George Eliot's flawed but passionate novel *Daniel Deronda* (1875), it produced one of the great positive appraisals of Judaism in English literature and an early intimation of

[21] See Harold Bloom, *A Map of Misreading*, New York, Oxford University Press, 1975.
[22] See, in detail, Gertrude Himmelfarb, *On Liberty and Liberalism: The Case of John Stuart Mill*, especially 143–68.

Zionism. Even Charles Dickens, who produced the most famous negative stereotype, Fagin in *Oliver Twist* (1837–8), later balanced it with a far more sympathetic portrayal of the Jew in the character of Mr Riah in *Our Mutual Friend* (1864–5). Victorian society was not free of racism and intolerance – no society is – but it contained little of the pervasive anti-Semitism that was later to mar the work of G. K. Chesterton, D. H. Lawrence, T. S. Eliot, Ezra Pound, Scott Fitzgerald and Graham Greene.[23] Other immigrant groups, arriving in Britain over the past fifty years, were less fortunate. Despite much-heralded advances in liberalisation and race relations, they found a less tolerant society.

There is a truth here, self-evident but rarely stated: that societies, like individuals, are more likely to be generous when they are self-confident, and more likely to be self-confident when they have a strong moral code, an ethic of self-reliance, and a clear sense of their own identity. The Jews who came to Britain in the 1880s, unlike their Asian counterparts a century later, found a culture sympathetic to their fundamental commitments. It respected family and tradition and religious worship. It valued self-discipline, less as a means to an end than as a quality of character valuable in its own right. Jews knew that the society around them was a Christian one: in London's East End and elsewhere they had to contend against Christian missionaries. But they also knew that a Christian society had a sense of the sacred, even if what was sacred was not the same in both faiths. They were not confronted with the fragmented culture of today, its violence, overt sexuality, its drug subcultures and its underlying bass-note of despair. As a result, the intergenerational gap – always a tragedy within immigrant families – was less severe than it is for new ethnic minorities today. Victorian society held forth rules for integration that were clear and simple to follow. They involved mastering a new language, a new culture and a new code of civility. When the domestic culture is fractured and incoherent it is much more difficult to integrate, or

---

[23] On this subject see Harold Fisch, *The Dual Image*, London, World Jewish Library, 1971; Linda Nochlin and Tamar Garb (eds), *The Jew in the Text*, London, Thames & Hudson, 1995.

even know whether integration is desirable. British and American societies since the 1960s have become markedly more abrasive in the encounters between ethnic groups.[24]

It is no part of my case to argue for a return to Victorian values. There is nothing to be said for marching boldly towards the past. Our concerns are different and our landscape has changed. The Victorians did not have to worry about environmental catastrophe, international terrorism or the globalisation of the economy. Their experience does however offer us a model and a hope. The hope lies in the fact that what has been done once can be done again. The model lies in the instrumentality of social change. What the Victorians taught us is that whatever we seek collectively to create, the way to do so is to focus on character and on the institutions that promote a strong sense of independent personhood and social concern. That is done less through governments than through the spontaneous associations of individuals which arise whenever there is widespread recognition that things are not as they should be, and that to make them different we have to join hands. Social change is always preceded by and works through moral change.

This, as Gertrude Himmelfarb reminds us, is what the Victorian example teaches, 'that the ethos of a society, its moral and spiritual character, cannot be reduced to economic, material, political or other factors' and that 'values – or better yet, virtues – are a determining factor in their own right'. If, during rapid economic and social change, 'the Victorians managed to achieve a substantial improvement in their "condition" and "disposition", it may be that economic and social change do not necessarily result in personal and public disarray'.[25] The Victorian model is not one to imitate, but it is one to inspire a sense of possibility. Theirs was a society as much informed by covenant as by contract, by moral character as by interests. That is why, as an example of what can be done, it is a testimony to hope.

---

[24] See, for example, Arthur Schlesinger, *The Disuniting of America*, and the vast literature generated by the controversy over Salman Rushdie's *The Satanic Verses*.

[25] Gertrude Himmelfarb, *The De-Moralization of Society*, 257.

22

Reclaiming the Ground of Hope

Perhaps life is not a race whose only goal is being foremost. Perhaps true felicity does not lie in continually outgoing the next before. Perhaps the truth lies in what most of the world outside the modern West has always believed, namely that there are practices of life, good in themselves, that are inherently fulfilling. Perhaps work that is intrinsically rewarding is better for human beings than work that is only extrinsically rewarded. Perhaps our enduring commitment to those we love and civic friendship toward our fellow citizens are preferable to restless competition and anxious self-defence. Perhaps common worship, in which we express our gratitude and wonder in the face of the mystery of being itself, is the most important thing of all. If so, we will have to change our lives and begin to remember what we have been happier to forget.

Robert Bellah[1]

THE HEBREW BIBLE has endowed Western civilisation with two different concepts of time. One is the apocalypse, the idea that we are heading towards a shattering cataclysm in which the universe will shake on its foundations before the moral order is restored. There will be a day of wrath, sun and moon will be darkened, the heavens will roll together and the earth will quake. Then, like sunshine after the storm, justice will reign, evil will be defeated and truth will prevail. This vision, to be found in the book of Daniel and the writings of sectarian groups during the last days of the Second Temple, resurfaces in Christianity, giving rise in one century after another during the course of the Middle Ages to a series of revolutionary and anarchic sects.[2]

[1] Robert Bellah et al., *Habits of the Heart*, 295.
[2] See Norman Cohn, *The Pursuit of the Millennium*, London, Paladin, 1970.

It is born in a strange mix of despair and certainty, certainty that good will triumph, despair that it will do so within the course of society as it is. So arises the belief in the end of history, and even, *in extremis*, a willingness to act to hasten that end. This, as Michael Walzer notes, is what lies behind 'the readiness of messianic militants to welcome, even to initiate, the terrors that precede the Last Days; and hence the strange politics of *the worse, the better*.'[3] In recent years we have been tragically reminded of such doomsday cults: Jonestown, the Branch Davidians of Waco, and the Church of the Solar Temple are three examples. More generally, apocalyptic thinking has entered the mainstream of cultural anxiety. It is to be found in Alasdair MacIntyre's prediction of the 'new dark ages' and the many other laments I chronicled in the first chapter. Apocalyptic time has a destination. It is called the Millennium.

But there is another Jewish tradition, not apocalyptic but prophetic. Its most famous image is the journey of the Israelites across the desert towards the promised land. Here too there is a destination, but it is to be reached, not by upheaval, but rather through a long, slow journey, by 'joining together and marching'. The way is rarely straight. There are digressions and diversions, blind alleys and false turnings, backslidings and rebellions. At times the people despair and long to go back to a misremembered past, an idealised Egypt, the 'world we have lost'. But somehow, through a combination of coaxing and persistence, they reach sight of their goal, even though Moses, who has led them there, will not live to cross the Jordan. 'It is not given to you to complete the task,' said a first-century rabbi, summarising the moral enterprise, 'but neither are you free to desist from it.'[4]

The prophetic dream is less about the end of history (the messianic age) than about how to move forward, step by step, towards the good society. It is not a cosmic vision; rather, it is a moral one. Isaiah's 'Seek justice, encourage the oppressed, defend the cause of the fatherless, plead the case of the widow', or Micah's 'What does the Lord require of you but to act justly, love mercy and

[3] Michael Walzer, *Exodus and Revolution*, 145.
[4] Mishnah, *Avot*, 2:21.

walk humbly with your God?' are not revolutionary programmes. They are reminders that with every act of kindness we undertake, every virtue we develop, every love we translate into life, we help to mend a fractured world and make society a little more just, a little less abrasive and inhumane. Its most striking expression in time is not the Millennium but the Jubilee: 'Consecrate the fiftieth year and proclaim liberty throughout the land to all its inhabitants. It shall be a jubilee for you, a time when everyone shall return to his inheritance and to his family' (Leviticus 25:10). The Jubilee is not the end of history. It is simply a reminder that wherever we are, we can begin again.

Throughout this book I have been arguing for a prophetic rather than apocalyptic view of society. Things may be bad; the social fabric may be frayed; but precisely because we are moral beings, we have every reason not to despair. It is no accident that what Alasdair MacIntyre calls 'hope as a social virtue'[5] makes its first appearance among the prophets of ancient Israel. It lies in the profound difference between prophecy and prediction. Foreseeing the future, the prophets did not predict what *would* happen, but warned of what *might* happen in the hope that people would change. In Judaism there is no inevitable future, and hence no tragedy in the classic sense, because the driving force of human history is not a power beyond our control, but our own responsible decisions. Through free will we overcome the present. Through repentance and forgiveness we overcome the past. That is the moral basis of hope.

My argument has been simple. A vision once guided us, one that we loosely call the Judaeo-Christian tradition. It was not a single ethical system, more a related family of them. It did not answer all questions, and even when it was at its height, there were vexed moral debates. But it taught us moral habits. It gave us a framework of virtue. It embodied ideals. It emphasised the value of institutions – the family, the school, the community – as vehicles through which one generation hands on its ideals to the next. In its broad outlines

[5] Alasdair MacIntyre, *Marxism and Christianity*, 88.

it was shared by poor and rich alike, by miners, labourers, politicians, teachers, the police, judges, fellows of Oxbridge colleges and children in the village school. You could catch traces of its influence from pubs to pulpits to cricket matches. It bound us together as a nation and gave an entire society its bearings.

That tradition has been comprehensively displaced. In its stead has come a variety of substitutes: ethics of work and success, cults of physical fitness, consumerism and salvation-by-shopping, therapies, new age mysticisms, alternative lifestyles, sub- and counter-cultures, resurgent ethnicities of multiple kinds, and internet-surfing as a mode of global identity. Never before have we been faced with such kaleidoscopic variety, but it fails to cohere. It does not provide us with the resources to connect our present with an identifiable past and future. It does not give unity to a life. It does not lend structure and stability to our relationships. It does not connect our private desires with a larger purpose of which we are a part. It is less like music, more like noise.

Behind these glittering surfaces, though, does lie a coherent picture of humanity. It sees each of us as part of a story, not of purpose and moral striving, but of physical and social causes and effects. There is the individual as a bundle of desires to be satisfied. There is the state as distributor of resources and the agent of social engineering. And there is the market – the place of free exchange of goods and services, ideas and identities – where we meet as buyer and seller, consumer or consumed. What is missing from this picture, comprehensive though it is, is any sustained attempt to understand the mechanisms through which we endow life with a meaning. That is a serious omission, for whatever else we are, we are meaning-seeking animals. We are the only beings yet known to science capable of self-consciousness, language, and sustained flights of the imagination. Rousseau once said that the first man who enclosed a piece of ground and said, 'This is mine' was the real founder of civil society. I prefer to trace its origins back further. The first person to use the first person singular and pronounce the word 'I' had already journeyed from loneliness to relationship to identity, and taken the initial steps on the road to trust and moral commitment.

The alternative world we have come to inhabit has its roots deep in history. I have followed it back to Hobbes in the seventeenth century. Others would date its genesis earlier still. It did not come into being solely as a result of Thatcherism or Reaganomics in the 1980s, or the 'permissive society' of the 1960s, or the welfare state of the 1940s. Each of these merely carried further tendencies that were present long before. That is why serious thinkers have understood that what is really at stake in the present debate is the Enlightenment itself as an adequate account of human nature and rationality.[6] Many aspects of that revolution in thought were necessary and beneficial. We could not undo them, nor should we wish to. But in one aspect it was simply wrong, in its attempt to assimilate our understanding of humanity to science. The belief was that just as science was opening the way to limitless progress in our understanding and control of the physical world, so a scientific morality would create an order of rational, tolerant and benevolent human beings, free of the conflicts and prejudices of the past. That was a noble undertaking, but like the Tower of Babel it was aimed too high, and the result is that we find it increasingly difficult to communicate with one another. We are left, like the builders of the tower, isolated and confused.

Fortunately, we are not without hope. The Judaeo-Christian heritage never disappeared, and it exists today as a great reservoir of moral energy and aspiration. Nor are we called on to abandon the heritage of the Enlightenment, for it taught us two things that must never be forgotten: that religion is not science, neither is it politics. Religion is not the best way of understanding *what is*; its domain is in the realm of *what ought to be*. Nor is it an appropriate vehicle of power. Politics is the art of mediating between what is and what ought to be, and calls for compromises that faith cannot make. In two ways religion

[6] See Alasdair MacIntyre, *After Virtue*; John Gray, *Enlightenment's Wake*.

had trespassed beyond its borders, and the Enlightenment was a necessary corrective. Sacred texts do not exclude scientific knowledge. Ecclesiastical rule, in this less-than-perfect world, is no substitute for democratically accountable government. In these respects the Enlightenment was closer to truth than the religious establishments of the day.

But in one respect it simply failed to understand the nature of human society. We are not atoms, held together by the force-field of the state. We are children and parents, neighbours and friends. We are self-conscious beings, knowing what it is to feel the pain of loneliness, yet not willing to abdicate our selfhood in total fusion with others. We seek individuality and relationship – individuality through relationship. We learn to pronounce the 'We' the better to be able to say 'I'. Thus is born the intricate dynamic of society, beginning with the family and extending outward, through which we learn to trust others and to act so that others can trust us. This requires us to internalise a complex of rules, virtues, dispositions and habits mediating between the self and others, allowing us to sustain relationships without the use or threat of force. As John Macmurray reminds us, these habits are precarious and need constant renewal. 'The institutions by which society maintains itself are not natural,' he writes. '[T]hey are artifacts, and they are maintained by effort in order to sustain the personal life of men and women, and to prevent a relapse into . . . barbarism'.[7] As we have come to know all too well in the twentieth century, civilisation has a thin skin, and is easily wounded.

I have told the long story of the interplay between Enlightenment philosophy and libertarian politics because only thus can we gain a sense of the intellectual momentum which lay behind the remarkable failure of successive generations to understand the importance of the *social* as opposed to the individual and the universal. Morality, like language, is a social phenomenon. It is something we enter, not something we make. The family and its concentric circles of community are where we learn to

[7] John Macmurray, *Persons in Relation*, 153.

speak, to share, to love, to trust, where we discover where we came from and of what history we are a part. They are where we acquire the arts of relationship without which we cannot survive for long. Hobbes, Locke, Rousseau and others believed that individuals could act together on the basis of a contract which brought into being a state. They discounted the social in favour of the political.

This was a great error. For without trust there can be no contracts, and without moral relationships there can be no trust. Politics is then confronted with a breakdown in the social order which it cannot solve because its methods are universal and impersonal, when what is needed is personal and particular. For a long time, it made little difference. Philosophers speculated, and people got on with their lives. But in the quarter of a century after the Second World War, Western governments enacted a series of measures which for the first time made it legally possible and financially viable for large numbers of people to live by these values. The procedural state supplied the means, the autonomous individual made the choices, and the model of human interaction became the market exchange. This was, quite simply, the de-moralisation of society, an unprecedented experiment in conducting a large-scale human environment without recourse to shared values and institutions. Within a single generation the costs have become high, even unsustainable.

There are times when any great system of thought encounters a crisis. That is the situation of liberal democratic politics today. Crime is rising, abusiveness and violence are on the increase, schools face problems of illiteracy and absenteeism, unemployment has become endemic, poverty has not disappeared, our expectations of the state grow while our willingness to pay for them declines, cynicism about politicians is at a historic high and there is a general awareness of a breakdown of authority. These are problems for which there is a solution, and only a blind spot in our culture prevents us from seeing what it is. The historic route out of such crises has been the strengthening of social institutions, beginning with the family. This does not necessarily mean less government, or more government, but a different kind of government, one which works with the grain of families and communities, giving them work to do rather than taking it away.

I believe that collectively we have delegated away too much of what matters in our lives: to governments, police forces, judges, courts, social workers, managers, teachers, therapists and gurus, each of whom, we suspect, can manage our affairs or conflicts or emotions better than we can. This was understandable, but in hindsight it was wrong. When my car breaks down, I take it to a mechanic because he can diagnose the fault and put it right faster and more accurately than I can. But my car is something I own. My life is something I am, and in handing much of it away I am diminished. There has been prolonged public debate about the rights and wrongs of giving away part of British sovereignty to a European parliament. But there has been almost no debate about the unprecedented handing over of sovereignty over large tracts of our lives to other agencies and experts. It has happened exactly as Tocqueville predicted it would, slowly, tacitly and without resistance. When the system breaks down – as it must – we are liable to despair, because our destiny now rests in other hands, not our own. That is when the politics of delegation must turn again to the politics of responsibility, and of moral institutions.

Morality is the antidote to despair because it locates social change at a level at which we, as individuals, can make a difference – in the acts we do and the relationships we create. Its problems are unlike those of politics – the environment, for example, or the economy or a choice of government. A decision on our part not to use leaded fuel makes no measurable difference to levels of pollution. A day's work or absence does not affect the rate of gross national product. A single vote rarely makes a difference to the outcome of a general election. That is not to say that these issues, and our participation in them, are not immensely important. They are, but to have an effect, our decisions must be mirrored in a million others not under our control. By contrast, a promise kept, a kindness rendered, praise given, understanding shown: these touch the lives of others and may change them. Certainly they change us.

Morality is the language of hope, for it presupposes that in a critical respect, man is not a part of nature. Because we are speakers of a language we are capable of imagination, of envisaging a reality other than that currently present to the senses. So, for us, there is a difference between 'is' and 'ought', between the world we observe and the world to which we aspire, and in aspiring begin to make. None of us can make that world alone, but we are not condemned to live alone. Nor, if we are part of a moral community, are we dependent on the whims and passing interests of others. Marriage gives permanence to love. Loyalty gives strength to parenthood. Education becomes a conversation between the generations. Kinship and covenant link us to our fellow human beings so that they know they can rely on us and we know we can rely on them. The knowledge that we are strangers teaches us to reach beyond the boundary of 'us' and extend friendship and reciprocity to 'them'. The knowledge, too, that the earth is not ours, that we are temporary residents, heirs of those who came before us and guardians for those who will come after us in turn, steers us away from the destructive impulse – whether to war or excessive exploitation – which may sometimes come to those who have no stake in a future beyond their lifetime.

Christopher Lasch has written wisely on the difference between the leading value of the Enlightenment, progress, and the Judaeo-Christian concept of hope. Progress is the belief that through science, observation and reason, open-ended advance can be achieved in the control of nature, including human nature. It rests ultimately on 'a denial of the natural limits on human power and freedom' and it cannot survive indefinitely in a world in which 'an awareness of those limits has become inescapable'.[8] Hope, by contrast:

[8] Christopher Lasch, *The True and Only Heaven*, 530.

implies a deep-seated trust in life that seems absurd to those who lack it. It rests on confidence not so much in the future as in the past. It derives from early memories ... in which the experience of order and contentment was so intense that subsequent disillusionments cannot dislodge it. Such experience leaves as its residue the unshakable conviction, not that the past was better than the present, but that trust is never completely misplaced.[9]

The belief in progress gives rise to optimism, and the loss of optimism all too easily shades into despair and the apocalyptic imagination. Hope leads to something different: to courage. For though it does not protect us against calamity, we know that if it strikes we will not be alone. If our moral environment is in a state of health, we are surrounded by family and friends, colleagues and neighbours. We know that they will be there for us as we would be for them. They will give us the strength to grieve, to endure, to recover our independence, to reaffirm life. In its most human and yet most religious expression, it is the trust that lies behind the words 'I will fear no evil, for Thou art with me.'

Hope – not optimism – is what empowers us to take risks, to offer commitment, to give love, to bring new life into the world, to comfort the afflicted, to lift the fallen, to begin great undertakings, to live by our ideals. It is to be found in families and communities, in the great religious traditions and certain of their humanist counterparts.[10] It is sustained by them, as they are sustained by it. As so much in our world, privately, nationally and globally, becomes uncertain, it is the best way, perhaps the only way, of retaining our sense of the underlying goodness of the world and the miraculous gift of life itself.

It may seem naive to suggest that the recovery of hope through the re-moralisation of society can solve problems that have defeated some of the world's most powerful governments. But it did so in

---

[9] Ibid., 81.

[10] On hope as a 'signal of transcendence', see Peter Berger, *A Rumour of Angels: Modern Society and the Rediscovery of the Supernatural*, London, Allen Lane, 1970, 66–96.

the past – in nineteenth-century Britain and America, and at many other moments of social crisis. I find it strangely moving that the Judaeo-Christian tradition, predicated on the sanctity of life, the priority of right over might, and the imperatives of justice and compassion for the vulnerable and disenfranchised, has survived for almost four thousand years while the great empires that persecuted its adherents have crumbled and vanished from the stage of history. Societies built on trust have a resilience and adaptability that no political order in and of itself can create. That is why totalitarianisms on the one hand, libertarian cultures on the other, initially dazzle by their power or creativity, but rapidly expend their energies and inevitably suffer death through decadence.

To be a Jew as the twentieth century reaches its close – remembering my people's recent history from the pogroms of Russia to the anti-Semitism which swept through Europe to the Holocaust in which some two-thirds of Europe's Jews were murdered – is not to speak lightly of hope. But neither is it accidental that the Hebrew word for hope – *Hatikvah* – gave its name to the national anthem of the reborn Jewish state. The fact that Jews and Judaism survive today is sufficient testimony to the strength of the human spirit, for what Jews can do, so can others.

Slowly we are beginning to realise that the story of man-the-political-and-economic-animal is only one half of the truth of our human situation. Without a strong civil society, political and economic structures fail. Even businesses cannot thrive without long-term relationships of trust between producer and consumer, employer and employee. We know that schools fail without the support of families. We know that families fail without the support of communities. We know that communities fail without neighbourly virtues and the obligations that flow from fellow-feeling. Neither the free market nor the democratic state can survive in the long run without internalised constraints which prevent us – from a sense of honour or fidelity or decency or habit – from doing certain things which it may be to our advantage to do.

Civil society rests on moral relationships. They are covenantal rather than contractual. They belong to a liberal, not libertarian, social order. They are brought about not by governments but by us, as husbands and wives, parents, friends and citizens, and by the knowledge that what we do and what we are makes a difference to those around us. We can change the world if we can change ourselves. Indeed that is the only way the world is changed, for politics ultimately works through people and our acceptance of responsibility. That is why morality is prior to politics, and why it remains the only secure base of freedom and dignity. Renewing society's resources of moral energy is the programme, urgent but achievable, of a new politics of hope.

Bibliography

Acton, Lord, *Essays in the History of Liberty*, ed. J. Rufus Fears, Indianapolis, Liberty, 1985.

Anderson, Digby (ed.), *The Loss of Virtue: Moral Confusion and Social Disorder in Britain and America*, London, Social Affairs Unit, 1992.

— (ed.), *This Will Hurt: The Restoration of Virtue and Civic Order*, London, Social Affairs Unit, 1995.

— (ed.), *Gentility Recalled: 'Mere' Manners and the Making of Social Order,* London, Social Affairs Unit, 1996.

Aristotle, *The Politics*, Cambridge, Cambridge University Press, 1988.

Arnold, Matthew, *Culture and Anarchy and other writings*, ed. Stefan Collini, Cambridge, Cambridge University Press, 1993.

Ashdown, Paddy, *Beyond Westminster*, London, Simon & Schuster, 1994.

Atkinson, Dick, *The Common Sense of Community*, London, Demos, 1994.

—, *Radical Urban Solutions: Urban Renaissance for City Schools and Communities*, London, Cassell, 1994.

— (ed.), *Cities of Pride*, London, Cassell, 1995.

Avineri, S., and de-Shalit, A. (eds), *Communitarianism and Individualism*, Oxford, Oxford University Press, 1992.

Ayer, A. J. *Language, Truth and Logic*, New York, Dover, 1946.

Beiner, Ronald, *What's The Matter with Liberalism?*, Berkeley, University of California Press, 1995.

Bell, Daniel, *The Cultural Contradictions of Capitalism*, London, Heinemann, 1979.

Bell, Daniel A., *Communitarianism and its Critics*, Oxford, Clarendon Press, 1993.

Bellah, Robert N., et al., *Habits of the Heart*, London, Hutchinson, 1988.

—, et al., *The Good Society*, New York, Vintage, 1992.

Bennett, William J. *The De-Valuing of America*, New York, Touchstone, 1992.

— (ed.), *The Book of Virtues*, New York, Simon & Schuster, 1993.

—, *Index of Leading Cultural Indicators*, New York, Simon & Schuster, 1994.

Berlin, Isaiah, *Four Essays on Liberty*, Oxford, Oxford University Press, 1969.

—, *The Crooked Timber of Humanity*, London, Fontana, 1991.

—, *The Sense of Reality*, London, Chatto & Windus, 1996.

Blair, Tony, *New Britain*, London, Fourth Estate, 1996.

Bloom, Allan, *The Closing of the American Mind*, London, Penguin, 1988.

—, *Giants and Dwarfs,* New York, Touchstone, 1991.

Bodin, Jean, *The Six Bookes of a Commonweale*, trans. Richard Knolles (1606), ed. Kenneth D. McRae, Cambridge, Harvard University Press, 1962.

—, Six Books of the Commonwealth, abridged and trans. M. J. Tooley, Oxford, Blackwell, 1955.

—, *On Sovereignty*, ed. and trans. Julian H. Franklin, Cambridge, Cambridge University Press, 1992.

Burke, Edmund, *Reflections on the Revolution in France*, Oxford, Oxford University Press, 1993.

—, *Further Reflections on the Revolution in France*, ed. Daniel Ritchie, Indianapolis, Liberty, 1992.

Clark, Henry, *The Church Under Thatcher*, London, SPCK, 1993.

Clinton, Bill, *Between Hope and History*, New York, Times Books, 1996.

Clinton, Hillary, *It Takes A Village*, New York, Simon & Schuster, 1996.

Cohen, Stuart A., *The Three Crowns: Structures of Communal Politics in Early Rabbinic Jewry*, Cambridge, Cambridge University Press, 1989.

Conway, David, *Classical Liberalism*, London, Macmillan, 1995.

D'Ancona, Matthew, *The Ties that Bind*, London, Social Market Foundation, 1996.

Darlington, C. D., *The Evolution of Man and Society*, London, George Allen & Unwin, 1969.

Darwin, Charles, *The Descent of Man*, Princeton, N. J., Princeton University Press, 1981.

Davies, Jon (ed), *God and the Marketplace*, London, IEA Health and Welfare Unit, 1993.

— (ed), *The Family: Is it just another lifestyle choice?*, London, IEA Health and Welfare Unit, 1993.

Dawson, Christopher, *Religion and the Modern State,* London, Sheed & Ward, 1936.

Dennis, N., *Rising Crime and the Dismembered Family*, London: IEA Health and Welfare Unit, 1993

—, and Erdos, G., *Families without Fatherhood*, London, IEA Health and Welfare Unit, 1992

—, and Halsey, A. H., *English Ethical Socialism*, Oxford, Clarendon Press, 1988.

Devlin, Patrick, *The Enforcement of Morals*, Oxford, Oxford University Press, 1965.

Dixon, Patrick, *The Rising Price of Love*, London, Hodder & Stoughton, 1995.

Duncan, Alan, and Hobson, Dominic, *Saturn's Children*, London, Sinclair-Stevenson, 1995.

Dworkin, Ronald, *Taking Rights Seriously*, London, Duckworth, 1978.

—, *Law's Empire*, London, Fontana, 1986.

—, *A Matter of Principle*, Oxford, Clarendon Press, 1986.

—, *Life's Dominion*, London, HarperCollins, 1993.

Elazar, Daniel J., *People and Polity: The Organizational Dynamics of World Jewry*, Detroit, Wayne State University Press, 1989.

— (ed.), *Kinship and Consent: The Jewish Political Tradition and its Contemporary Uses*, London, Turtledove, 1981.

—, and Cohen, Stuart A., *The Jewish Polity*, Bloomington, Indiana University Press, 1985.

Eliot, T. S., *The Idea of a Christian Society*, London, Faber & Faber, 1939.

—, *Notes Towards the Definition of Culture*, London, Faber & Faber, 1948.

—, *Selected Prose*, edited by Frank Kermode, London, Faber & Faber, 1975.

—, *To Criticize the Critic*, London, Faber & Faber, 1978.

Etzioni, Amitai, *The Spirit of Community*, New York, Crown, 1993.

—, *The New Golden Rule: Morality and Community in a Democratic Society,* New York, BasicBooks.

Field, Frank, *An Agenda for Britain*, London, HarperCollins, 1993.

—, *Making Welfare Work: Reconstructing Welfare for the Millennium*, London, Institute of Community Studies, 1995.

—, *How to Pay for the Future: Building a Stakeholders' Welfare*, London, Institute of Community Studies, 1996.

Flew, Anthony, *Self-Improvement and Social Action*, London, Social Affairs Unit, n.d.

Foucault, Michel, *The Order of Things: An Archeology of the Human Sciences,* New York, Vintage, 1973.

Fukuyama, Francis, *Trust: The Social Virtues and the Creation of Prosperity*, London, Hamish Hamilton, 1995.

—, *The Great Disruption*, London, Profile, 1999.

Fuller, Lon, *The Morality of Law*, New Haven, Yale University Press, 1969.

Galbraith, John Kenneth, *The Culture of Contentment*, London, Sinclair-Stevenson, 1992.

Gellner, Ernest, *Nations and Nationalism*, Oxford, Blackwell, 1983.

—, *Postmodernism, Reason and Religion*, London, Routledge, 1992.

—, *Conditions of Liberty: Civil Society and its Rivals*, London, Hamish Hamilton, 1994.

Giddens, Anthony, *Beyond Left and Right: The Future of Radical Politics*, Cambridge, Polity, 1994.

Gingrich, Newt, *To Renew America*, New York, HarperCollins, 1995.

Glendon, Mary Ann, *Rights Talk*, New York, Free Press, 1991

Glyn-Jones, Anne, *Holding Up a Mirror: How Civilizations Decline*, London, Century, 1996.

Graeff, Roger, *Living Dangerously*, London, HarperCollins, 1993.

Gray, John, *Liberalisms*, London, Routledge, 1989.

—, *Liberalism*, Milton Keynes, Open University Press, 1993.

—, *Beyond the New Right*, London, Routledge, 1993.

—, *The Undoing of Conservatism*, London, Social Market Foundation, 1994.

—, *Enlightenment's Wake*, London, Routledge, 1995.

—, *Isaiah Berlin*, London, HarperCollins, 1995.

—, *After Social Democracy*, London, Demos, 1996.

Green, Damien, *Communities in the Countryside*, London, Social Market Foundation, 1996.

Green, David G., *Reinventing Civil Society*, London, IEA Health and Welfare Unit, 1993.

—, *Community Without Politics*, London, IEA Health and Welfare Unit, 1996.

Hailsham, Lord, *Values: Collapse and Cure*, London: HarperCollins, 1994.

Hampshire, Stuart, *Morality and Conflict*, Oxford, Blackwell, 1983.

—, *Innocence and Experience*, London, Penguin, 1989.

— (ed.), *Public and Private Morality*, Cambridge, Cambridge University Press, 1978.

Handy, Charles, *The Age of Unreason*, London, Arrow, 1990.

—, *The Empty Raincoat*, London, Hutchinson, 1994.

Hart, H. L. A., *Law, Liberty and Morality*, Oxford, Oxford University Press, 1963.

Havel, Vaclav, *Living in Truth*, London, Faber & Faber, 1987.

Hayek, F. A., *The Constitution of Liberty*, London, Routledge & Kegan Paul, 1976.

—, *The Fatal Conceit*, London, Routledge, 1990.

Himmelfarb, Gertrude, *On Liberty and Liberalism: The Case of John Stuart Mill*, New York, Knopf, 1974.

—, *Marriage and Morals Among the Victorians*, London, Faber and Faber, 1986.

—, *Poverty and Compassion: The Moral Imagination of the Late Victorians*, New York, Knopf, 1991.

—, *On Looking into the Abyss*, New York, Vintage Books, 1994.

—, *The De-Moralization of Society*, New York, Knopf, 1995.

Hobbes, Thomas, *Leviathan*, Cambridge, Cambridge University Press, 1991.

Hobhouse, L. T., *Liberalism and other writings*, ed. James Meadowcroft, Cambridge, Cambridge University Press, 1994.

Hobsbawm, Eric, *Age of Extremes*, London, Michael Joseph, 1994.

Hughes, Robert, *Culture of Complaint*, New York, Oxford University Press, 1993.

Hutton, Will, *The State We're In*, London, Jonathan Cape, 1995.

Ionescu, Ghita, *Politics and the Pursuit of Happiness*, London, Longman, 1984.

Jacobs, Jane, *The Death and Life of Great American Cities*, London, Jonathan Cape, 1962.

James, Oliver, *Britain on the Couch*, London, Century, 1997.

Jenkins, Simon, *Accountable to None: The Tory Nationalization of Britain*, London, Hamish Hamilton, 1995.

Johnson, Paul, *Wake Up Britain*, London, Weidenfeld & Nicolson, 1994.

Kaus, Mickey, *The End of Equality*, New York, Basic Books, 1992.

Kristol, Irving, *Reflections of a Neoconservative*, New York, Basic Books, 1983.

—, *Neo-Conservatism*, New York, Free Press, 1995.

Kymlicka, Will, *Liberalism, Community and Culture*, Oxford, Clarendon, 1989.

— (ed.), *The Rights of Minority Cultures*, Oxford, Oxford University Press, 1995.

Landes, David, *The Wealth and Poverty of Nations*, London, Little, Brown, 1998.

Larmore, Charles, *Patterns of Moral Complexity*, Cambridge, Cambridge University Press, 1987.

Lasch, Christopher, *Haven in a Heartless World*, New York, Basic Books, 1977.

—, *Culture of Narcissism*, New York, Norton, 1979.

—, *The Minimal Self*, New York, Norton, 1984.

—, *The True and Only Heaven: Progress and Its Critics*, New York, Norton, 1991.

—, *The Revolt of the Elites and the Betrayal of Democracy*, New York, Norton, 1995.

Leach, Penelope, *Children First*, London, Michael Joseph, 1994.

Letwin, Shirley Robin, *The Anatomy of Thatcherism*, London, Fontana, 1992.

Lewis, C. S., *The Abolition of Man*, London, Collins, 1978.

Locke, John, *Political Writings*, ed. David Wootton, London, Penguin, 1993.

Lukes, Steven, *Individualism*, Oxford, Blackwell, 1973.

Macedo, Steven, *Liberal Virtues: Citizenship, Virtue and Community in Liberal Constitutionalism*, Oxford, Clarendon Press, 1990.

MacIntyre, Alasdair, *A Short History of Ethics*, London, Routledge, 1967.

—, *Marxism and Christianity*, Harmondsworth, Penguin, 1971.

—, *After Virtue*, London, Duckworth, 1981.

—, *Whose Justice? Which Rationality?*, London, Duckworth, 1988.

—, *Three Rival Versions of Moral Enquiry*, London, Duckworth, 1990.

Maclean, Anne, *The Elimination of Morality: Reflections on Utilitarianism and Bioethics*, London, Routledge, 1993.

Macmurray, John, *The Self as Agent*, London, Faber & Faber, 1957.

—, *Persons in Relation*, London, Faber & Faber, 1961.

Magnet, Myron, *The Dream and the Nightmare: The Sixties' Legacy to the Underclass*, New York, 1993.

Maimonides, Moses, *The Guide of the Perplexed*, trans. Shlomo Pines, 2 vols., Chicago, University of Chicago Press, 1963.

Mandelson, Peter, and Liddle Roger, *The Blair Revolution*, London, Faber & Faber, 1996.

Marenbom, John, *Answering the Challenge of Communitarianism*, London, Politeia, 1996.

Marquand, David, *The Unprincipled Society*, London, Fontana, 1988.

McLennan, Gregor, Held, David, and Hall, Stuart, *State and Society in Contemporary Britain*, Cambridge, Polity Press, 1984.

Mendus, Susan, and Edwards, David (eds), *On Toleration*, Oxford, Clarendon Press, 1987.

Midgley, Mary, *Heart and Mind*, London, Methuen, 1983.

—, *Wickedness*, London, Routledge & Kegan Paul, 1984.

—, *Can't We Make Moral Judgements?* Bristol, The Bristol Press, 1991.

Miles, Rosalind, *The Children We Deserve*, London, HarperCollins, 1994.

Mill, J. S. *Utilitarianism, On Liberty and Considerations on Representative Government*, ed. H. B. Acton, London, Dent, 1972.

—, *Essays on Politics and Culture*, ed. Gertrude Himmelfarb, New York, 1962.

—, *Essays on Ethics, Religion and Society*, ed. J. M. Robson, Toronto, University of Toronto Press, 1969.

Mitchell, Basil, *Morality: Religious and Secular*, Oxford, Clarendon Press, 1985.

—, *Why Social Policy Cannot be Morally Neutral*, London, Social Affairs Unit, 1989.

Morgan, Patricia, *Farewell to the Family?*, London, IEA Health and Welfare Unit, 1995.

Mount, Ferdinand, *The Subversive Family*, London, Jonathan Cape, 1982.

Mulhall, Stephen, and Swift, Adam, *Liberals and Communitarians*, Oxford, Blackwell, 1992.

Murray, Charles, *Losing Ground: American Social Policy 1950–1980*, New York, Basic Books, 1984.

—, *In Pursuit of Happiness and Good Government*, New York, Simon and Schuster, 1988.

—, *The Emerging British Underclass*, London, IEA Health and Welfare Unit, 1990.

—, et al., *Underclass: The Crisis Deepens*, London, IEA Health and Welfare Unit, 1994.

—, and Herrnstein, Richard, *The Bell Curve*, New York, Free Press, 1994.

Nagel, Thomas, *Mortal Questions*, Cambridge, Cambridge University Press, 1979.

—, *The View from Nowhere*, New York, Oxford University Press, 1986.

—, *Equality and Partiality*, New York, Oxford University Press, 1991.

Neuhaus, Richard John, *The Naked Public Square*, second ed., Michigan, Eerdmans, 1995.

Niebuhr, Reinhold, *Moral Man and Immoral Society*, New York, Charles Scribner's, 1947.

Nisbet, Robert, *The Quest for Community*, New York, Oxford University Press, 1953.

—, *Twilight of Authority*, London, Heinemann, 1976.

—, *Conservatism: Dream and Reality*, Milton Keynes, Open University Press, 1991.

Novak, Michael, *Free Persons and the Common Good*, Lanham, Madison Books, 1989.

—, *The Spirit of Democratic Capitalism*, London, IEA Health and Welfare Unit, 1991.

—, *This Hemisphere of Liberty*, Washington, AEI Press, 1992.

—, *The Catholic Ethic and the Spirit of Capitalism*, New York, Free Press, 1993.

—, *Awakening from Nihilism*, London, IEA Health and Welfare Unit, 1995.

—, and Preston, Robert, *Christian Capitalism or Christian Socialism?*, London, IEA Health and Welfare Unit, 1994.

Nozick, Robert, *Anarchy, State and Utopia*, Oxford, Basil Blackwell, 1974.

O'Brien, Conor Cruise, *On the Eve of the Millennium*, New York, Free Press, 1994.

Oakeshott, Michael, *Rationalism in Politics and other essays*, Indianapolis, Liberty Press, 1991.

—, *Religion, Politics and the Moral Life*, ed. Timothy Fuller, New Haven, Yale University Press, 1993.

Olasky, Marvin, *The Tragedy of American Compassion*, Washington, Regnery Publishing, 1992.

Osborne, David, and Gaebler, Ted, *Reinventing Government*, New York, Plume, 1993.

Passmore, John, *Man's Responsibility for Nature*, London, Duckworth, 1980.

Patten, John, *Things to Come*, London, Sinclair-Stevenson, 1995.

Paul, E., Miller, F., and Paul J. (eds), *Altruism*, Cambridge, Cambridge University Press, 1993.

Peters, Richard, *Hobbes*, Harmondsworth, Penguin, 1956.

Phillips, Melanie, *All Must Have Prizes*, London, Little, Brown, 1996.

Plamenatz, John, *Man and Society*, vol. 1, London, Longman, 1963.

Prager, Dennis, *Think a Second Time*, New York, ReganBooks, 1995.

Prochaska, Frank, *Royal Bounty: The Making of a Welfare Monarchy*, New Haven, Yale University Press, 1995.

Rawls, John, *A Theory of Justice*, Oxford, Clarendon Press, 1972.

—, *Political Liberalism*, New York, Columbia University Press, 1993.

Raz, J., *The Morality of Freedom*, Oxford, Clarendon Press, 1986.

Ridley, Matt, *The Origins of Virtue*, London, Viking, 1996.

Rieff, Philip, *The Triumph of the Therapeutic*, London, Chatto & Windus, 1966.

Riesman, David, Glazer, Nathan and Denney, Reuel, *The Lonely Crowd*, New York, Doubleday Anchor, 1954.

Rorty, Richard, *Contingency, Irony and Solidarity*, Cambridge, Cambridge University Press, 1989.

Rousseau, Jean-Jacques, *The Social Contract*, Harmondsworth, Penguin, 1968.

Russell, Bertrand, *History of Western Philosophy*, London, George Allen & Unwin, 1962.

Sacks, Jonathan, *Wealth and Poverty: a Jewish Analysis*, London, Social Affairs Unit, 1985.

—, *The Persistence of Faith*, London, Weidenfeld & Nicolson, 1991.

—, *Faith in the Future*, Darton, Longman & Todd, 1995.

—, *Community of Faith*, London, Peter Halban, 1995.

—, 'The Role of Religions in the Transmission of Moral Values: A Jewish Perspective', *World Faiths Encounter*, 12, November 1995, 4–9.

—, 'Social Contract or Social Covenant', *Policy Review*, 78, July–August 1996, 54–7.

Sandel, Michael, *Liberalism and the Limits of Justice*, Cambridge, Cambridge University Press, 1982

—, *Democracy's Discontent: America in Search of a Public Philosophy*, Cambridge, Mass., Harvard University Press, 1996.

— (ed.), *Liberalism and its Critics*, Oxford, Blackwell, 1984.

Schlesinger, Arthur M., *The Disuniting of America*, New York, Norton, 1992.

Schumpeter, Joseph, *Capitalism, Socialism and Democracy*, London, George Allen & Unwin, 1947.

Scruton, Roger, *The Philosopher on Dover Beach*, Manchester, Carcanet, 1990.

—, *The Meaning of Conservatism*, London, Macmillan, 1994.

—, *The Conservative Idea of Community*, London, The Conservative 2000 Foundation, 1996.

—, *Animal Rights and Wrongs*, London, Demos, 1996.

Selbourne, David, *The Spirit of the Age*, London, Sinclair-Stevenson, 1993.

—, *The Principle of Duty*, London, Sinclair-Stevenson, 1994.

Seligman, Adam B., *The Idea of Civil Society*, Princeton, Princeton University Press, 1992.

Sennett, Richard, *The Fall of Public Man*, London, Faber & Faber, 1986.

—, *Authority*, London, Faber & Faber, 1993.

Shils, Edward, *Tradition*, London, Faber & Faber, 1981.

Shtromas, Alexsandras (ed.), *The End of 'Isms'? Reflections on the Fate of Ideological Politics after Communism's Collapse*, Oxford, Blackwell, 1994.

Sirico, Robert, et al., *A Moral Basis for Liberty*, London, IEA Health and Welfare Unit, 1994.

Smith, Adam, *The Wealth of Nations*, London, Penguin, 1986.

—, *The Theory of Moral Sentiments*, Oxford, Oxford University Press, 1976.

Soros, George, *The Crisis of Global Capitalism*, London, Little, Brown, 1998.

Spinoza, Benedict de, *A Theologico-Political Treatise*, trans. R. H. M. Elwes, New York, Dover, 1951.

Stephen, James Fitzjames, *Liberty, Equality, Fraternity*, Indianapolis, Liberty, 1993.

Stivers, Richard, *The Culture of Cynicism*, Oxford, Blackwell, 1994.

Stout, Jeffrey, *Ethics After Babel: The Languages of Morals and Their Discontents*, Boston, Beacon Press, 1988.

Strauss, Leo, *Liberalism Ancient and Modern*, Chicago, University of Chicago Press, 1989.

Sykes, Charles, *A Nation of Victims: The Decay of the American Character*, New York, St Martin's Press, 1992.

—, *Dumbing Down Our Kids: Why American Children Feel Good About Themselves But Can't Read, Write, or Add*, New York, St Martin's Press, 1995.

Tawney, R. H., *The Acquisitive Society*, London, Fontana, 1961.

Taylor, Charles, *The Ethics of Authenticity*, Cambridge, Mass., Harvard University Press, 1991.

—, *Sources of the Self*, Cambridge, Cambridge University Press, 1992.

Templeton, Kenneth (ed.), *The Politicization of Society*, Indianapolis, Liberty, 1979.

Tocqueville, Alexis de, *Democracy in America*, abridged with an introduction by Thomas Bender, New York, The Modern Library, 1981.

Trilling, Lionel, *Beyond Culture*, New York, Viking, 1965.

—, *Sincerity and Authenticity*, Cambridge, Mass., Harvard University Press, 1971.

Waldegrave, William, *The Binding of Leviathan*, London, Hamish Hamilton, 1978.

Walden, George, *We Should Know Better: Solving the Education Crisis*, London, Fourth Estate, 1996.

Waldron, Jeremy (ed.), *Theories of Rights*, Oxford, Oxford University Press, 1984.

Walsh, David, *Selling Out America's Children*, Minneapolis, Fairview Press, 1994.

Walzer, Michael, *Spheres of Justice*, Oxford, Blackwell, 1983.

—, *Exodus and Revolution*, New York, Basic Books, 1985.

—, *Citizenship and Civil Society*, Rutgers, N. J., New Jersey Committee for the Humanities Series on the Culture of Community, 1992.

— (ed.), *Toward a Global Civil Society*, Oxford, Berghahn Books, 1995.

Weber, Max, *The Protestant Ethic and the Spirit of Capitalism*, trans. Talcott Parsons, London, Unwin, 1985.

Whelan, Robert, *The Corrosion of Charity*, London, IEA Health and Welfare Unit, 1996.

— (ed.), *Teaching Right and Wrong: Have the Churches Failed?* London, IEA Health and Welfare Unit, 1994.

— (ed.), *Just a Piece of Paper?*, London, IEA Health and Welfare Unit, 1995.

Will, George, *Statecraft as Soulcraft*, London, Weidenfeld and Nicolson, 1984.

Willetts, David, *Modern Conservatism*, Harmondsworth, Penguin, 1992.

—, *Civic Conservatism*, London, Social Market Foundation, 1994.

Williams, Bernard, *Morality*, Harmondsworth, Penguin, 1973.

—, *Moral Luck*, Cambridge, Cambridge University Press, 1981.

—, *Ethics and the Limits of Philosophy*, London, Fontana, 1985.

—, *Shame and Necessity*, Berkeley, University of California Press, 1993.

—, *Making Sense of Humanity*, Cambridge, Cambridge University Press, 1995.

Williams, Raymond, *Culture and Society 1780–1950*, Harmondsworth, Penguin, 1963.

—, *Keywords: A Vocabulary of Culture and Society*, London, Fontana, 1983.

Wilson, James Q., *The Moral Sense*, New York, Free Press, 1993.

—, and Herrnstein, Richard, *Crime and Human Nature*, New York, Simon & Schuster, 1985.

Wright, Robert, *The Moral Animal*, London, Little, Brown, 1995.

Index